Lecture Notes of the Institute for Computer Sciences, Social-Informatics and Telecommunications Engineering 41

Dasun Weerasinghe (Ed.)

Information Security and Digital Forensics

First International Conference, ISDF 2009
London, United Kingdom, September 7-9, 2009
Revised Selected Papers

Volume Editor

Dasun Weerasinghe
City University
School of Engineering and Mathematical Sciences
Northampton Square, London, EC1V 0HB, United Kingdom
E-mail: dasun.weerasinghe@city.ac.uk

Library of Congress Control Number: 2009943128

CR Subject Classification (1998): D.4.6, K.6.5, E.3, C.2, C.2.2, C.3, C.1.3

ISSN 1867-8211
ISBN-10 3-642-11529-2 Springer Berlin Heidelberg New York
ISBN-13 978-3-642-11529-5 Springer Berlin Heidelberg New York

springer.com

Printed in Germany

Typesetting: Camera-ready by author, data conversion by Scientific Publishing Services, Chennai, India
Printed on acid-free paper SPIN: 12829897 06/3180 5 4 3 2 1 0

Preface

ISDF 2009, the First International Conference on Information Security and Digital Forensics, was held at City University London during September 7-8, 2009. The conference was organized as a meeting point for leading national and international experts of information security and digital forensics. The conference was rewarding in many ways; ISDF 2009 was an exciting and vibrant event, with 4 keynote talks, 25 invited talks and 18 full-paper presentations and those attending had the opportunity to meet and talk with many distinguished people who are responsible for shaping the area of information security.

This conference was organized as part of two major research projects funded by the UK Engineering and Physical Sciences Research Council in the areas of Security and Digital Forensics.

I would like to thank all the people who contributed to the technical program. The most apparent of these are the Indian delegates who all accepted our invite to give presentations at this conference. Less apparent perhaps is the terrific work of the members of the Technical Program Committee, especially in reviewing the papers, which is a critical and time-consuming task. I would like to thank Raj Rajarajan (City University London) for making the idea of the ISDF 2009 conference a reality with his hard work. Last but not least, I would like to thank all the authors who submitted papers, making the conference possible, and the authors of accepted papers for their cooperation.

Dasun Weerasinghe

Table of Contents

Analysis of Denial of Service Attacks in IEEE 802.11s Wireless Mesh Networks

Divya[*] and Sanjeev Kumar[**]

Computer Science & Enginee
Punjab Engineering College,
Chandigarh. India
{divya,sanjeevsofat}@pec.edu.in

Abstract. Unlike wired networks, wireless networks do not have well-defined physical boundaries, which makes them prone to several security threats. As various wireless networks evolve into the next generation to provide better services, a key technology in the form of wireless mesh networks (WMNs) has emerged recently. Wireless Mesh Networks hold the promise of facilitating large-scale community networks in complex environments. There are number of issues in deploying WMNs, amongst others, security is a very serious issue. In these and other vital or security-sensitive deployments, keeping the network available for its intended use is essential. Without proper security mechanisms, networks will be confined to limited, controlled environments, negating much of the promise they hold. One of the major loop-holes in the security of WMNs is that management frames are not authenticated, and hence can be easily spoofed to cause DoS or Denial of Service attacks. We analyze the existing schemes and the proposed protocols to authenticate Disassociation and Deauthentication management frames. In this paper an original scheme is proposed that can be used to prevent DoS attacks over 802.11i security standard.

Keywords: Advanced Encryption Standard (AES), Wired Equivalent Privacy (WEP), 802.11i, WMNs, Denial of Service, 802.11w.

1 Introduction

Denial of Service (DoS) refers to a form of attack in computer systems over a network. DoS is normally a malicious attempt to render a networked system unusable (though often without permanently damaging it). Denial of Service (DoS) attacks prevents legitimate users from the use or management of a network asset. A denial of service attack may target a user, to prevent him from making outgoing connections on the network. A denial of service may also target an entire organization, to either prevent outgoing traffic or to prevent incoming traffic to certain network services, such as the organizations web page.

---

[*] Lecturer and Associate Coordinator, Cyber Security Research Centre.
[**] Professor and Coordinator, Cyber Security Research Centre.

D. Weerasinghe (Ed.): ISDF 2009, LNICST 41, pp. 1–10, 2010.

DoS attacks usually consist of frequency jamming whereby the attacker interferes with the whole of frequency band used in transmission of data by sending signals with more power at the same frequency. Also DoS attacks can be launched exploiting the manner in which channels are allocated to WLAN nodes wishing to transmit data. The attacker can cause the client device to think the channel is busy and defer sending data waiting for the channel to be idle. Furthermore, DoS attacks against a network can be launched by saturating a network devise with requests such that it cannot respond to legitimate traffic and therefore making the particular device unavailable to legitimate users. Denial of service attacks are much easier to accomplish than remotely gaining administrative access to a target system. Because of this, Denial of Service attacks have become very common on the Internet. Several security protocols have been proposed to prevent DoS attacks, most of which include modification of management frames in order for them to be authenticated.

1.1 Types of Dos Attacks

Probe Request Flood
Probe request frames are used by stations to actively scan an area in order to discover existing wireless networks. Any AP receiving a probe request frame must respond with a proper probe response frame that contains information about the network, to allow the station to associate. By sending a burst of probe request frames very quickly, each with a different MAC address (MAC spoofing) to simulate the presence of a large number of scanning stations in the area, the attacker can induce a heavy workload on the AP, resulting in a wastage of computing and memory resources which cannot be used for normal operations.

Denial of Service (DoS) Attack
In this attack, the intruder sends continually stream of different kinds of management frames to the WLAN. An attacker can spoof MAC address of a client and flood the WLAN with different kinds of forgery de-authentication, disassociation, association, or beacon management frames by using both directions of the communication. In this case, the WLAN overloads and will be unusable for even legitimate users.

Power Saving Attacks
The power conservation functions of 802.11 also prevent several identity-based vulnerabilities. To conserve energy, clients are allowed to enter a sleep state during which they are unable to transmit or receive. Before entering the sleep state, the client announces its intention so the access point can start buffering any inbound traffic for the node. Occasionally, the client awakens and polls the access point for any pending traffic. If there is any buffered data at this time, the access point delivers it and subsequently discards the contents of its buffer. By spoofing the polling message on behalf of the client, an attacker may cause the access point to discard the client's packets while it is asleep. Along the same vein, it is potentially possible to trick the client node in to thinking that there are no buffered packets as indicated in a periodically broadcast packet called the traffic indication map, or TIM. If the TIM message itself is spoofed, an attacker may convince a client that there is no pending data for it, and the client will immediately revert back to the sleep state. Finally, the power conservation mechanisms

rely on time synchronization between the access point and its clients so clients know when to awake. Key synchronization information, such as the period of TIM packets and a time-stamp broadcast by the access point, are sent unauthenticated and in the clear. By forging these management packets, an attacker can cause a client node to fall out of synch with the access point and fail to wake up at the appropriate times.

De-authentication attack

After an 802.11 client has selected an access point to use for communication, it must first authenticate itself to the AP before further communication may commence. Moreover, part of the authentication framework is a message that allows clients and access points to explicitly request de-authentication from one another. Unfortunately, this message itself is not authenticated using any keying material. Consequently, the attacker may spoof this message, either pretending to be the client or AP as shown in fig 1. In response, the AP or client will attempt to re-authenticate and any higher level time-outs or back-offs that may suppress the demand for communication. By repeating the attack persistently, a client may be kept from transmitting or receiving data indefinitely. One of the strengths of this attack is its great flexibility: an attacker may elect to deny access to individual clients, or even rate limit their access, in addition to simply denying service to the entire channel. However, accomplishing these goals efficiently requires the attacker to promiscuously monitor the channel and send deauthentication messages only when a new authentication has successfully taken place (indicated by the client's attempt to associate with the access point).

Disassociation Attack

A very similar vulnerability may be found in the association protocol that follows authentication. Since a client may be authenticated with multiple access points at

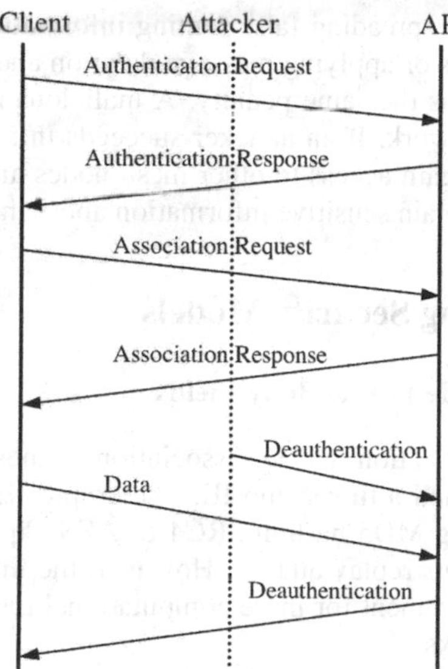

Fig. 1. De-authentication attack

once, the 802.11 standard provides a special association message to allow the client and access point to agree which access point shall have responsibility for forwarding packets to and from the wired network on the client's behalf. As with authentication, association frames are unauthenticated, and 802.11 provides a disassociation message similar to the deauthentication message described earlier. Exploiting this vulnerability is functionally identical to the deauthentication attack. However, it is worth noting that the disassociation attack is slightly less efficient than the deauthentication attack. This is because deauthentication forces the victim node to do more work to return to the associated state than disassociation, ultimately requiring less work on the part of the attacker. Association frames are unauthenticated and 802.11 provide a disassociation message similar to the de-authentication message [8, 9].

1.2 DoS Attacks in WMNs

One of the most severe threats on wireless mesh networks will be Denial of Service (DoS) attacks. The attack slows down the system and ceases the network from working properly. Unfortunately, there is no possible way to completely avoid this attack. This phenomenon takes place at link layer, as an attacker or invader can inject the frames with high network allocation vectors. The result of such an attack is that the nodes receiving the frames will stay idle till the duration indicated by network allocation vector (NAV). DoS can be avoided to some degree using some cryptographic mechanisms and surplus paths. Unauthorized access to the mesh nodes is yet another security concern in WMNs. The key concern is that at which level can the nodes participating in the communication be trusted? Generally, mesh nodes are protected with some secure text like password. There are many way to find out or retrieve passwords. What may happen if an attacker gains access to a mesh node by retrieving the secure text or password? The possibilities to make use of the network are multiple like, get access to the network or obtain the rights of a mesh node or Perform DoS by refusing to forward data or spreading false routing information or conducting Man in the Middle (MITM) attacks or applying message deletion and modification. An attack like Node spoofing also has the same penalty. A malicious node can pretend to be a regular member of the network. If an attacker succeeds in injecting such a node into the network, he may also gain access to other mesh nodes and can redirect the traffic over the corrupt node to obtain sensitive information about the network.

2 Analysis of Existing Security Models

2.1 Addition of IEs Inside Frame Body Fields

To authenticate Deauthentication and Disassociation frames, [11] proposes addition of two IEs – a crypto IE and a timestamp IE. The crypto IE is of 128 bits and filled with octets generated using MD5 hashing, RC4 or AES Cipher, while the timestamp IE is of 40 bits and prevents replay attacks. However, the limitations of this proposal are increased length, requirement for more computational resources and compatibility with only 802.11w networks.

2.2 Addition of 11 Bit Code by Replacing Bits of Frame Control and Sequence Control

This scheme, proposed in [10], consists of addition of 11 bits, randomly generated by using a key as a seed for a random number generator algorithm. The 11-bit code is split into 7 bits and 4 bits. The 7-bit code is inserted into the Frame Control field and the 4-bit code is inserted into the Sequence Control field. The bits of the Frame control field used are (i) To DS (ii) From DS (iii)More fragmentation (iv) Power Management (v)More data (vi)Protected frame (vii)Order.

The part of the Sequence control field used is the fragment number. This scheme is implemented by adding new functions to the NS-2 simulator. First, the standard 802.11 De-authentication and Disassociation procedures are added and after that the proposed scheme is implemented.

The proposed scheme can work since the problem is that of authentication of management frames and by deciding a code through which the access point and the station can authenticate each other, the problem is solved to some extent.

However, the drawbacks or weaknesses of the scheme are:

(i) Since a limited number of random numbers exist, i.e. 2^{11}, spoofing is possible.

(ii) The fields that have been deemed as unused may actually be of much use. In the frame control field, the To DS and from DS fields tell whether the station and the access point belong to the same BSS or different ones. The retry field instructs retransmission, the power management field indicates the power management mode and so on. Similarly, in the Sequence control field, the fragment number is important.

(iii) Since there is no private key exchange using a cryptographic algorithm, there is nothing to guarantee that the frame indeed has been sent by the station in question and has not been spoofed.

2.3 Proposed Draft as IEEE 802.11w

This scheme works for management frames in a way similar to the 802.11i standard for data frames. 802.11w will define the management frame protection scheme. Thus, the aim is to utilize existing security mechanisms rather than creating new ones or new Management frame format.

Protection-capable Management Frames are protected by the same cipher suite as an ordinary Data MPDU

- MPDU payload is TKIP or CCMP encrypted
- MPDU payload and header are TKIP or CCMP integrity protected

The MIC Key, the sender's MAC address, the receiver's MAC address and the frame are used to generate the Message Integrity Code (MIC), which is appended to the management frame. To prevent replay attacks, the IV (Initialization Vector) is used as part of the 802.11i header. The headers and the management frame body are authenticated by MIC, while the frame body and MIC are in encrypted format as shown in Fig 2.

As in the case of 802.11i, the cryptographic algorithm used is AES, which is a significant improvement over RC4 which is used in WEP. The use of TKIP ensures that the same encryption key is not used again. [12].

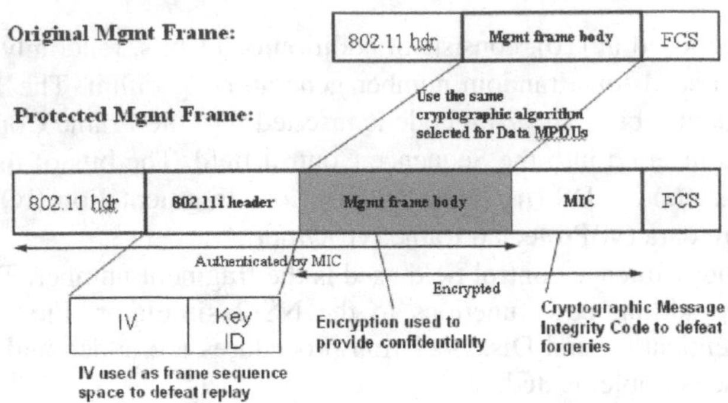

Fig. 2. Protected Management frame format in 802.11w

Since the scheme works for the authentication of normal data frames, and the same mechanism is applied to management frames, it is bound to work. MIC provides security against forgery attacks. The IV and the sequence counter prevent replay attacks.

However, just like in data frames, the problems for the implementation in case of management frames is the replacement of existing access points which are WEP compatible in order to be able to implement the more complex AES algorithm.

2.4 Other Related Work

Investigation of access point invulnerabilities to DoS attacks in 802.11 networks has been carried out in [16]. It describes possible denial of service attacks to infrastructure wireless 802.11 networks. To carry out such attacks only commodity hardware and software components are required. It identified some simple attack schemes that might lead to a **DoS** effect and observes the reactions of various types of infrastructure networks to these attacks. It identifies the message sequences that could lead to an attack towards an AP. The paper discusses probe request flood (PRF) , Authentication Request Flood (ARF), Association request flood (ASRF) and response by the AP to each of these attacks and how each of these attacks may bring the AP down to a level where all resources of AP are consumed to saturation level. It discussed the mechanism how to forge arbitrary 802.11 management frames and injecting them in the medium, regardless of protocol rules and constraints using Netgear MA401 PCMCIA card and Host AP driver and presented various attack statistics for different network configurations. The paper explains why the DoS effect does not appear when MAC spoofing is disabled. In the end it concluded that PRF, ARF and ASRF flooding attacks can be executed by any malicious station in the area of a wireless infrastructure network, without being neither associated nor authenticated to the access point and **AP's** main vulnerability to these flooding attacks seems to reside in unacknowledged frame retransmission, which causes memory buffers exhaustion and freezes AP functionalities

An analysis and cryptographic solution to two Denial of Service (DoS) attacks: Deauthentication flooding (DeauthF) and disassociation flooding (DisassF) attacks has been presented in [11].To authenticate deauthentication and disassociation frames; it adds two IEs inside their frame body fields. One is the crypto IE, and the other is the timestamp IE. The crypto IE is used to hold crypto information for authenticating deauthentication and disassociation frames. Timestamp is used to prevent the replay attack. The crypto field has a fixed length of 128 bits, which is filled with octets generated by MD5 hashing, RC4 or AES cipher. The timestamp field has a length of 40 bits. It Implements 802.11w cryptographic mechanisms to protect deauthentication and disassociation frames using NS-2.But the limitation is that this proposed solution is only compatible with 802.11w networks. Other limitations of the protocol are increased length and requirement of more computation resources.

A three bit random bit authentication mechanism to protect 802.11 networks from DoS attacks has been proposed in [13]. Random bits are placed into unused fields of the management frames. AP and STA can then authenticate each other according to these authentication bits. The experimental results are shown are using Prism/2/2.5/3 802.11b PCMCIA cards and Host AP driver.

A model for Management Frames with Authentication and Integrity (MFIA) has been proposed in [15]. According to the proposed model, when a sender wants to send each kind of management frame, first by using MAC algorithm, key (*k*), header and body of the MF, the Sender Code (S-code) is computed and is connected to the MF then this new protected MF is transmitted (FCS is appended after S-code). When receiver takes this protected MF, first computes Receiver Code (R-code), by using the received MF, *k* and MAC algorithm. If S-code and R-code match together, so receiver understands the management frame has not been changed during transmission and also understands it has been transmitted by a legitimate user who knows the key, so will implement the MF. However, issues with the protocol are increased size of frame and additional computation time.

Based on hash chains technique, a new authentication and key management scheme for WLAN has been proposed in [14], which achieves authenticating the main entity STA in the foremost time and negotiating and refreshing session keys efficiently. A hash chain is generated by multiple iterations of a secure hash function upon a secret seed and tip of the chain is used as a key. The scheme named fast WLAN authentication infrastructure (FWAI) includes five protocol flows or conversation messages between two stations.

Some implementation changes to mitigate the underlying vulnerabilities have been proposed in [17].The paper provides an experimental analysis of 802.11-specific attacks – their practicality, their efficacy. It discusses deauthentication, disassociation and power saving attacks and evaluates the practicality of implementing them and how well they perform in practice. The paper proposes a queuing mechanism to deal with deauthentication attacks, where it delays the effects of deauthentication or disassociation requests (e.g., by queuing such requests for 5-10 seconds) an AP has the opportunity to observe subsequent packets from the client. If a data packet arrives after a deauthentication or disassociation request is queued, that request is discarded – since a legitimate client would never generate packets in that order. However, our proposed solution is has certain drawbacks. It may lead to more severe DoS attacks. In particular; it opens up a new vulnerability at the moment in which mobile clients roam between access points. The association message is used to determine which AP should receive packets destined for the mobile client. In certain circumstances leaving the old association established for an additional period of time may prevent the routing updates necessary to deliver packets through the new access point. Or, in the case of an adversary, the association could be kept open indefinitely by spoofing packets from the mobile client to the spoofed AP by keeping the association current.

A central Manager Solution to prevent Dissociation attacks has been proposed in [18].But the drawbacks of the solution is that it requires a single dedicated node to counter the attacks.

3 Proposed Scheme

The scheme that we have thought of is a modification of the *Scheme C* proposed. The *Scheme B* was ruled out for modifications because it used fields that may be of use, and adding an extra 11-bit code to the existing frame is a considerable over-head and would not provide much security.

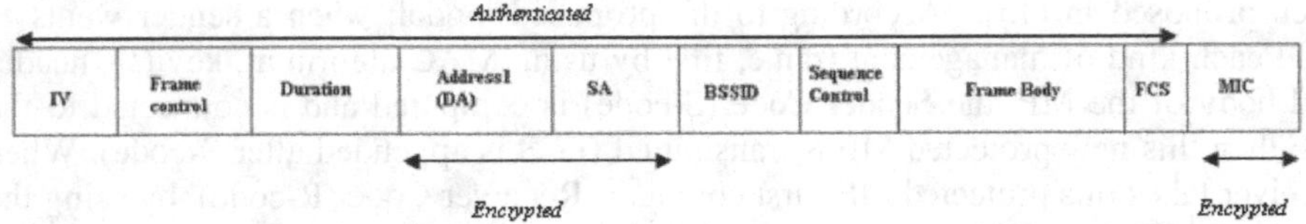

Fig. 3. Modified frame under proposed scheme

We propose that the de-authentication be performed in a way similar to the authentication in the case of 802.1X, i.e. Key in a pass phrase (master key) is used at both the client end and AP end. The pass phrases should match in case the key is correct. In addition to that, we propose that a MIC (Message Integrity Code) be added to the frame, but in order to simplify process involved, entire management frame body need not be encrypted (unlike 802.11i in which the entire data frame body is encrypted). The encryption is to be carried out using AES algorithm. We propose that management frames need not be completely protected unlike as proposed in the draft standard 802.11w as encrypting the entire header adds to overheads reducing the capacity of the mesh network.

3.1 Advantage over the Proposed Draft

To establish a connection with a legitimate station concerned only the MAC addresses needs to be secured. It is therefore sufficient to encrypt only the source and destination address fields in the frame. This makes the process less time-consuming and more efficient. We propose that management frames need not be completely protected unlike as proposed in the draft standard 802.11w. For the disassociation and de-authentication frames to be authenticated, the fields that need to be protected are the MAC addresses. The MAC addresses carry the information about the source and the destination. By spoofing the MAC address of a different station to send information can lead to de-authentication and disassociation attacks.

3.2 Shortfalls of 802.11w

As soon as IEEE 802.11w gets ratified it will become widely accepted and will offer better security to the users. However the standard will still not be able to mitigate the DoS attacks. DoS attacks can be mitigated through strong systems practices but DoS attacks against wireless networks can still not be stopped. The following attacks will still be prevalent on Wireless Mesh Networks:

- Net Allocation Vector(NAV) DoS:
  802.11w does not provide protection against attacks based on control frames. An attacker can manipulate the Network Allocation Vector (NAV) using RTS/CTS frames to force other stations to back-off, preventing them from transmitting on the network.
- Exposed Node Problem:
  Using RTS/CTS problem does provide solution in case of hidden node problem. However there is no solution for exposed node problem.
- Beacon invalid channel DoS:
  Many wireless cards will follow whatever channel is specified in spoofed beacon frames, allowing an attacker to manipulate the station into switching to channel "0", for example.
- EAPOL Start DoS & Logoff DoS:
  In an EAPOL Start DoS, an attacker rapidly hides the AP and RADIUS server with EAP Start requests. This can cause an AP to exhaust all memory and reboot, and it can cause severe performance degradation on the RADIUS server. In EAPOL logoff attack, the adversary sends EAP Logoff messages to a target station, impersonating the RADIUS server/AP. The station disconnects, and the user loses connectivity.
- PEAP Account Lockout:
  Since PEAP networks transmit the username information in plaintext, an attacker can capture valid PEAP usernames and attempt to login as that user with randomly selected passwords. This will often trigger account lockout policies from multiple failed authentication attempts, resulting in DoS for the end-user.

4 Conclusion

The draft standard 802.11w solves the problem of unprotected management frames to quite some extent with the use of MIC and IV along with sequence counter. However, protecting the entire header adds to considerable overheads. In this paper we have proposed a modified scheme which utilizes the advantages offered by the draft standard 802.11w and also makes the process less time-consuming and hence more efficient. It is evident from this study that many of the DoS attacks can still not be prevented by the new standards and the impact of such an attack is significant as it can be achieved using only commodity based hardware and software. Further such attacks can be executed with minimal chance of detection and localization. These concerns are most pronounced in network environments that rely on the correct behavior of participating nodes for continued operation. There is a dire need to develop adequate strategies to mitigate the significant threat of denial of service in current IEEE 802.11s WMN technology, the application of this technology should be precluded from use in safety-critical environments which may typically have stringent availability requirements.

References

1. IEEE 802.11 Architecture, `http://www.tutorial-reports.com/wireless/wlanwifi/wifi_architecture.php`
2. Fogie, S.: Maximum Wireless Security by Cyrus PeiKari. Sams Publishing, ISBN:0-672-32488-1
3. Wang, Y.: A Tutorial of 802.11 Implementation in NS-2
4. Zhang, H., Zhu, Y.: A New Authentication and Key Managemtn Scheme of WLAN
5. Ergen, M.: University of California Berkley, IEEE 802.11 Tutorial (June 2002)
6. Gast, M.: 802.11 Wireless Networks. O'Reilly & Associates, Inc., Sebastopol (2002)
7. Miller, S.S.: Wi-Fi Security. Tata McGraw Hill Publication, New York
8. Liu, C., Yu, J.T.: An Analysis of DoS Attacks on Wireless LAN. In: IASTED International Conferences on Wireless Networks and Emerging Technologies (WNET 2006), Banff Canada (2006)
9. Liu, C., Yu, J.T.: A Solution to Wireless LAN Authentication and Association DoS Attacks. In: Second International Conference on Computer Science and Engineering (JICCSE 2006) (December 2006)
10. A Protocol to defend Against Deauthentication and Disassociation Attacks, A Dissertation submitted to PEC (Deemed University) for Masters of Engineering in Computer Science and Engineering (2008)
11. Liu, C., Yu, J.: Rogue Access Point Based DoS Attacks against 802.11 WLANs. In: Fourth Advanced International Conference on Telecommunications
12. Qi, E.H., Walker, J.: Management frame protection. Intel Corporation (2005)
13. Lee, Y.-S., Chien, H.-T., Tsai, W.-N.: Using Random Bit Authentication to Defend IEEE 802.11 DoS Attacks
14. Zhang, H., Zhu, Y.: A New Authentication and Key Management Scheme of WLAN
15. Malekzadeh, M., Ghani, A.A.A., Zulkarnain, Z.A., Muda, Z.: Security Improvement for Management Frames in IEEE 802.11 Wireless Networks. IJCSNS International Journal of Computer Science and Network Security 7(6) (June 2007)
16. Ferreri, F., Bernaschi, M., Valcamonici, L.: Access points vulnerabilities to DoS attacks in 802.11 networks. In: WCNC 2004. IEEE Communications Society, Los Alamitos (2004)
17. Bellardo, J., Savage, S.: 802.11 Denial-of-Service Attacks. Real Vulnerabilities and Practical Solutions. In: Proceedings of the 12th USENIX Security Symposium, Washington, D.C, August 4-8 (2003)
18. Ding, P., Holliday, J., Celik, A.: Improving the Security of Wireless LANs by Managing 802.1X Disassociation. In: Proceedings of the IEEE Consumer Communications and Networking Conference, Las Vegas, NV, January 2004, pp. 53–58 (2004)

A Semi-fragile Watermarking Algorithm for Authenticating 2D Engineering Graphics Based on Log-Polar Transformation

Fei Peng[1], Re-Si Guo[1], Chang-Tsun Li[2], and Min Long[3]

[1] College of Computer and Communication, Hunan University, Changsha, PRC, 410082
[2] Department of Computer Science, University of Warwick, Coventry, UK, CV47 AL
[3] College of Computer and Communication Engineering, Changsha University of Science and Technology, Changsha, PRC, 410076
pengfei@hnu.cn, hnu_grs@163.com, c-t.li@warwick.ac.uk, longm@tom.com

Abstract. A semi-fragile watermarking algorithm for authenticating 2D engineering graphics based on log-polar coordinates mapping is proposed. Firstly, the coordinates of vertices of entities are mapped to the log-polar coordinate system to obtain the invariance of translation, scaling and rotation. Then the watermark is embedded in the mantissa of the real-valued log-polar coordinates via bit substitution. Theoretical analysis and experimental results show that the proposed algorithm is not only robust against incidental operations such as rotation, translation and scaling, but can also detect and locate malicious attacks such as entity modification, entity addition/deletion.

Keywords: semi-fragile watermarking, integrity verification, data hiding, content authentication, engineering graphics.

1 Introduction

Nowadays, copyright violation and illegal manipulation of multimedia are becoming serious problems in the cyberspace. Traditional cryptographic systems can protect the information to a certain degree, but it still has some drawbacks [1]. On the other hand, watermarking has been viewed as an efficient solution to protect the copyright and the integrity of digital data, thus has been paid significant attention in recent years [2, 3].

The functions of semi-fragile watermarking are similar to those of the digital signatures used in cryptosystems. However, for many multimedia applications, semi-fragile watermarking is superior to digital signature [4].

Since the publication of the first paper on watermarking for 3D models by Ohbuchi [5], many watermarking schemes [6-8] have been proposed to serve the similar purpose. However, little work has been done in watermarking for 2D vector graphics[9-11], which are commonly used in geographical information systems (GIS) and computer aided design (CAD). At the same time, current semi-fragile watermarking researches on vector graphics are mainly focused on 3D models. Therefore, it is our intention in this work to propose a semi-fragile watermarking scheme for verifying the integrity of 2D vector graphics.

D. Weerasinghe (Ed.): ISDF 2009, LNICST 41, pp. 11–18, 2010.

The remainder of the paper is organized as follows. 2D engineering graphics and log-polar coordinate transformation are introduced in Section 2. In Section 3, the watermarking algorithm is described in detail. The analyses of experimental results and performance are conducted in Section 4. Finally, Section 5 concludes the work.

2 2D Engineering Graphics and Log-Polar Transformation

2.1 2D Engineering Graphics

A 2D engineering graphics is a vector graphics composed of entities such as points, lines, arcs, polygons, circles, elliptic circles, etc, and vertex is a basic element of the entities. Every entity also has its own properties such as handle value, color, line type and etc. The characteristics of 2D engineering graphics are as following [12]:

- The data of 2D engineering graphics include geometry and topology information.
- The redundancy of 2D engineering graphics is less than that of raster image.
- There is no concept of sampling rate in 2D engineering graphics, and mathematical operations such as DFT, DCT and DWT cannot be applied to its data directly.

Considering the afore-mentioned characteristics, approaches to watermarking for authenticating 2D engineering graphics is different from those to the watermarking of raster images, audio and video.

2.2 Log-Polar Transformation

Given a point (x_0, y_0) in the Cartesian coordinate system, if it is the origin of the polar coordinate system after transformation, any Cartesian coordinates (x, y) can be transformed into polar coordinates (r, θ) according to Eq. (1) [13]

$$\begin{cases} r = \sqrt{(x-x_o)^2 + (y-y_0)^2} \\ \theta = \tan^{-1} \dfrac{y-y_0}{x-x_0} \end{cases} , \tag{1}$$

where r represents the radial distance from the origin and θ represents the angle. It can be described as a complex number z,

$$z = x + iy = r(\cos\theta + i\sin\theta) = re^{i\theta} . \tag{2}$$

Applying log operation to Eq. (2), i.e.,

$$\ln z = \ln r + i\theta = u(r,\theta) + iv(r,\theta) .$$

We get the transformation from the polar coordinate system to the log-polar coordinate system as formulated in Eq. (3).

$$\begin{cases} u(r,\theta) = \ln r \\ v(r,\theta) = \theta \end{cases} . \tag{3}$$

If a pair of Cartesian or polar coordinates is scaled and rotated by a factor of r_0 and θ_0, respectively, then new polar coordinates would become $(r_0 r, \theta + \theta_0)$. Applying logarithm operation to $(r_0 r, \theta + \theta_0)$, we get

$$\ln z = \ln(r_0 r e^{i(\theta+\theta_0)}) = \ln r + \ln r_0 + i(\theta + \theta_0) = u(r,\theta) + iv(r,\theta) , \tag{4}$$

where

$$\begin{cases} u(r,\theta) = \ln r + \ln r_0 \\ v(r,\theta) = \theta + \theta_0 \end{cases} . \tag{5}$$

This indicates that scaling and rotation in the Cartesian coordinate system are equivalent to translation in the radial and angular axes in the log-polar coordinate system, respectively. Specially, if the centre of the log-polar system corresponds to the origin of the Cartesian coordinate system, r is invariant to rotation, θ is invariant to scaling, and both are invariant to translation in the log-polar system.

3 Semi-fragile Watermarking for 2D Engineering Graphics

Given a 2D engineering graphics G, where V represent the vertex set in G. In the proposed watermarking scheme, the vertices in V are first divided into n groups and then a vertex V_W is selected under the control of a secret key as watermarkable while the rest of the group are seen as non-watermarkable $\overline{V_w}$. Finally a content-dependent watermark w_i is embedded into the watermarkable vertex V_W of the corresponding group i. In a 2D engineering graphics, usually the coordinates of the vertices are represented in IEEE-754 double-precision format, as illustrated in Fig. 1.

	Sign	Exponent	Mantissa
bits	63	62 ~ 52	51 ~ 0

Fig. 1. IEEE-754 double-precision floating-point format

3.1 Generation of Watermark

Because each entity in a 2D engineering graphics has a unique handle value, and it is not changed even the entity is modified, so we use the handle values to construct the watermark. In order to improve the accuracy of tamper localization, topological information is considered in the generation of watermark information. Assuming the entity groups is a circular linked list, the generation of a b-bit watermark to be embedded in the ith group of entity E_i is described in Eq. (6),

$$w_i = Intcp((hash(H(V_{W_{i-1}})) \text{ XOR } hash(H(V_{W_i}))), b, K) \tag{6}$$

where $H(\cdot)$ is the method for acquiring the handle value , *hash*( ) represents a hash operation (MD5 is used in our algorithm) and *Intcp*(*A*, *b*, *K*) is a function that returns *b*(*b*>0, *b* is an even integer) bits from a string *A* in a random fashion under the control of a secret key *K*.

3.2 Watermark Embedding

The watermark embedding algorithm is presented as follows.

Step 1. Represent each entity of an *N*-entity 2D engineering graphics with the centroid of its vertices and store all centroids in an *N*-element array *E*. For example, given an entity E_i with *k* vertices $V_{E_i} = \{V_{E_i}^1, V_{E_i}^2, ..., V_{E_i}^k\}, k \geq 1$, the entity is represented by the centroid $(\frac{1}{k}\sum_{j=1}^{k}(V_{E_i}^j)_x, \frac{1}{k}\sum_{j=1}^{k}(V_{E_i}^j)_y)$, where $(V_{E_i}^j)_x$ and $(V_{E_i}^j)_y$ are the *x* and *y* coordinates of vertex $V_{E_i}^j$.

Step 2. Divide *E* into groups, each composed of *n* entities, and identify one vertex from each group as watermarkable vertex V_W and denote the non-watermarkable vertices as $\overline{V_M}$. The entity grouping and watermarkable entity identification are both under the control of the secret key *K*.

Step 3. Generate watermark w_i according to method described in Section 3.1.

Step 4. For each entity group, apply log-polar transformation to the watermarkable vertex V_W such that

$$\begin{cases} r_{V_M} = \sqrt{((E_V)_x - x_c)^2 + ((E_V)_y - y_c)^2} \\ \theta_{V_M} = \tan^{-1}\dfrac{(V_M)_y - y_c}{(V_M)_x - x_c} \end{cases}, \tag{7}$$

where $x_c = \frac{1}{n-1}\sum_{j \in \overline{V_M}}(V_j)_x$ and $y_c = \frac{1}{n-1}\sum_{j \in \overline{V_M}}(V_j)_y$ .From Eq. (7), we can see that the origin of the log-polar coordinate systems corresponds to the geometrical centre (x_c, y_c) of the *n*-1 non-watermarkable vertices in the Cartesian coordinate system.

Step 5. For each entity group, select *b* bits each, at random according to the secret key *K*, from the mantissa parts of r_{V_M} and θ_{V_M} , and substitute them with the watermark bit sequences w_i. Denote the watermarked vertex as V'_W.. For the convenience of verification, a new line type is used to mark the embedded entity that the watermarked vertex belongs to.

Step 6. For each entity group, perform the reverse log-polar transformation to the watermarked vertex E'_W.

Step 7. For each entity group, select one vertex at random according to the secret key *K* and adjust its coordinates so that the change to the centroid (See Step 1) due to watermark embedding is compensated for. This step is to ensure that the same centroid of each group can be obtained at the watermark verification stage.

3.3 Watermarks Verification

Given a 2D engineering graphics G' as input, the following algorithm is performed to extract and verify the embedded watermark based on the same secret key K used by the Watermark Embedding algorithm.

Step 1. Repeat Step 1 of Watermark Embedding algorithm to form a centroid array E'.

Step 2. According to the line type of the entities, divide E' into several groups, and identify one vertex from each group as watermarked vertex V'_W and denote the non-watermarkable vertices as $\overline{V_M}$. The entity grouping and watermarkable vertex identification are both under the control of the secret key K and a pre-defined line type.

Step 3. Generate watermark w_i according to method described in Section 3.1.

Step 4. For each entity group, apply log-polar transformation to the watermarked vertex V'_W according to Eq. (7)

Step 5. For each entity group, take b bits each, at random according to the secret key K, from the mantissa parts of r'_{v_w} and θ'_{v_w} as the watermark bit sequences w'_{i1} and w'_{i2}. If $w'_{i1} = w_i$ or $w'_{i2} = w_i$ the ith entity group is deemed authentic. Otherwise the group seen as tampered.

4 Experimental Results and Discussion

4.1 Experimental Results

The experiments are carried out on a PC with CPU P4 2.2G, RAM 1G, WinXP Professional, AutoCAD2006,VC++6.0 and DWGDirect 4.2. The results show the watermarking algorithm has a good performance in imperceptibility, robustness and ability of tampering location.

4.2 Discussion of the Robustness and Ability of Tamper Location

A. Analysis of robustness against translation, rotation and scaling
According to the properties of Log-polar transformation described in 2.2, it is easy to find the watermarking algorithm is robust against translation, rotation and scaling.

B. Analysis of ability of tamper localization
1). *Modification.* Generally, modification to entities can be classified into two categories: one is modification of vertices in E_W (watermarked), the other is modification of vertices in $\overline{E_W}$ (non-watermarked). As for the former, it may lead to modification of (r_{E_M} , θ_{E_M}) directly, while the later may lead to modification of coordinates (x_c, y_c), which will also change the value of (r_{E_M} , θ_{E_M}). As a result, the extracted watermark will be different from the original, thus the modification is detected.
2). *Entity addition.* For the entities in a 2D engineering graphics is traversed in temporal order, the newly added entities will be traversed last, and classified into the last

group. During the watermarks verification, the extracted watermark will be different from the generated watermark, thus the added entities are detected.
3). *Entity Deletion.* Entity deletion changes the topology of the 2D engineering graphics. Generally, entity deletion can be classified into three categories. The first category is that all deleted entities are only in $\overline{V_W}$ (non-watermarked). The second category is that some deleted entities are in V_W while some in $\overline{V_W}$. The third category is that the deleted entities form one or more complete embedding group. According to the grouping method described in Section 3.2, the first category only destroys the topology of the group and there is no influence to the relation between groups, which is similar to entity modification. The second category changes the grouping at Step 2 of the verification algorithm and as a result the extracted watermark is different from the original. As for the third category, the extracted watermark in the adjacent groups will be different from the original ones. For all situations will lead to incorrect verification, thus entity deletion is detected.

4.3 Performance Discussion

A. The relationship between embedding distortion and n
We use *root mean square* (*RMS*), as formulated in Eq. (8), to represent distortion inflicted on the graphics by the watermarking algorithm

$$RMS = \frac{1}{N}\left\| V - V' \right\| \tag{8}$$

where V' and V are the sets of vertices in the original 2D engineering graphics and its watermarked counterpart, respectively, and N is the number of vertices. The relationship of *RMS* and n is shown in Fig.2. With the increase of n, *RMS* decrease greatly, which means *RMS* is inversely proportional to n.

B. The relation between RMS and b and the relation between RMS and embedding positions
The bit positions where the watermarks are embedded and the length b of the watermark embedded in each group are another two factors affecting the embedding distortion. A small value of b leads to lower distortion. Theoretically, the embedding distortion would be less perceptible if the watermark is embedded in the least significant bits of the mantissa, but it may also reduce the scheme's authentication power in detecting malicious attacks because a floating number is not an accurate number, especially the value of the end part of the mantissa. On the other hand, embedding watermark in the most significant bits of the mantissa may cause visible distortion to 2D engineering graphics, so, the middle bits of the mantissa is a reasonable compromise between false-negative rate and distortion.

Given fixed watermark length b, the relation between *RMS* and embedding positions is shown in Fig. 3, where *SIM* represents the start embedding position. With the same *SIM*, *RMS* is proportional to b, which demonstrates our analysis above. The *RMS-SIM* relationships when the proposed algorithm is applied to 4 different graphics with b = 8 and n = 5 are shown in Fig. 4. After many experiments, we recommend that *SIM* should take value between 41 and 26, and b between 5 and 8 to ensure a good performance of the algorithm.

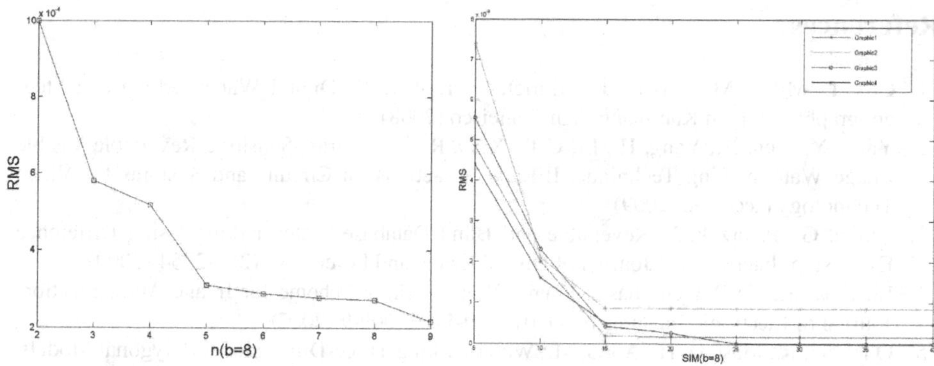

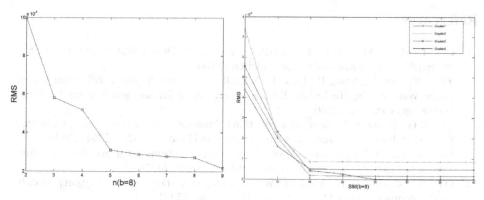

Fig. 2. Relationship between *RMS* and *n*

Fig. 4. Different *RMS* – *SIM* relationships of 4 different graphics given $b = 8$ and $n = 5$

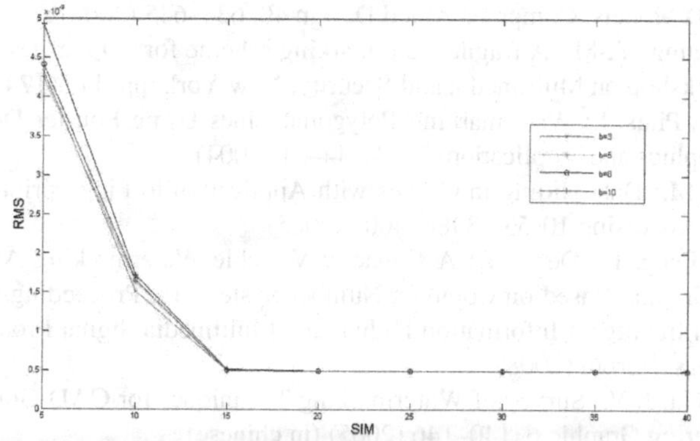

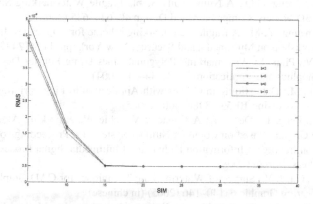

Fig. 3. Relationship between *RMS*- and *b*

5 Conclusions

A semi-fragile watermarking algorithm for verifying the content integrity of 2D engineering graphics is proposed in this work. To strike a good balance between the contradicting requirements of high authentication power, low embedding distortion and high accuracy of tamper localization, the watermark is generated by hashing the content of the graphics and embedded in the middle bits of the mantissa parts of the coordinates of graphical entities. Because the entity coordinates are transformed from the Cartesian system into the log-polar system before the watermark embedding takes place, the algorithm is tolerant to some incidental operations such as rotation, translation and scaling, but sensitive to malicious attacks.

Acknowledgement

This work is supported by Hunan Provincial Natural Science Foundation of China (09JJ4032, 08JJ4020).

References

1. Cox, I., Miller, M., Bloom, J., Fridrich, J., Kalker, T.: Digital Watermarking and Steganography. Morgan Kaufmann, San Francisco (2008)
2. Yang, Y., Sun, X., Yang, H., Li, C.T., Xiao, R.: A Contrast-Sensitive Reversible Visible Image Watermarking Technique. IEEE Transactions on Circuits and Systems for Video Technology (accepted, 2009)
3. Gupta, G., Pieprzyk, J.: Reversible and Blind Database Watermarking Using Difference Expansion. International Journal of Digital Crime and Forensics 1(2), 42–54 (2009)
4. Li, C.T., Si, H.: Wavelet-based Fragile Watermarking Scheme for Image Authentication. Journal of Electronic Imaging 16(1), 013009-1–013009-9 (2007)
5. Ohbuchi, R., Masuda, H., Aono, M.: Watermarking Three-Dimensional Polygonal Models. In: Proceeding of the ACM Multimedia 1997, pp. 261–272 (1997)
6. Chou, C.M., Tseng, D.C.: A Public Fragile Watermarking Scheme for 3D Model Authentication. Computer-Aided Design 38(11), 1154–1165 (2005)
7. Wang, W.B., Zheng, G.Q.: A Numerically Stable Fragile Watermarking Scheme for Authenticating 3D Models. Computer-Aided Design 40, 634–645 (2008)
8. Wu, H.T., Cheung, Y.-M.: A fragile watermarking scheme for 3D meshes. In: Proceedings of the 7th Workshop on Multimedia and Security, New York, pp. 117–124 (2005)
9. Solachidis, V., Pitas, I.: Watermarking Polygonal Lines Using Fourier Descriptors. IEEE Computer Graphics and Applications 3(24), 44–51 (2004)
10. Gou, H., Wu, M.: Data Hiding in Curves with Application to Fingerprinting Maps. IEEE Trans. Signal Processing 10(53), 3988–4005 (2005)
11. Huang, X.F., Peng, F., Deng, T.: A Capacity Variable Watermarking Algorithm for 2D Engineering Graphic Based on Complex Number System. In: Proceedings of International Conference on Intelligent Information Hiding and Multimedia Signal Processing, pp. 339–342. IEEE Press, Harbin (2008)
12. Huang, X.S., Gu, J.W.: Survey of Watermarking Techniques for CAD Graphic Data. Journal of Engineering Graphic 6, 140–146 (2005) (in chinese)
13. Zhang, W., Ren, X.Y., Zhang, G.L.: An Robust Object Locating Method Based On Log-polar Transform and Affine Transform. Journal of Image and Graphics 11(9), 1255–1259 (2006) (in Chinese)

On the Repudiability of Device Identification and Image Integrity Verification Using Sensor Pattern Noise

Chang-Tsun Li, Chih-Yuan Chang, and Yue Li

Department of Computer Science
University of Warwick
Coventry CV4 7AL
UK
{ctli,cyc,yxl}@dcs.warwick.ac.uk

Abstract. In this work we study the power of the methods for digital device identification and image integrity verification, which rely on sensor pattern noise as device signatures, and the repudiability of the conclusions drawn from the information produced by this type of methods. We prove that the sensor pattern noise existing in the original images can be destroyed so as to confuse the investigators. We also prove that sensor pattern noise of device A can be easily embedded in the images produced by another device B so that the device identifier would mistakenly suggest that the images were produced by device A, rather than by B, and mislead forensic investigations.

Keywords: Digital Device Identification, Digital Forensics, Digital Investigation, Digital Evidence, Sensor Pattern Noise, Integrity Verification.

1 Introduction

While digital imaging devices, such as digital cameras and scanners, bring unquestionable convenience of image acquisition, powerful image processing software also provides means for editing images so as to serve good and malicious purposes. To combat image manipulations for malicious purposes, researchers have proposed ways of verifying the integrity of images based on the detection of local inconsistencies of device attributes or data processing related characteristics, such as sensor pattern noise [1], camera response function [3], resampling artifacts [7], color filter array (CFA) interpolation artifacts [8, 12], and JPEG compression [10]. Similar device attributes and data processing related characteristics have also been exploited to identify and classify the source devices in aiding forensic investigation [2, 5, 6, 9, 11]. While many methods [3, 7, 8, 12] require that specific assumptions be satisfied, methods based on sensor pattern noise have drawn much attention due to the relaxation of the similar assumptions. The deterministic component of pattern noise is mainly caused by imperfections during the sensor manufacturing process and different sensitivity of pixels to light due to the inhomogeneity of silicon wafers [4]. It is because of the inconsistency and the uniqueness of manufacture imperfections and sensitivity to light that even sensors made from the same silicon wafer would possess uncorrelated pattern noise, which can be extracted from the images produced by the devices. This

D. Weerasinghe (Ed.): ISDF 2009, LNICST 41, pp. 19–25, 2010.

property makes sensor pattern noise a robust signature for identifying the origin and verifying the integrity of images.

Although good performance of source identification and integrity verification has been reported [1, 2, 5, 6, 9, 11], we observed that, due to the fact that sensor pattern noise is treated as additive signal to images during its extraction process, sensor pattern noise can be manipulated and substituted to confuse investigators and mislead forensic investigations. Therefore, the conclusions made by these methods can only be useful in aiding forensic investigations by narrowing down cases under investigation, but further research is necessary to enhance the non-repudiability of their findings before they can be accepted as admissible evidence in the court of law.

The rest of this work is organised as follows. We discuss the way digital source identifiers and integrity verifiers using sensor pattern noise work in Section 2 and prove how sensor pattern noise can be manipulated in Section 3. Section 4 concludes this work.

2 Device Identification and Image Integrity Verification Using Sensor Pattern Noise

Although the use of sensor pattern noise, $\boldsymbol{n}_D$, in different methods is slightly different, sensor pattern noise is commonly treated as an additive high-frequency signal to an image, $\boldsymbol{I}_D$, and the way it is extracted is similar to that used in [6], which is formulated as

$$\boldsymbol{n}_D = \boldsymbol{I}_D - F(\boldsymbol{I}_D) \tag{1}$$

where F is a denoising filtering function which filters out the sensor pattern noise. The subscript, D, indicates that $\boldsymbol{I}_D$ is an image taken by device D and $\boldsymbol{n}_D$ is the sensor pattern noise extracted from $\boldsymbol{I}_D$. Although various denoising filters can be used as F, the wavelet-based denoising filter described in [6] has been reported as effective in producing good results and our experiments confirm with the report. Therefore, this filter is used in the current work. We use the *average* of the sensor pattern noise, $\boldsymbol{P}_D$, of a set of images taken by a particular device D to represent that device. In this work, we call this *average* sensor pattern noise, $\boldsymbol{P}_D$, *signature* of sensor D in order to differentiate it from sensor pattern noise, $\boldsymbol{n}_D$, extracted from *individual* photos. The correlation of ρ_{AB}, as formulated in Eq. (2), between the sensor pattern noise $\boldsymbol{n}_A$ of an image $\boldsymbol{I}_A$ and $\boldsymbol{P}_B$ is used to decide whether image $\boldsymbol{I}_A$ is taken by device B.

$$\rho_{AB} = \frac{(\boldsymbol{n}_A - \overline{\boldsymbol{n}}_A)\cdot(\boldsymbol{P}_B - \overline{\boldsymbol{P}_B})}{\left\|\boldsymbol{n}_A - \overline{\boldsymbol{n}}_A\right\|\cdot\left\|\boldsymbol{P}_B - \overline{\boldsymbol{P}_B}\right\|} \tag{2}$$

where $\overline{\boldsymbol{n}}_A$ and $\overline{\boldsymbol{P}_D}$ are the means of $\boldsymbol{n}_A$ and $\boldsymbol{P}_D$, respectively. A large value of ρ_{AB} indicates high likelihood that $\boldsymbol{I}_A$ is taken by device B. We could expect that $\rho_{AA} > \rho_{AB}$ and $\rho_{BB} > \rho_{AB}$ if A and B are two different devices because ρ_{AA} and ρ_{BB} are *intra-class* metrics of similarity while ρ_{AB} indicates *inter-class* similarity.

On the other hand, methods for image integrity verification using sensor pattern noise, such as [1], are based on detecting local inconsistencies of sensor pattern noise blocks introduced into the forged images. The basic way of making use of sensor pattern noise is the same as that of device identifiers except that sensor pattern noise is extracted from each individual image *blocks* and compared to the corresponding blocks of the device signature, rather than the *whole* signature.

3 Potential Attacks

From the presentation in Section 2 and Eq. (1), we can see that digital device identifiers and image integrity verifiers using sensor pattern noise consider the sensor pattern noise as an additive signal to images. However, it is this additive nature of the sensor pattern noise that opens gap for potential attacks and manipulations. We present some experiments in the next two sub-sections to demonstrate how attacks with two different malicious intentions could be launched on photos taken by digital cameras. We call the first attack *Signature Removal*, which could be maliciously carried out to confuse investigators while the other attack –*Signature Substitution*, as we call it, could be applied to mislead forensic investigations.

3.1 Signature Removal

We define *Signature Removal* as an attack of removing the sensor signature $\boldsymbol{P}_A$ of image $\boldsymbol{I}_A$, taken by device A, using Eq. (3) so that the device identifiers cannot extract the sensor pattern noise.

$$\boldsymbol{I}_{A'} = \boldsymbol{I}_A - \alpha \boldsymbol{P}_A \tag{3}$$

where α is a positive strength factor determining the amount of sensor signature to be removed.

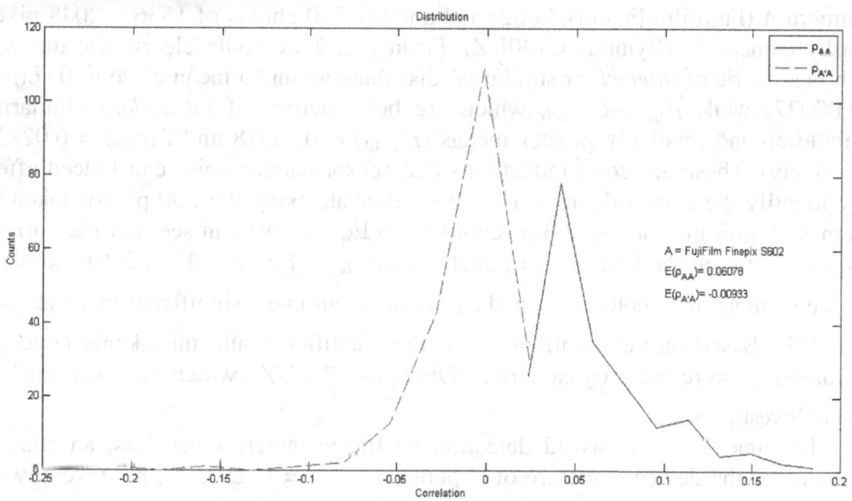

Fig. 1. Demonstration of *Signature Removal* attack

To evaluate the effect of *Signature Removal* attack, we apply Eq. (3) to 200 photos of 1536 × 2048 pixels taken by camera *A* (FujiFilm Finepix S602) in our experiment and demonstrate the results in Fig. 1. The blue solid curve is the distribution of the correlations between the sensor pattern noise of the 200 photos and the signature, $\boldsymbol{P}_A$, of camera *A*, with a mean $E(\rho_{AA})$ equal to 0.06078. After manipulating those 200 photos we extract the fake sensor pattern noise $\boldsymbol{n}_{A'}$ from each of them using Eq. (1) and then calculate the correlations $\rho_{A'A}$ according to Eq. (3), with $\alpha =$ 0.75. We can see from Fig. 1 that $\rho_{A'A}$, illustrated with red dashed curve, distribute around $E(\rho_{A'A})$ = -0.009334 (≈ 0), which far less than $E(\rho_{AA})$ (= 0.06078) of ρ_{AA}. This is a clear indication that the original sensor pattern noises, $\boldsymbol{n}_A$, have been removed from their corresponding host photos. This may well lead the forensic investigators to think that the photos in question were taken by some unknown cameras, but not by camera *A*.

3.2 Signature Substitution

We define *Signature Substitution* as an attack of removing signature, $\boldsymbol{P}_A$, of device *A* from image $\boldsymbol{I}_A$ taken by device *A* and then embedding the signature, $\boldsymbol{P}_B$, of device *B* so that device identifiers would mistakenly suggest that the manipulated image, $\boldsymbol{I}_{A'}$, were taken by device *B*, rather than by device *A*. The operation is as follows.

$$\boldsymbol{I}_{A'} = \boldsymbol{I}_A - \alpha \boldsymbol{P}_A + \beta \boldsymbol{P}_B \tag{4}$$

where α, like in Eq. (3), is a positive strength factor determining the amount of sensor signature of device *A* to be removed and β is also a positive strength factor determining the amount of sensor signature of device *B* to be embedded.

Fig. 2 demonstrates our experimental results when *Signature Substitution* (i.e., Eq. (4)) is applied, with $\alpha = \beta = 1$. In this experiment, we use the same 200 photos taken by camera *A* (FujiFilm Finepix S602) and another 200 photos of 1536 × 2048 pixels taken by camera *B* (Olympus C730UZ). From Fig. 2 we could clearly see that ρ_{AB}, which is a metric of *inter-class* similarity, distribute around a mean close to 0 ($E(\rho_{AB})$ = -0.00027) while ρ_{AA} and ρ_{BB}, which are both metrics of *intra-class* similarity, distribute around relatively greater means ($E(\rho_{AA})$ = 0.06078 and $E(\rho_{BB})$ = 0.02823, respectively). These are good indications that sensor pattern noise can indeed effectively identify the source devices. However, after attacking the 200 photos taken by camera *A* (FujiFilm Finepix S602) according to Eq. (4), we can see that the correlations, $\rho_{A'B}$, between the fake sensor pattern noise, $\boldsymbol{n}_{A'}$, (i = 1, 2, 3,…, 200), extracted from the manipulated photos, $\boldsymbol{I}_{A'}$, and $\boldsymbol{P}_B$ distribute around a significant mean ($E(\rho_{A'B})$ = 0.06723). Based on the significant $\rho_{A'B}$, the identifier would mistakenly conclude that images $\boldsymbol{I}_{A'}$ were taken by camera *B* (Olympus C730UZ), which may well mislead forensic investigations.

By the same token, to avoid detection by image integrity verifiers, an attacker could remove the device signature of *K* photos, $\boldsymbol{I}_{A_k}$ (k = 1, 2, 3, …, *K*), taken by the same or different devices using Eq. (3) to create $\boldsymbol{I}_{A'_k}$ before carrying out a forgery

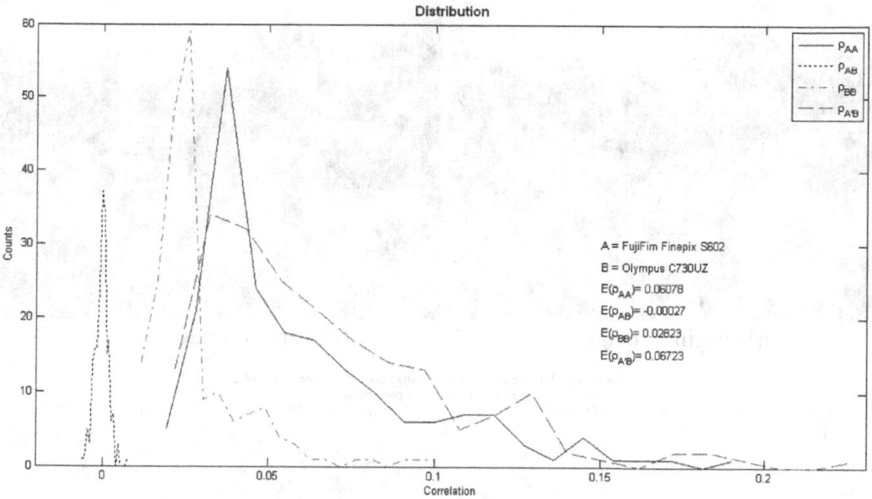

Fig. 2. Demonstration of *Signature Substitution* attack

operation to create a fake image $I_{A'}$. Finally, the attacker could embed the signature, P_B, of a specific device B to make the fake image $I_{A''}$ appear to be created by device B. The attack can be formulated as

$$I_{A''} = \sum_{k=1}^{K} I_{A'_k} + \beta P_B \tag{5}$$

where $I_{A'_k} = I_{A_k} - \alpha_k P_{A_k}$ (see Eq. (3)) and $\sum_{k=1}^{K}$, not to be taken as summation, is an arbitrary forgery operation, such as splicing and cut-and-paste, involving K images. Fig. 3 illustrates an original photo (Fig. 3(a)) and a forged image (Fig. 3(b)) with a car inserted in the foreground of the scene. Two photos (i.e., K = 2) taken by camera A (Olympus C730UZ) are used for forging Fig. 3(b). To avoid detection by the image integrity identifier, we applied Eq. (5) to make the device identifier believe that the forged photo was taken by another camera B after the forgery is done. Fig.3(c) illustrates the correlation $\rho_{A''B}$ when the signatures of six different cameras (Canon IXUS850IS, Canon PowerShot A400, Canon IXY DIGITAL 500, FujiFilm Finepix S602, FujiFilm Finepix A920 and Olympus FE210) are embedded. The significant correlations, which are close to the mean correlations between the signatures of the cameras and the photos they take suggest that the attack has been successful. Note that in our experiments involving the seven cameras mentioned in this work, the means of the intra-class correlation are all greater than 0.02, indicating that any correlation greater than 0.02 are significant.

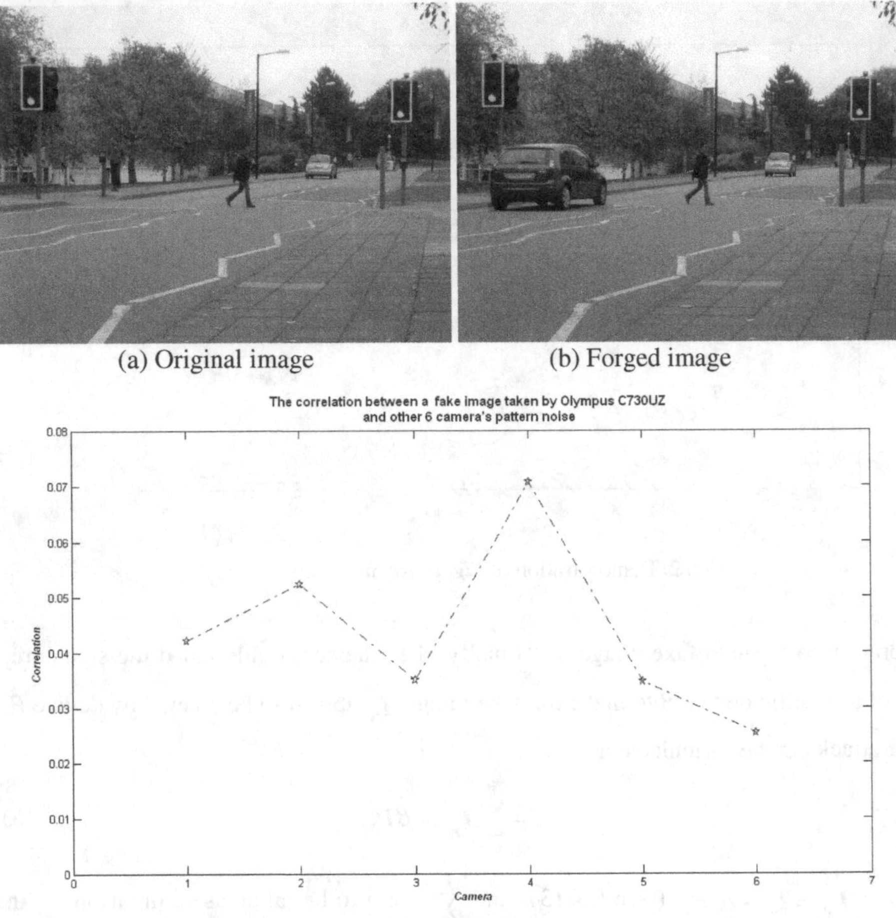

(c) correlation

Fig. 3. Demonstration of image forgery and Signature Substitution attack. a) The original image taken by an Olympus C730UZ camera. b) A forged image using photos taken by the same Olympus C730UZ camera with the sensor signature of FujiFilm Finepix S602 camera embedded. c) The correlations between the sensor pattern noises $n_{A''}$ extracted from Fig. 3(b) and the signatures of six cameras.

4 Conclusions

Sensor pattern noise has been reported in many articles as a robust signature of images produced by various digital devices, with great potential for device identification and integrity verification in the context of digital forensics. However, in this work, we have demonstrated that, due to its additive nature, the sensor pattern noise of an image can be manipulated to confuse forensic investigators or mislead investigations by applying the two attacks that we devised and presented in Section 3. We conclude that device identifiers and image integrity verifiers using sensor pattern noise are effective tools in aiding forensic investigations. Nevertheless, without further research to make the conclusions drawn by these methods non-repudiatable, it is unlikely that their conclusions will be accepted in the court of law as admissible evidence.

References

1. Chen, M., Fridrich, J., Goljan, M., Lukáš, J.: Determining Image Origin and Integrity Using Sensor Noise. IEEE Transactions on Information Forensics and Security 3(1), 74–90 (2008)
2. Gloe, T., Franz, E., Winkler, A.: Forensics for Flatbed Scanners. In: Proc. SPIE, Electronic Imaging, Security, Steganography, and Watermarking of Multimedia Contents IX, San Jose, CA, January 29-February 1, vol. 6505, pp. 1I–1J (2007)
3. Hsu, Y.F., Chang, S.F.: Image Splicing Detection Using Camera Response Function Consistency and Automatic Segmentation. In: Proc. IEEEInternational Conference on Multimedia and Expo., Beijin, China, July 2-5 (2007)
4. Janesick, J.R.: Scientific Charge-Coupled Devices, vol. PM83. SPIE, Bellingham (2001)
5. Khanna, N., Chiu, G.T.C., Allebach, J.P., Delp, E.J.: Forensic techniques for Classifiying Scanner, Computer Generated and Digital Camera Images. In: Proc. IEEE International Conference on Acoustics, Speech, and Signal Processing, Las Vegas, USA, 30 March-4 April, pp. 1653–1656 (2008)
6. Lukáš, J., Fridrich, J., Goljan, M.: Digital Camera Identification from Sensor Pattern Noise. IEEE Transactions on Information Forensics and Security 1(2), 205–214 (2006)
7. Popescu, A.C., Farid, H.: Exposing Digital Forgeries by Detecting Traces of Resampling. IEEE Transactions on Signal Processing 53(2), 758–767 (2005)
8. Popescu, A.C., Farid, H.: Exposing Digital Forgeries in Color Filter Array Interpolated Images. IEEE Transactions on Signal Processing 53(10), 3948–3959 (2005)
9. Sankur, B., Celiktutan, O., Avcibas, I.: Blind Identification of Cell Phone Cameras. In: Proc. SPIE, Electronic Imaging, Security, Steganography, and Watermarking of Multimedia Contents IX, San Jose, CA, January 29-February 1, vol. 6505, pp. 1H–1I (2007)
10. Sorell, M.J.: Digital Camera Source Identification through JPEG Quantisation. In: Li, C.-T. (ed.) Multimedia Forensics and Security. Information Science Publishing, Hershey (2008)
11. Sutcu, Y., Batram, S., Sencar, H.T., Memon, N.: Improvements on Sensor Noise based Source camera Identification. In: Proceeding of IEEE International Conference on Multimedia and Expo., Beijing, China, July 2-5, pp. 24–27 (2007)
12. Swaminathan, A., Wu, M., Liu, K.J.R.: Nonintrusive Component Forensics of Visual Sensors Using Output Images. IEEE Transactions on Information Forensics and Security 2(1), 91–106 (2007)

Virtualization Efficacy for Network Intrusion Detection Systems in High Speed Environment

Monis Akhlaq, Faeiz Alserhani, Irfan U. Awan, John Mellor, Andrea J. Cullen, and *Pravin Mirchandani

Informatics Research Institute, University of Bradford, Bradford, BD7 1DP, United Kingdom and
*Syphan Technologies (www.syphan.com)
{m.akhlaq2,f.m.f.alserhani,i.u.awan,j.e.mellor}@bradford.ac.uk,
a.j.cullen@braford.ac.uk, *pmirchandani@syphan.com

Abstract. The virtualization concept was developed a few decades back to facilitate the sharing of expensive and robust main-frame hardware among different applications. In the current scenario, virtualization has gone through a conceptual transformation from cost effectiveness to resource sharing. The research community has found virtualization to be reliable, multipurpose and adaptable. This has enabled a single system to dynamically map its resources among multiple instances of operating systems running numerous applications. The concept has been adopted on platforms dealing with network performance, application analysis, system design, network security and storage issues. This research work has focussed on analysing the efficacy of the virtualization concept for Network Intrusion Detection Systems (NIDS) in the high-speed environment. We have selected an open source NIDS, Snort for evaluation. Snort has been evaluated on virtual systems built on Windows XP SP2, Linux 2.6 and Free BSD 7.1 platforms. The test-bench is considered to be extremely sophisticated, ensuring current day network requirements. The evaluation has been targeted at the packet-handling capacity of operating systems/ applications (Snort) under different traffic conditions and on similar hardware platforms. Our results have identified a strong performance limitation of NIDS running on virtual platforms. It can be easily ascertained that virtual platforms are not ideal for NIDS in high-speed environments. Finally, the analysis has also identified the factors responsible for the unsatisfactory performance of IDS (Snort) on a virtual platform.

Keywords: Network intrusion detection systems, operating systems, performance evaluation, Snort, virtualization.

1 Introduction

Virtualization is a framework for abstracting the resources of a PC into multiple execution platforms by creating multiple machines on a single computer. Each machine operates on the allocated hardware and can afford multiple instances of applications [1]. This

D. Weerasinghe (Ed.): ISDF 2009, LNICST 41, pp. 26–41, 2010.

concept has been successfully incepted within the industry/ business community. The mechanics of system virtualization to implement network security tools has been considered as an appropriate choice for academia dealing with information security [2, 3].

Network Intrusion Detection Systems (NIDS) are considered to be an important security tool in any organization [4]. The effectiveness of any Intrusion Detection Systems (IDS) depends on its ability to handle various traffic-loads at maximum speed with minimal packet loss. The consequences of packet loss in any NIDS can be ascertained by considering the damages caused by single packet attacks-Witty worms [5]. Witty was the first widespread internet worm to attack a security product. It uses buffer overflow technique [6] to exploit a flaw in the firewall software [7]. From any perspective, packet capturing and handling are considered as major factors in deciding the efficiency of an IDS. Packet handling assumes an additional importance in relation to the use of virtual machines, where resources are shared between multiple platforms.

Snort [8], an open source NIDS has been selected because of its popularity and status as a de facto IDS standard. Snort relies on the packet capturing libraries (libpcap and winpcap) [9]. The libraries act as packet capturing interfaces to the underlying operating system [9]. Snort is a signature based IDS; it uses rules to detect hostile attempts to intrude onto a the network. The rules are a set of requirements created to generate an alert and have a particular syntax. On successful detection of a hostile intrusion, the detection engine sends an alert to a log file/storage resource [10].

Our research work focuses on evaluating the virtualization concept for NIDS in high-speed networks. Virtualization has found its acceptance in NIDS; however no comprehensive evaluation has done before. Mostly, the concept has been debated on perceived logics of resource conservation in virtualization without any experimental proof. We have analyzed the concept by utilizing open source NIDS- Snort under high-speed multi-Gbps environment. Our concept is unique in the sense that we have incorporated three different OS platforms and the evaluation criteria is based on packet handling capacity of Snort. The results are based on the response of Snort for different packet sizes and bandwidths representing actual network traffic.

The test-bench is built on VMware Server [11]; the VMware performs CPU virtualization by employing direct execution and binary translation. The software executes CPU instructions with minimum overheads. A guest operating system (OS) can run on the server without modification, thus ensuring a high degree of system compatibility.

Throughout the testing phase, VMware was installed on Windows Server 2008 [12]. Three virtual platforms were built on different OS platforms (Windows XP SP2 [13], Linux 2.6 [14] and Free BSD 7.1 [15]). These platforms were provided in all cases with equal hardware resources and subjected to similar traffic conditions. The responses of each platform were recorded and analyzed to reach the conclusions presented here.

This paper has been organized into sections; section 2 gives an overview of the virtualization concept employed, section 3 analyzes the factors affecting packet handling and section 4 describes the test-bench. Section 5 shows the results and finally in section 6 we present our analysis.

2 Virtualization

The concept has been developed to address the issues related to reliability, security, cost and complexity of the network/systems. It has successfully been used for the processing of legacy applications, ensuring load balancing requirements, resource sharing and tasking among virtual machines by using autonomic computing techniques. The technique has also shown merits in the situation where an application failure on one machine does not affect the other. In addition, ease of isolation allows multiple OS platforms to be built on one machine running variable instances of applications. This has made the concept quite fascinating for the research community [16].

Virtualization in information technology is the technique of creating a number of machines (guest machines) running on top of a physical machine (host machine). The guest machines use the hardware of the host machine and can manage multiple instances of applications running guest operating systems. Currently there are two kinds of server virtualization [17]:

2.1 Hosted Virtualization

This is also called as operating system (OS) based virtualization because the virtual layer on the host OS runs multiple instances of the guest OS. The guest OS operates as an independent platform and manages multiple applications as shown in Figure 1 [17].

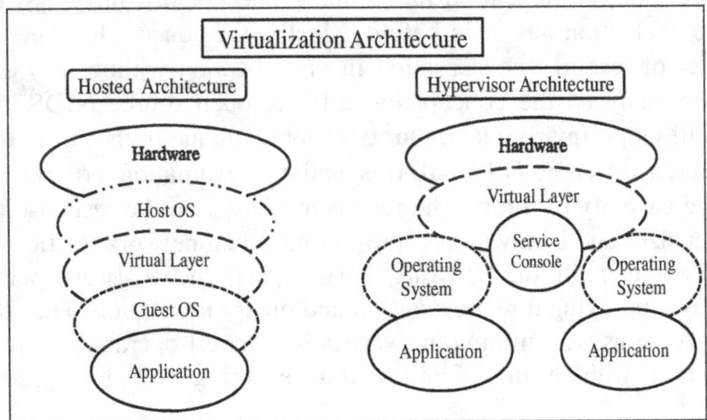

Fig. 1. Virtualization Architecture

2.2 Hypervisor Virtualization

Hypervisor; software manages the physical resources of the server by allocating the hardware resources of the machine to multiple virtual platforms. This concept uses two interfaces, a virtual layer and a service console. The virtual layer enables OS installation and the service console manages user applications as shown in Figure 1 [17].

3 Packet Handling

Packet capturing and handling is vital requirement for a NIDS. A good packet capturing response by the NIDS towards variant traffic reduces the probability of a system becoming compromised. Factors that affect the packet capturing performance of a NIDS in a Gigabit Ethernet environment include host configuration parameters (hardware and software) and application-specific parameters (NIDS).

3.1 System Hardware

3.1.1 Processor Speed and Architecture

The clock speed and the architecture of the processor directly impact the performance of a NIDS. Multi core and multithreaded architectures provide few performance gains in comparison with single processor as, many applications such as Snort Version 2.6 developed and optimized for legacy architectures fail to maximize these architectural advances [9].

3.1.2 PCI Bus and Disk Input/ Output (I/O) Operations

PCI bus architecture directly influences the operational efficiency of memory and storage devices. Current system architectures identify two bottlenecks in packet capturing accuracy – bus bandwidth and disk throughput. When writing to a disk, packet capture libraries pass data to the system bus twice, once from the network interface card to memory, and secondly from memory to disk. Thus the actual bandwidth available to the PCI bus is half that of the traffic bandwidth [18].

Table 1. PCI Buses and Disk System

Bandwidth – Current PCI Buses	
PCI Bus Parameters	Bandwidth
Standard 32 bit, 66 MHz	264 Mbytes/s
Standard 64 bit, 133 MHz	1,066 Mbytes/s
PCIexpress x 1	250 Mbytes/s
PCIexpress x 16	4000 Mbytes/s
PCIexpress x 32	8000 Mbytes/s

Bandwidth – Disk System	
Type	Transfer Rate
ATA/ATAPI Interface	133 Mbytes/s
SATA	**300 Mbytes/s**
SCSI (320)	320 Mbytes/s
Fiberchannel	512 Mbytes/s
SCSI (SAS)	348 Mbytes/s
SAS 2	768 Mbytes/s
SAS 3	1563 Mbytes/s

Data intensive applications and the huge amounts of data required to be stored in enterprise networks demand highly efficient I/O operations to avoid performance bottlenecks. The invention of multi-core processors has enhanced the capability of systems to support multiple virtual machines, yet system performance in relation to disk I/O operations remains limited [19]. Table 1 shows the types of I/O devices and their data transfer rates. The performance of these I/O devices in high-speed Gbps networks needs evaluation.

3.1.3 Memory

Alongside CPU capabilities, memory is another major factor affecting packet-handling ability. The memory controller is a part of the CPU sub-system and establishes information flow between memory and the CPU. The CPU sends a signal to the memory within a system clock cycle, which varies depending upon the speed of memory and bus speed. System performance is also affected by the speed at which the data can be transferred between system memory and the CPU. System bus and memory are the critical components when it comes to the efficiency of system in relation to packet handling [9].

When the system does not have enough main memory resources, virtual memory is used [9]. Virtual memory is allocated on the system hard disk. The performance of virtual memory in comparison to main memory is considered as a weak link in system performance [17].

3.1.4 Network Interface Card (NIC)

This component is directly connected to the physical media to interface to the data flow. The chosen NIC should correspond to the system capacity and network requirements. NICs are designed to offload the packet-capturing overhead by removing the system's CPU from this process. These devices are also capable of filtering, load balancing and regular expression functionality at hardware level [9].

The capacity of traditional NICs can also be enhanced by using specialized techniques such as [1]NAPI [20] and [2]PF_RING [21].

3.2 Operating System

The performance of an application also depends on the host operating system. In order to maximise performance gains, a suitable operating systems that supports the processor architectures is recommended. Ideally system performance can be increased by using an operating system with multithreaded kernel architecture on a multiprocessor machine.

3.3 NIDS and Packet Capturing Libraries

Snort has been selected as the target IDS platform for this research; this section describes the packet processing capabilities of Snort with an emphasis on its packet capture libraries [9].

- It calls libpcap by using the pcap_dispatch function to process waiting packets.
- For each available packet, libpcap calls the PcapProcessPacket function to perform packet processing. This function resets several per-packet counters, collects packet statistics and calls ProcessPacket.
- The ProcessPacket function handles all the actions involved in decoding the packet and printing in verbose mode. It can also call the logging functions if running in logger mode or call the pre-processors if running in IDS mode.

---

[1] NAPI ("New Application Programming Interface") is a modification to the device driver packet processing framework, which is designed to improve the performance of high-speed networking.

[2] Type of socket (PF_RING) optimization for packet capturing techniques based on a circular buffer.

A limitation of Snort is that it can only process a single packet at a time. Its pcap and inline API (Inline application programming interface) provide buffering resources; however any prolonged processing causes the buffers to fill and packets start to be dropped as a result. Additionally, the [3]Frag3 and [4]Stream4 pre-processors deal with multiple packets received by the system. Any missing packet forces Snort to wait till the session time out thus causing memory and CPU drain. This also creates a feedback loop where lost packet cause additional packet loss causing overall system degradation.

Another area that has an impact on packet drop rates is the technique of retrieving packets from the network interface using the pcap API (Packet Capturing application Programming interface). A few improvements in these techniques have been suggested in [21], [22] and [23], however increases in traffic-loads and speed considerably reduce the positive impact of these modifications.

4 Performance Test

4.1 Test-Bench

The test-bench is distributed into three parts and configured around a ProCurve series 2900 switch [24] as shown in Figure 2.

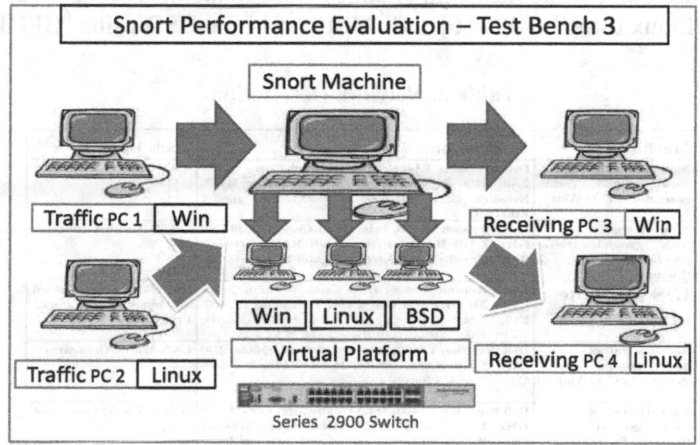

Fig. 2. Test-bench

The basic idea of the evaluation process revolves around packet capturing and evaluation by virtual platforms and Snort. We have selected two machines for traffic generation: Linux 2.6 and Windows XP SP2 platforms respectively. Similarly, the traffic reception machines were also deployed to fulfil network requirements. Details of the traffic generation tools are shown in Table 2.

[3] IP defragmentation preprocessor in Snort.

[4] Verify & reassembles TCP sessions in Snort.

The virtual platform running Snort has been configured on a dual quad-core processor. The machine hardware details are listed in Table 2. The system is built on the Windows 2008 Server platform and three separate virtual platforms have been created- Windows XP SP2, Linux 2.6 & Free BSD 7.1. Snort is running simultaneously on all the virtual machines and similar traffic-loads and type are injected onto all platforms.

4.2 Evaluation Methodology

In order to ascertain the capability of Snort to handle high-speed network traffic on virtual platforms we proceeded as follows:

- Parallel Snort sessions were run on all virtual machines.
- The machines were injected with similar traffic-load characteristics (UDP and TCP Traffic) for 10 minutes.
- Different packet sizes (128, 256, 512, 1024 and 1460 bytes) were generated and Snort's performance at the following traffic-load was evaluated: 100 Mbps, 250 Mbps, 500 Mbps, 750 Mbps, 1.0 Gbps and 2.0 Gbps respectively.
- Snort's performance characteristics were evaluated - packets received, packets analysed, packets dropped and CPU usage at various packet sizes and band widths levels.
- Packets received were compared at both the host OS and the virtual platforms running the Snort applications.
- During the course of the tests, no changes were made in OS implementation specifically Linux using NAPI [16] and [5]MMP and Free BSD using [6]BPF [27].

Table 2. Network Description

Machine Type	Description	Tools Used
Network traffic/ back ground traffic generator- PC 1 (Win)	Dell Precision T3400, Intel D Quad-Core, Q6600 2.40 GHz. 2 GB RAM, PCIe, 1Gb/s RJ45, Network Card (Broadcom NetXtremo gigabit Ethernet).	LAN Traffic Generator [25]
Network traffic/ back ground traffic generator - PC 2 (Linux)	Dell Precision T3400, Intel Quad-Core, Q6600 2.40 GHz. 2 GB RAM, PCIe, 1Gb/s RJ45, Network Card (Broadcom NetXtremo gigabit Ethernet).	D-ITG Traffic Generator [26]
IDS Machine (Snort)	Dell Precision T5400, Intel (Xenon) Dual Quad-Core, 2.0 GHz. 4.0 GB RAM, L2 Cache 12 MB, PCIe, Network Card , 10 GB Chelsio. Hard Disk: 1000 GB, Buffer 32 MB, SATA 300.	VM Ware Server, Virtual Machines (Win, Linux, Free BSD)
Network traffic/ back ground traffic Receiver- PC 3 (Win)	Dell Precision T3400, Intel Quad-Core, Q6600 2.40 GHz. 2 GB RAM, PCIe, 1Gb/s RJ45, Network Card , 10 GB Chelsio.	LAN Traffic Generator
Network traffic/ back ground traffic Receiver- PC 4 (Linux)	Dell Precision T3400, Intel Quad-Core, Q6600 2.40 GHz. 2 GB RAM, PCIe, 1Gb/s RJ45, Network Card (Broadcom NetXtremo gigabit Ethernet).	D-ITG Traffic Generator
Switch	ProCurve Series 2900, 10Gb/s switch with 24x1 Gb/s ports and 2x10 Gb/s 3CR17762-91-UK ports.	

5 Results

The results are distributed over UDP and TCP traffic types respectively. It was observed that the total packets transmitted from the traffic-generating PCs was

[5] Modified device drivers packet handling procedures.
[6] Berkley Packet filter.

Table 3. Packets Received at Host Operating Systems

Total Packets Received at OS (Millions) – UDP

Bandwidth	128 Bytes	256 Bytes	512 Bytes	1024 Bytes	1460 Bytes
100 MB	60	35.82	17.77	10.56	6.96
250 MB	178.1	94.14	48.00	18.34	20.22
500 MB	358.3	148.29	92.56	46.2	39.00
750 MB	System Non Responsive		144.72	91.56	45.23
1.0 GB	System Non Responsive			167.40	78.00
2.0 GB	System Non Responsive				

Total Packets Received at OS (Millions) – TCP

Bandwidth	50 Connections	100 Connections	200 Connections
100 MB	10	26.7	21.60
250 MB	31.86	39.763	48.69
500 MB	67.90	108.56	84.098
750 MB	80.29	113.72	124.58
1.0 GB	102.51	118.144	148.982
2.0 GB	147.54	170.994	221.28

equivalent to the number of packets received at the host machine/ OS running virtual platforms as shown in Table 3; however this is not the case once the system found [7]non responsive.

5.1 UDP Traffic

The results below are described in relation to packet size, bandwidth (i.e. traffic-load), and the virtual OS platform running the Snort application:

5.1.1 Snort Response for Packet Sizes – 128 & 256 Bytes

- Linux shows quite good performance for these packet-sizes upto 250 Mbps traffic-load; its performance declined at higher bandwidth levels as shown in Figure 2. The system found non responsive at the traffic-loads of 750 Mbps and above.

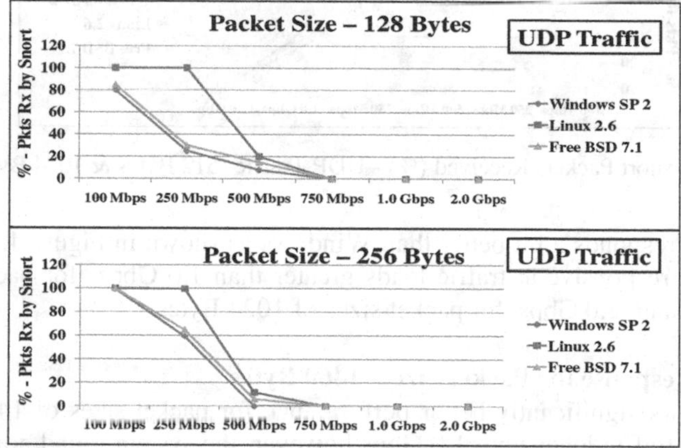

Fig. 3. Snort Packets Received (%) - UDP Traffic (128 Bytes & 256 Bytes)

[7] In non responsive situation we consider 100% packet loss.

- Windows shows good performance for 128 Bytes packet sizes at 100 Mbps loading only. Its performance is compromised at higher loading levels as shown in Figure 3. The system also found non responsive at traffic-loads of 750 Mbps and above.
- Free BSD performs slightly better than Windows as shown in Figure 3. The system also found non responsive at traffic-loads of 750 Mbps and above.

5.1.2 Snort Response for Packet Size – 512 & 1024 Bytes

- Linux shows quite good performance for traffic-load upto 500 Mbps for all packet sizes as shown in Figure 4. The Linux however system found non responsive at traffic-loads of 1.0 Gbps and above for 512 Bytes packet sizes and at 2.0 Gbps for packet sizes of 1024 Bytes.
- Windows also performed satisfactorily at traffic-loads of 250 Mbps and 500 Mbps for packet sizes of 512 Bytes and 1024 Bytes respectively as shown in Figure 4. The system found non responsive at traffic-loads of 1.0 Gbps and above for packet size of 512 Bytes and 2.0 Gbps for packet sizes of 1024 Bytes.

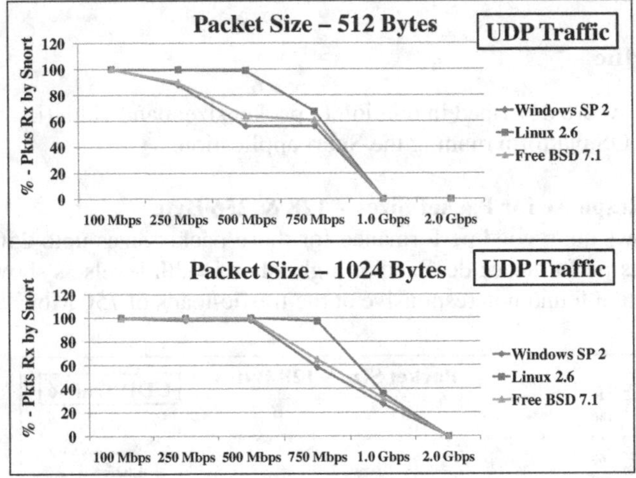

Fig. 4. Snort Packets Received (%) - UDP Traffic (512 Bytes & 1024 Bytes)

- Free BSD responds a bit better than Windows as shown in Figure 4. The system found non responsive at traffic-loads greater than 1.0 Gbps for packet sizes of 512 Bytes and 2.0 Gbps for packet sizes of 1024 Bytes.

5.1.3 Snort Response for Packet Size – 1460 Bytes

- Linux shows significantly better performance for packet sizes of 1460 Bytes of packet for traffic-loads upto 1.0 Gbps however, the system found non responsive at 2.0 Gbps loading as shown in Figure 5.
- Windows also shows good performance upto750 Mbps loading. The system found non responsive at 2.0 Gbps traffic-load as shown in Figure 5.

- Free BSD responds a bit better than Windows as shown in Figure 5. The system found non responsive at 2.0 GB traffic-load as shown in Figure 5.

5.2 TCP Traffic

We have included the results of 512 Bytes packet sizes in this section due to paucity of space. The results have been accumulated on the basis of successful connections (50, 100 and 200 respectively). Packets received at the host platform/ OS are shown in Table 3.

5.2.1 Snort Response for 50 Connections – 512 Byte

- Linux exhibits quite good performance upto 750 Mbps loading however, its performance declined at higher traffic-loads as shown in Figure 5.
- Windows was acceptable upto 250 Mbps loading and its performance reduced for higher traffic-loads as shown in Figure 5.
- Free BSD performed a bit better than Windows as shown in Figure 5.

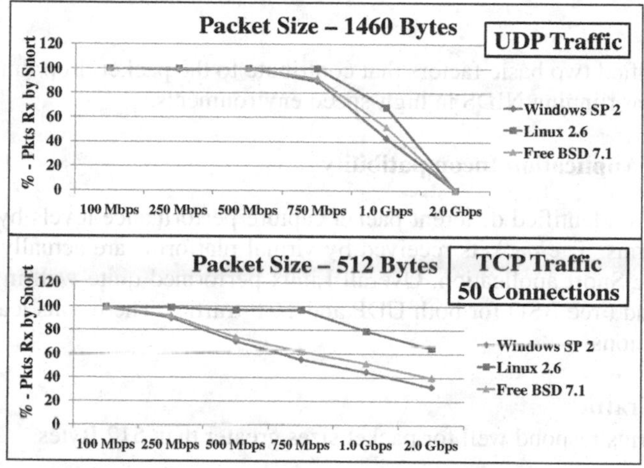

Fig. 5. Snort Packets Rx (%) - UDP (1460 Bytes) & TCP (50 Connections)

5.2.2 Snort Response for 100/ 200 Connections – 512 Bytes

- Linux exhibits quite good performance upto 250 Mbps loading with minimum packet loss, however, its response linearly declined for higher traffic-loads as shown in Figure 6.
- Windows also exhibits a similar performance level upto 250 Mbps loading levels and its performance declined for higher traffic-loads as shown in Figure 6.
- Free BSD performs a bit better than Windows as shown in Figure 6.

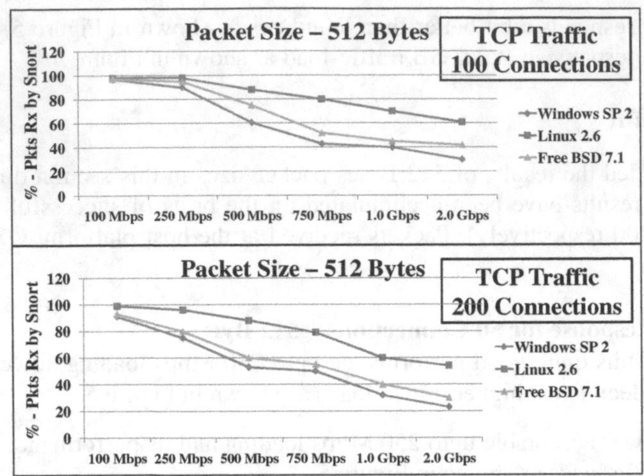

Fig. 6. Snort Packets Received (%) - TCP Traffic (100 & 200 Connections)

6 Analysis

We have identified two basic factors that contribute to the packet-drop limitation in virtual platforms running NIDS in high-speed environments.

6.1 OS and Application Incompatibility

The results have identified different packet capture performance levels by the respective OS platforms. The packets received by virtual platforms are actually the packets received by the Snort application. Overall Linux performed quite well in comparison to Windows and Free BSD for both UDP and TCP traffic. The results lead to the following conclusions:

6.1.1 UDP Traffic

- All platforms respond well for packet sizes greater than 512 Bytes.
- For packet sizes of 128 Bytes and 256 Bytes, Linux performs significantly better than others; however its performance declines above 250 Mbps loading. Windows and Free BSD performed well for 128 Bytes at 100 Mbps traffic-load only.
- All OS platforms non responsive at packet sizes of 128 Bytes and 256 Bytes above 500 Mbps of traffic-loads.
- There were practically no measurable results from all the platforms at 2.0 Gbps loading for all packet sizes.
- The overall performance standing measured was Linux, followed by Free BSD, with Windows in last position.

6.1.2 TCP Traffic

- The systems remain alive for all packet sizes and number of connections for traffic-loads upto 2.0 Gbps.
- The performance of the systems linearly declined in response to increases in the number of connections and traffic-loads.
- Linux outperforms Windows and Free BSD in all the tested scenarios.

6.1.3 Evaluating OS Packet Handling Competency

In order to reach a definite conclusion concerning OS incompatibility as regards the virtualization of NIDS in high-speed networks environments, we extended the research to conduct some additional tests. These tests comprised of three virtual machines built on the same OS platform (Free BSD). The Snort application was activated on all platforms and similar tests were conducted as described in section 4.2. In the first scenario, three machines were operational and in the second one, two were running. The performance of the system was analysed to reach a conclusion.

6.1.4 OS Performance Analysis

In the first scenario, with Free BSD configured on three parallel virtual platforms similar performance metrics were observed. As such the performance of Free BSD was found to be quite similar to the previously executed test-bench scenario and only a small amount of variation was observed. In the second two-machine scenario, an improvement in performance was observed; however performance levels declined at higher traffic-loads. Due to a paucity of space we have only included the results of 512 Bytes of packet size for UDP Traffic as shown in Figure 7. The graph shows the average performance of systems in each scenario.

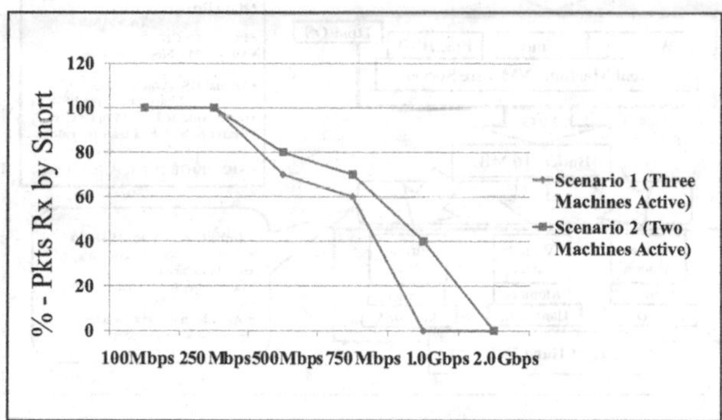

Fig. 7. Snort Packet Received (%) – Free BSD on Three/ Two virtual platforms

The performance of Free BSD in the two scenarios has identified a direct link between packet capturing ability of the system and the use of hardware resource sharing. The results shows that two platforms perform significantly well in comparison to the use of three virtual machines. Thus, it can be concluded that the packet capturing performance for NIDS when run as multiple virtual instances is limited due to the impact of hardware resource sharing and there is no direct relationship to OS itself. Similar tests were also conducted on Linux and Windows platforms; due to space restrictions we have not included the results here. Both platforms behaved in a similar patter as that of Free BSD thus confirming the hardware resource sharing limitation.

6.2 Hardware Incompatibility in Virtualization

The dynamics of virtualization requires the Host OS and the Virtual Machine software (VMware Server) to be stored in the physical memory (RAM) of the host machine. The virtual machines (Windows XP SP 2, Linux 2.6 and Free BSD 7.0) running on VMware Server have been respectively allocated virtual RAM and disk space on the physical hard drive of the host machine. The processes/ applications running on the virtual machines use these simulated virtual RAMs and hard disks for the various operations shown in Figure 8.

Our test-bench has multiple instances of Snort and packet-capture libraries running on different virtual platforms each with a different OS. The packets captured by each virtual machine are less than the packets received by the NIC, thus identifying packet loss somewhere in between. The basic cause of packet loss at each OS apart from the losses incurred by Snort during evaluation is the bottleneck caused by a low disk data transfer rate. The disk I/O statistics as shown in Figure 9 reflects the hardware limitations in handling multiple read/write operations. At 300 Mbps of traffic-load, the disk I/O capacity touches 100% thus its performance at higher loads can be easily ascertained.

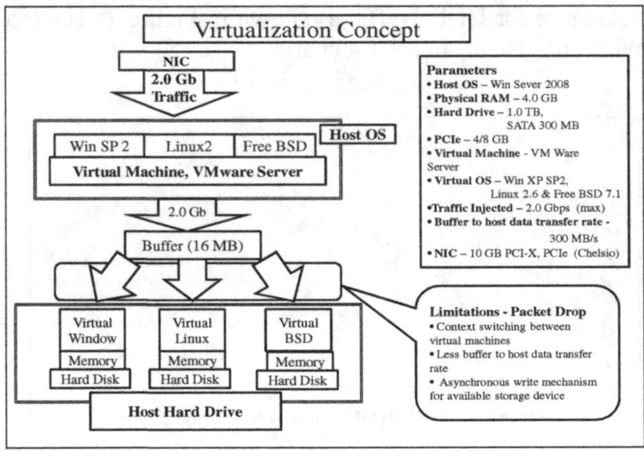

Fig. 8. Virtualization Concept

The memory and storage for each virtual machine has actually been allocated on the physical storage resources (i.e. hard disk) of the host machine. Packets received by the NIC without any loss are transferred to the hard disk buffer at the PCI rate (4/8 Gbps). From this buffer, these packets are required to be written to the disk at the buffer- to-host transfer rate of 300 MB/sec (SATA Hard Drive [28]); thus a huge gap between the disk-transfer rate and the incoming traffic load exists. In addition, traffic

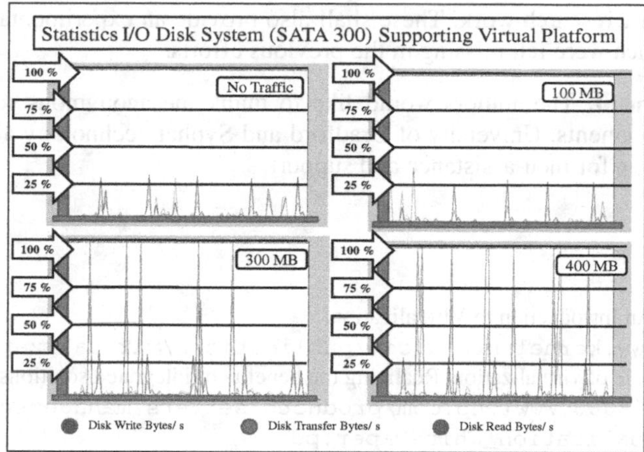

Fig. 9. Statistics I/O System (SATA 300) Hard Drive

is fed to all virtual machines simultaneously (in parallel mode), the disk is physically only able to write to one location at a time. Thus any disk-write instance to a virtual machine, will cause packet drops on another. There are also some additional packet losses due to context switching within the hard disk.

In order to augment our analytical stance of showing hardware as one of the major bottlenecks for the efficacy of the virtualization concept for NIDS in high-speed networks we have utilized the disk queue length counter as shown in Figure 10. In normal circumstances, the average disk queue length should be three or less (its ideal value) [29]. However; in our test network, it is observed to be always greater than the ideal value for the traffic ranges measured at 2.0 Gbps.

7 Conclusion

This research has focused on ways of determining the efficacy of the virtualization concept for NIDS in high-speed network environments. The test scenarios employed involved the use of the widely deployed open-source NIDS, namely Snort. The results obtained have shown a number of significant limitations in the use of virtual NIDS, where both packet-handling and processing capabilities at different traffic loads were used as the primary criteria for defining system performance. We have confirmed that the underlying host hardware plays a prominent role in determining overall system performance. We have further shown that performance is further degraded as the number of virtual instances of NIDS is increased, irrespective of the virtual OS used. Furthermore, we have demonstrated a number of significant differences in the performance characteristics of the three different virtual OS environments in which Snort was run.

This work has identified specific and replicable bottlenecks in commonly used implementations of virtualization for a widely used NIDS in high-speed networks. The results obtained can be taken as a benchmark for improving the performance of these systems in future research work. These shall also provide an experimental data to the researchers which were felt missing in the previous efforts.

Acknowledgement. The authors would like to thank the anonymous reviewers for their insight comments. University of Bradford and Syphan technology also deserved deep appreciation for their assistance and support.

References

1. Singh, A.: An Introduction to Virtualization, `http://www.kernelthread.com/publications/virtualization`
2. Business value of virtualization: Realizing the benefits of integrated solutions, `http://h18000.www1.hp.com/products/servers/management/vse/Biz_Virtualization_WhitePaper.pdf`
3. Virtualization, `http://www.windowsecurity.com/whitepapers/Virtualization.html`
4. Inella, P.: An Introduction to IDS, `http://www.securityfocus.com/infocus/1520`
5. Shannon, C., Moore, D.: The spread of the Witty Worm. IEEE Security and Privacy 2(4), 46–50 (2004)
6. Buffer overflow, `http://www.mcafee.com/us/local_content/white_papers/wp_ricochetbriefbuffer.pdf`
7. The spread of Witty worms, `http://www.caida.org/research/security/witty`
8. Snort, `http://www.Snort.org/`
9. Baker, A.R., Esler, J.: Snort IDS and IPS Toolkit, Syngress, Canada (2007)
10. Alserhani, F., Akhlaq, M., Awan, I., Cullen, A., Mellor, J., Mirchandani, P.: Evaluating Intrusion Detection Systems in High Speed Networks. In: Fifth International Conference of Information Assurance and Security (IAS 2009). IEEE Computer Society, Los Alamitos (in press, 2009)
11. VMware Server, `http://www.vmware.com/products/server/`
12. Windows Server (2008), `http://www.microsoft.com/windowsserver2008/en/us/default.aspx`
13. Windows XP SP2, `http://www.softwarepatch.com/windows/xpsp2.html`
14. Linux 2.6, `http://www.kernel.org/`
15. Free BSD 7.1, `http://www.freebsd.org/where.html`
16. Xu, J., Zhao, M., Fortes, J.A.B., Carpenter, R., Yousif, M.: On the Use of Fuzzy Modelling in Virtualized Data Center Management. In: Proceedings of 4th International Conference on Autonomic Computing, ICAC 2007 (June 2007)
17. Virtualization and disk performance /pdf/Virtualization_, `http://files.diskeeper.comPerformance.pdf`
18. Schneider, F., Wallerich, J., Feldmann, A.: Packet capture in 10-gigabit ethernet environments using contemporary commodity hardware. In: Uhlig, S., Papagiannaki, K., Bonaventure, O. (eds.) PAM 2007. LNCS, vol. 4427, pp. 207–217. Springer, Heidelberg (2007)

19. Optimizing network infrastructure for virtualization, `http://www.dell.com/downloads/global/power/ps3q08-20080375-Intel.pdf`
20. Salim, J.H., Olsson, R., Kuznetsov, A.: Beyond Softnet. In: Proceedings of USENIX 2001, November 2001, pp. 165–172 (2001)
21. Deri, L.: Improving Passive Packet Capture: Beyond Device Polling. In: Proceedings of the 4th International System Administration and Network Engineering Conference, Amsterdam (September 2004)
22. Biswas, A., Sinha, P.: A high performance packet capturing support for Alarm Management Systems. In: 17th International conference on Parallel and Distributed Computing and Systems (PDCS), Phoenix (2005)
23. Salah, K., El-Badawi, K.: Performance Evaluation of Interrupt-Driven Kernels in Gigabit Networks. In: The IEEE Global Telecommunications Conference, GLOECOM 2003, December 2003, pp. 3953–3957 (2003)
24. ProCurve Series 2900 switch, `http://www.hp.com/rnd/products/switches/HP_ProCurve`
25. LAN Traffic V 2, `http://www.topshareware.com/lan-traffic-v2/downloads/1.html`
26. D-ITG V 2.6, `http://www.grid.unina.it/Traffic/index.php`
27. Berkley Packet Filter, `http://www.freebsd.org/releases/7.1R/relnotes.htm`
28. SATA Technology, `http://www.serialata.org/`
29. Disk Queue Length Counter, `http://www.windowsnetworking.com/articles_tutorials/Windows-Server-2003-PerfTuning.html`

Face Recognition Using Balanced Pairwise Classifier Training

Ziheng Zhou, Samuel Chindaro, and Farzin

School of Engineering and Digital Arts, University of Kent, Canterbury, UK
{z.zhou,s.chindaro,f.deravi}@kent.ac.uk

Abstract. This paper presents a novel pairwise classification framework for face recognition (FR). In the framework, a two-class (intra- and inter-personal) classification problem is considered and features are extracted using pairs of images. This approach makes it possible to incorporate prior knowledge through the selection of training image pairs and facilitates the application of the framework to tackle application areas such as facial aging. The non-linear empirical kernel map is used to reduce the dimensionality and the imbalance in the training sample set tackled by a novel training strategy. Experiments have been conducted using the FERET face database.format.

Keywords: face recognition, classification, aging.

1 Introduction

Face recognition (FR) has become one of the most important application areas for image analysis and understanding. Various feature-extraction techniques have been introduced and very often, large sets of features are extracted from a facial image (e.g., the Gabor features [1-3]) for classification. The question remains in how to best exploit the richness of such large feature sets and increasingly large training data sets to answer some of the challenging FR applications, such as compensating for the facial changes caused by aging [4].

The traditional approach to using large feature sets [5] is to find a subspace of the original feature space, which preserves as much subject-invariant information as possible. In other words, after a linear transformation from the original feature space to the subspace, the mapped feature points calculated from the images of the same person are made to be as close to each other as possible. By doing so, the intra-personal variations remaining in the feature sets are minimized and the distances between feature points are used to quantify the similarities between faces. Unlike other biometric modalities such as fingerprint and iris, human faces keep changing over our life time. In such a traditional FR approach, as the difference caused by aging becomes large, it becomes difficult to determine whether two images belong to the same person only by their measured distance.

Instead of ignoring the intra-personal variations within face images, we want to build an FR system that models the variations to handle facial aging. To do that, it needs to define a feature-extraction function $f: \mathfrak{I} \times \mathfrak{I} \rightarrow \mathbb{R}^m$ to explicitly characterize the difference between two faces. Here $\mathfrak{I}$ is the image domain and $\mathbb{R}^m$ denotes the

D. Weerasinghe (Ed.): ISDF 2009, LNICST 41, pp. 42–49, 2010.

feature space with dimension m. It can be seen that any set of features $\boldsymbol{x} = f(I_1, I_2)$, $I_1, I_2 \in \mathfrak{T}$ can be classified either as *intra-personal,* if images I_1 and I_2 are from the same person, or *inter-personal* otherwise. Therefore, the FR problem is turned into a supervised two-class classification problem. When someone uses the system, a feature vector is calculated from his (her) current captured facial image and a previously-enrolled stored image. The feature vector is then classified into one of the two classes, telling whether or not the two images are from the same person.

One attractive advantage of this approach is that the FR system can be built in such a way that our prior knowledge can be incorporated in the selection of the training pairs from which the features are extracted. The guiding knowledge for this selection can be any desired characteristic of the image pairs to be classified. For instance, when comparing two facial images, the information about when they are taken is a source of prior knowledge that can be used. Here the training set presented to the classifier is called the feature training set (FTS) and consists of the feature vectors calculated from the selected image pairs chosen from the training set (TS) of facial images. Note that although considering FR as a two-class classification problem [6] is not new, the idea of incorporating prior knowledge within such an approach as presented here is novel.

Although the classification methods can be used to tackle facial aging, there are difficulties in building such aging-adaptive FR systems. First, as mentioned above, the number of features extracted from images could be very large making the search for a classification solution in such a high-dimensional feature spaces very difficult. Secondly, since in the proposed approach image pairs are selected to calculate feature sets for training, there could be a large imbalance between the number of intra-personal pairs and the number of inter-personal pairs. Fig. 1 illustrates this imbalance.

In this paper, we propose a novel pairwise classification framework (PCF) that tackles the difficulties mentioned above. To demonstrate the framework's capability of handling high-dimensional feature vectors, the Gabor wavelets are used to calculate features from image pairs. To solve the two-class classification problem, we first reduce the dimensionality of the feature vectors using the non-linear empirical kernel map [7]. The Fisher's discriminant analysis is then used to find a classification

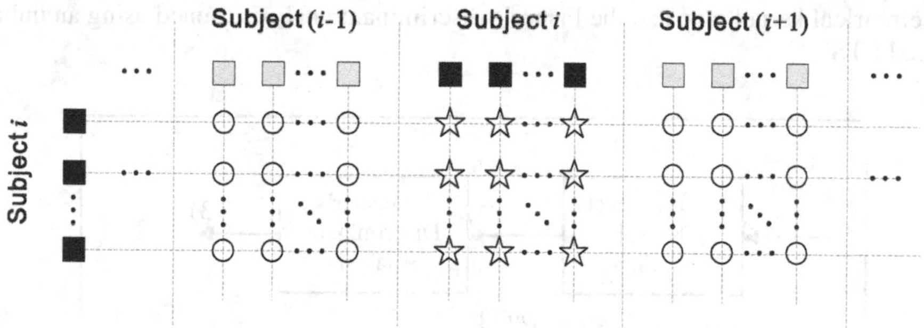

Fig. 1. An example showing the imbalance between the number of intra-personal pairs and the number of inter-personal pairs that can be sampled for Subject ***i***. The black squares represent images of Subject ***i*** and rest of the squares stand for other images. The stars mark all possible intra-personal image pairs for Subject ***i***, while the circles locate the inter-personal image pairs.

solution. A novel training strategy is proposed to tackle the imbalance within the training data. The FERET face database [8] is used for testing.

The rest of the paper is organized as following: Sections 2 and 3 describe the feature-extraction method and classifier training. Section 4 and 5 give details about the experiments and results with concluding remarks presented in Section 6.

2 Gabor Feature Extraction

Gabor wavelets have been successfully used in face recognition applications [1-3] and mathematically, can be defined as:

$$\Psi_{u,v}(\mathbf{z}) = \frac{\|k_{u,v}\|^2}{\sigma^2} e^{-(\|k_{u,v}\|^2\|\mathbf{z}\|^2/2\sigma^2)}\left[e^{ik_{u,v}\mathbf{z}} - e^{-(\sigma^2/2)}\right] \quad (1)$$

where $u = 0, \ldots, 7$ and $v = 0, \ldots, 4$ define the scale and orientation of the wavelet, $\mathbf{z}$ is the xy coordinates and $k_{u,v}$ is defined as $k_{u,v} = 2^{-\frac{2+v}{2}}\pi\, e^{i\frac{u}{8}\pi}$. Features are obtained by convolving a given image with each of the Gabor wavelets.

Let $\boldsymbol{y}_{\mathrm{amp}}$ and $\boldsymbol{y}_{\mathrm{pha}}$ be the vectors that store the amplitude and phase values from an image using all the 40 wavelets defined by Equation 1. The total Gabor feature vector $\boldsymbol{y}$ is constructed as $\boldsymbol{y} = \left(\boldsymbol{y}_{\mathrm{amp}}^{\mathrm{T}}, |\boldsymbol{y}|_{\mathrm{pha}}^{\mathrm{T}}\right)^{\mathrm{T}}$. We then define the feature-extraction function f as:

$$\boldsymbol{x} = f(I_1, I_2) = |\boldsymbol{y}_1 - \boldsymbol{y}_2| \quad (2)$$

where $\boldsymbol{y}_1$ and $\boldsymbol{y}_2$ are the feature vectors calculated from image I_1 and I_2, and $\boldsymbol{x}$ is the feature vector characterizing the difference between image I_1 and I_2, which will be used to determine whether these two images are from the same person.

3 Classifier Training

In the proposed approach two main steps are included in the training process (Fig. 2): the empirical kernel map and the Fisher's discriminant analysis trained using an unbalanced FTS.

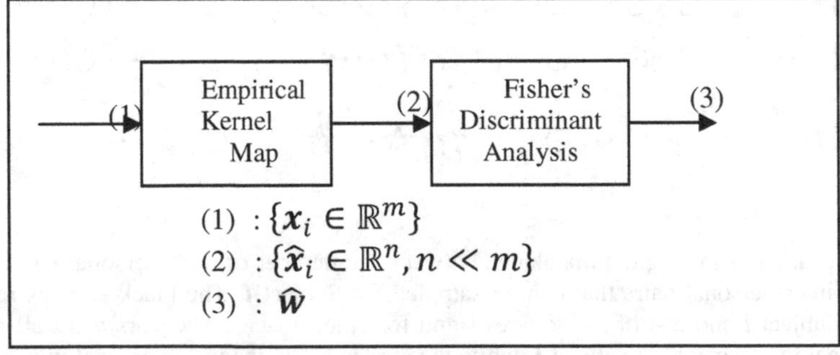

Fig. 2. Block diagram of classifier training

3.1 Empirical Kernel Map

The empirical kernel map (EKM) which is an approximation of the reproducing kernel map [7], is used to establish a non-linear map $g: \mathbb{R}^m \to \mathbb{R}^n$ which generates a new vector $\hat{\boldsymbol{x}}$ which has a much lower dimension. Given a set of feature vectors $\boldsymbol{\mathcal{X}} = \{\boldsymbol{x}_i \in \mathbb{R}^m\}_{i=1}^n$, the empirical kernel map can be defined as:

$$\hat{\boldsymbol{x}} = g(\boldsymbol{x}) = \begin{bmatrix} k(\boldsymbol{x}, \boldsymbol{x}_1) \\ \vdots \\ k(\boldsymbol{x}, \boldsymbol{x}_n) \end{bmatrix} \tag{3}$$

where k is a positive definite function. It can be seen that the size of $\boldsymbol{\mathcal{X}}$ decides the dimensionality of the new feature space. If $\boldsymbol{\mathcal{X}}$ includes all the training feature vectors, the training process shown in Fig. 2 is equivalent to the training process of the kernel discriminant analysis [7]. However, $\boldsymbol{\mathcal{X}}$ is chosen as a subset of all the training feature vectors in this work. It can be seen that the size of $\boldsymbol{\mathcal{X}}$, n decides the dimension of the new feature space which determines the computational complexity of the classification problem to be solved in the new feature space. Moreover, recent work [9] has shown that good performance can be achieved with lower values of n.

3.2 Training Strategy for Fisher's Discriminant Analysis on an Unbalanced Feature Training Set

Having reduced the feature dimension using EKM, the Fisher's discriminant analysis (FDA) is used in the new feature space to find the direction $\hat{\boldsymbol{w}}$ along which the intra- and inter-personal feature points are maximally separated. As mentioned in Section 1, there could be an imbalance (see Fig. 1 for an example) in the FTS since the training samples (feature vectors) are calculated from image pairs rather than single images.

Since the system is to be tested on the standard FERET database, the image set defined in FERET for training is used as the TS. For this data set when selecting image pairs to compute the FTS, it is found out that the number of intra-personal samples, n^1 (approximately less than a thousand) is much less than the number of inter-personal samples, n^0 (approximately more than 500 thousands). If prior knowledge is incorporated (e.g., if it is known that the two images to be matched are taken in different sessions), a more restricted rule will be used to select image pairs (that is, every one of them will have two images taken in different sessions), possibly resulting in a much smaller n^1. Moreover, it is found that n^1 could also be much smaller than the dimension of feature vectors, n. Therefore, we need to perform the FDA under the condition that $n^1 \ll n \ll n^0$.

In the following, a novel training strategy is introduced to deal with the above-mentioned situation. It is well known that the solution of the FDA can be obtained by maximizing function $\mathcal{J}(\boldsymbol{w})$:

$$\mathcal{J}(\boldsymbol{w}) = \frac{\boldsymbol{w}^{\mathrm{T}} \boldsymbol{S}_{\mathrm{B}} \boldsymbol{w}}{\boldsymbol{w}^{\mathrm{T}} (\boldsymbol{S}_{\mathrm{w}}^1 + \boldsymbol{S}_{\mathrm{w}}^0) \boldsymbol{w}} \tag{4}$$

where $\boldsymbol{S}_{\mathrm{B}}$ is between-class scatter matrix and $\boldsymbol{S}_{\mathrm{w}}^1$ and $\boldsymbol{S}_{\mathrm{w}}^0$ are the scatter matrices for the intra- and inter-personal training samples, respectively (see [7] for the detailed definitions). Given that $n^1 \ll n^0$, it may be desirable not to misclassify any of the intra-personal samples, which means there will be a zero false reject rate on the training data. This can be achieved by restricting every possible $\boldsymbol{w}$ to be within the null space of $\boldsymbol{S}_{\mathrm{w}}^{1}$, $N(\boldsymbol{S}_{\mathrm{w}}^{1})$, or equivalently, $\boldsymbol{w}^{\mathrm{T}}\boldsymbol{S}_{\mathrm{w}}^{1}\boldsymbol{w}=0$. Let $\boldsymbol{V}=[\boldsymbol{v}_1,\dots,\boldsymbol{v}_r]^{\mathrm{T}}$ be an orthonormal basis of the range of $\boldsymbol{S}_{\mathrm{w}}^{1}$ where r is the rank of $\boldsymbol{S}_{\mathrm{w}}^{1}$. The linear transformation from the feature space $\mathbb{R}^n$ onto $N(\boldsymbol{S}_{\mathrm{w}}^{1})$ can be established by using the matrix $\boldsymbol{P}=\boldsymbol{I}-\boldsymbol{V}\,\boldsymbol{V}^{\mathrm{T}}$ where $\boldsymbol{I}$ is the identity matrix. It is known that matrix $\boldsymbol{V}$ can be formed by the eigenvectors of $\boldsymbol{S}_{\mathrm{w}}^{1}$ with non-zero eigenvalues.

The problem of maximizing $\mathcal{J}(\boldsymbol{w})$ is then transformed into maximizing function $\mathfrak{J}(\boldsymbol{w}')$:

$$\mathfrak{J}(\boldsymbol{w}')=\frac{\boldsymbol{w}'^{\mathrm{T}}\boldsymbol{M}_{\mathrm{B}}\boldsymbol{w}'}{\boldsymbol{w}'^{\mathrm{T}}\boldsymbol{M}_{\mathrm{W}}^{0}\boldsymbol{w}'} \tag{5}$$

where

$$\boldsymbol{M}_{\mathrm{B}}=\boldsymbol{P}(\boldsymbol{\mu}^1-\boldsymbol{\mu}^0)(\boldsymbol{\mu}^1-\boldsymbol{\mu}^0)^{\mathrm{T}}\boldsymbol{P}^{\mathrm{T}} \tag{6}$$

$$\boldsymbol{M}_{\mathrm{W}}^{0}=\textstyle\sum_i \boldsymbol{P}(\widehat{\boldsymbol{x}}_i^0-\boldsymbol{\mu}^0)(\widehat{\boldsymbol{x}}_i^0-\boldsymbol{\mu}^0)^{\mathrm{T}}\boldsymbol{P}^{\mathrm{T}} \tag{7}$$

Here $\boldsymbol{w}'\in N(\boldsymbol{S}_{\mathrm{w}}^{1})$, $\boldsymbol{M}_{\mathrm{B}}$ and $\boldsymbol{M}_{\mathrm{W}}^{0}$ are the corresponding within-class and inter-personal scatter matrices in $N(\boldsymbol{S}_{\mathrm{w}}^{1})$, $\{\widehat{\boldsymbol{x}}_i^1\}$ are the inter-personal feature vectors after the EKM and $\boldsymbol{\mu}^0$ and $\boldsymbol{\mu}^1$ are the means. Let $\widehat{\boldsymbol{w}'}$ be the vector that maximizes $\mathfrak{J}(\boldsymbol{w}')$. The solution of the FDA, $\widehat{\boldsymbol{w}}$ can be calculated as $\widehat{\boldsymbol{w}}=\boldsymbol{P}\,\widehat{\boldsymbol{w}'}$.

4 Experimental Settings

The pairwise classification framework (PCF) was tested on two of standardized FERET experiments [8] which involved using some image subsets defined in the database, namely, the gallery set, FB probe set, Dup1 probe set and the training set (TS). The first experiment simulated an easy test scenario where every two image to be matched were taken around the same time. The second experiment represented a much harder scenario when every two images were taken on different days. The average time difference between two images is 251 days. The second experiment was designed to test the system's capability of handling facial aging and is used to demonstrate that by incorporating the prior knowledge a more effective FR system can be built to target such a difficult test scenario.

In the experiments, face images were normalized by the way described in [10], using the eye-coordinates provided in the FERET database. By using 40 Gabor wavelets defined by Equation (1) and (2), 1.64×10^5 features were calculated from each image pair. To reduce the dimension, a set of 2500 training samples were used to perform the EKM defined in Equation (3). Based on recent work [9] and the fact that $n^1\ll n\ll n^0$, the set was constructed in such a way that all the intra-personal samples in the FTS were included and the rest were randomly sampled from the population of the inter-personal samples. Finally, the RBF kernel function, $\mathcal{k}(\boldsymbol{x},\boldsymbol{x}')=\exp(-\|\boldsymbol{x}-\boldsymbol{x}'\|/2\sigma^2)$ was used in the EKM.

5 Results

In both experiments, the PCF was compared with other FR systems including the elastic bunch graph matching (EBGM) [1], the Gabor Fisher classifier (GFC) [2] and the Adaboost Gabor FR system (AGF) [3] using the features extracted by the same Gabor wavelets defined in (1). Table 1 shows the rank 1 recognition rate on the FB probe set (Results of EBGM and GFC were reported in [11]). It can be seen that all of the systems achieved recognition rates above 95% in this easy test scenario.

Table 1. Recogntion results on the FB probe set

FR System	Rank 1 Recognition Rate
EBGM	95.0%
GFC	96.3%
AGF	95.2%
PCF	97.8%

In the second experiment, systems were tested in a much harder test scenario. The prior knowledge used in selecting training image pairs is that the two images to be matched are taken on different days. To incorporate this knowledge, when selecting image pairs from the TS to calculate the FTS, we scanned all the possible image pairs and only used those whose images were taken on different days. Table 2 shows the rank 1 recognition results on the Dup1 probe set. It can be seen that the GFC outperformed the PCF. However, when closely looking at the TS, it was found out that only 244 intra-personal pairs satisfying the criterion could be formed from the images. Only 240 images from 60 subjects were involved in spite of the fact that there were 1002 images from 429 subjects in the TS. We believed that the small number of representative intra-personal image pairs caused the underperformance of the PCF system.

Table 2. Recogntion results on the Dup1 probe set

FR System	Rank 1 Recognition Rate
EBGM	59.1%
GFC	68.3%
AGFC	n/a
PCF	67.0%

To have more qualified intra-personal image pairs to train the PCF, we enlarged the TS by adding 72 images (10%) from the Dup1 probe set. The images were chosen in a way so that the number of intra-personal pairs that formed by two images taken on different days was maximized. In total, we managed to obtain 702 intra-personal image pairs using 320 images from 65 subjects. Instead of using all the images in the TS, the PCF was trained only on 320 images and tested on the reduced (90%) Dup1 probe set. To compare the results the system trained on the original TS was also tested on the reduced Dup1 probe set. Fig. 3 shows the cumulative match curves of the recognition results. The recognition rate for the PCF trained on 244 intra-personal samples was slightly higher (around 2%) from its figure (67%) in Table 2 due to the reduced size of the Dup1 probe set. For the PCF trained on the 703 intra-personal samples, the rank 1 recognition rate exceeded 75%. It can be seen that although the number of images used for training was much less than that in the original TS, the system performance was significantly improved in this difficult test.

6 Conclusion

We have presented a pairwise classification framework for face recognition. The novelty of this framework resides in providing a mechanism for incorporating prior knowledge through the selection of training data to tackle specific FR challenges such as facial aging and providing a novel training strategy to tackle the imbalance inherent in the training data available for pairwaise image classification. The experimental results have demonstrated the effectiveness of the proposed approach in incorporating prior knowledge, handling high-dimensional feature vectors and coping with the training data imbalance.

Acknowledgments. The authors would like to acknowledge the support of 3D FACE, a European Integrated Project funded under the European Commission IST FP6 program contract number 026845.

References

1. Wiskott, L., Fellous, J.-M., Küiger, N., von der Malsburg, C.: Face recognition by elastic bunch graph matching. IEEE Trans. PAMI 19(7), 775–779 (1997)
2. Liu, C., Wechsler, H.: Gabor Feature Based Classification Using the Enhanced Fisher Linear Discriminant Model for Face Recognition. IEEE Trans. IP 11(4), 467–476 (2002)
3. Yang, P., Shan, S., Gao, W., Li, Z., Zhang, D.: Face Recognition Using Ada-Boosted Gabor Features. In: Proc. IEEE Intl. Conf. Auto. Face and Gesture Recognition, pp. 356–361 (2004)
4. Patterson, E., Sethuram, A., Albert, M., Ricanek, K., King, M.: Aspects of Age Variation in Facial Morphology Affecting Biometrics. In: Proc. BTAS, pp. 1–6 (2007)
5. Cevikalp, H., Neamtu, M., Wilkes, M., Barkana, A.: Discriminative common vectors for face recognition. IEEE Trans. PAMI 27(1), 4–13 (2005)
6. Moghaddam, B., Wahid, W., Pentland, A.: Beyond eigenfaces: probabilistic matching for face recognition. In: Proc. IEEE Intl. Conf. Auto. Face and Gesture Recognition, pp. 30–35 (1998)
7. Schölkopf, B., Smola, A.J.: Learning with Kernels: Support Vector Machines, Regularization, Optimization and Beyond. MIT Press, Cambridge (2001)
8. Phillips, P.J., Moon, H., Rauss, P.J., Rizvi, S.: The FERET evaluation methodology for face-recognition algorithms. IEEE Trans. PAMI 22(10), 1090–1104 (2000)

9. Zhou, Z., Chindaro, S., Deravi, F.: Non-Linear Fusion of Local Matching Scores for Face Verification. In: Proc. IEEE Intl. Conf. Auto. Face and Gesture Recognition (2008)
10. Beveridge, J.R., Bolme, D.S., Draper, B.A., Teixeira, M.: The CSU face identification evaluation system: its purpose, features and structure. Machine Vision and Applications 16(2), 128–138 (2005)
11. Zhang, B., Shan, S., Chen, X., Gao, W.: Histogram of Gabor phase patterns (HGPP): A novel object representation approach for face recognition. IEEE Trans. IP 16(1), 57–68 (2007)

Forensic Investigation of the Soft-Modded PlayStation Portable (PSP)

Qin Zhou and Nigel Poole

Faculty of Engineering and Computing, Coventry University
Priory Street, Coventry, CV1 5FB, United Kingdom
{q.zhou,n.poole}@coventry.ac.uk

Abstract. The PlayStation Portable (PSP) is a popular handheld game console. The lack of a hard disk unit within the PSP does not imply a lack of stored data. It incorporates an onboard NAND flash memory and a memory card reader. This paper aims to raise awareness of the presence of custom firmware and identify possible data hiding places in the PSP. It discusses PSP forensics issues and proposes a possible technique for how such a PSP system may be forensically examined.

Keywords: PSP forensics, PlayStation Portable, Custom Firmware, forensic investigation.

1 Introduction

The PlayStation Portable (PSP) is a handheld game console manufactured by Sony Computer Entertainment. It is said that the console is "the most successful non-Nintendo handheld game system ever sold" [1]. Depending on the design version of a PSP system, it incorporates an onboard NAND flash memory offering 32MB or 64MB of storage holding its operating system (also referred to as firmware or system software) and persistent system/user settings like wallpaper or network settings [2]. The content of the onboard memory is hidden from the ordinary users by Sony's official firmware (OFW) but can be accessed with the use of custom firmware (CFW) such as M33 for storing extra data [3]. A reader compatible with Sony's Memory Stick Pro Duo (MS Pro Duo) flash cards is also found on the left edge of the PSP console. A new evolution of PSP, PSPgo is scheduled for release on 1st October, 2009 [4]. PSPgo replaces the UMD drive with 16GB of flash memory to store a variety of content [5].

It is possible to remove the optional extra MS Pro Duo card for external analysis, but the onboard flash memory cannot be easily removed for traditional write-blocked forensic imaging and analysis.

This paper intends to raise the awareness of the availability of CFW and identify places within the PSP memory where data could potentially be hidden. It also discusses PSP forensics issues and proposes a possible solution on how such a PSP system may be forensically examined.

D. Weerasinghe (Ed.): ISDF 2009, LNICST 41, pp. 50–56, 2010.

2 PSP Onboard Flash Memory and Custom Firmware

2.1 Data Storage Areas in the Onboard NAND Flash Memory

According to [6][7], the onboard NAND flash memory of a PSP system (either 32MB or 64MB in size depending on the model of the system) has been divided into three distinct areas: the Initial Program Load (IPL), the IDStorage, and the LFlash (or LFAT). All three areas are encrypted. The LFlash area consists of four FAT12 logical partitions, with Flash0 holding the actual firmware itself, Flash1 containing the system/user settings, Flash2 keeping data required for the PlayStation Network downloads and Flash3 storing extra undefined information. Table 1 shows the LFlash structure of a tested PSP system (Model: PSP2003). The IPL area stores the Initial Program Loader which boots the operating system firmware from the LFlash area. The IDStorage area keeps several hundred system-dependant keys for the PSP system.

Table 1. The LFlash structure of the test PSP system (PSP2003). Here, 1 sector = 512 bytes.

Partition Name	Size in Sectors	Purposes	Used Space	Free Space
Flash0	83936	firmware	24.3MB	16.6MB
Flash1	10208	System / user settings	752KB	4.18MB
Flash2	8160	Data for PlayStation Network downloads	0	3.92MB
Flash3	18656	For downloadable contents?	0	9.04MB

It is worth noting that PSP regularly reads/writes data to Flash1, making an imaging process not repeatable.

2.2 Custom Firmware (CFW)

A PSP system can be soft-modded to run custom firmware (CFW) [8]. CFW such as M33 [3][9] produced by unofficial developers allows users to run third-party software and have full read/write access to the four FAT12 partitions in the LFlash area of the onboard NAND flash memory via the PSP's USB interface. As shown in Table 1, there is typically more than 20MB free space in total available in these partitions which can be used to store extra data. The fact that these partitions can be configured from the Recovery Menu of the CFW such that they are invisible from the PSP's Home Menu makes them the ideal places to hide data. The Home Menu is also referred to as the system menu or the XMB (Cross Media Bar) interface [10].

The test PSP system used in the research was modded using the method of Pandora's battery and magic memory stick described in [3]. M33 CFW was installed on the system.

3 PSP Forensics Issues and Possible Solutions

If a PSP system has not been modded, the examination of the system is simple. An investigator can browse the Home Menu to obtain information about the system, such as system and network settings, web activities, etc.

A MS Pro Duo card found in the PSP system can be easily imaged with the use of a suitable external USB reader and disk imaging tool with a write-blocking mechanism. The fact that a standard FAT32 file system has been used for any memory stick card formatted by the PSP makes the media analysis of stored data straightforward.

Things get more interesting from a forensics point of view if a PSP system has been modded. The following sections explain how such a system may be examined with minimum modification to the system's contents.

3.1 Checking If the System Has Been Modded

First of all, the system information on a PSP system should be checked to decide if the system has been soft-modded. This can be done by navigating to **Settings → System Settings → System Information** from the Home Menu. An original PSP system running OFW should display its system information in the following order:

```
    MAC Address    XX:XX:XX:XX:XX:XX
System Software    Version X.XX (e.g. Version 2.71)
       Nickname    PSP
```

A different presentation order of the system information display suggests that the system has been modded, as illustrated in figure 1. The version of the CFW in the test system was 4.01M33-2.

It is notable that the version of the system software and MAC address can be spoofed by tools like the one in [11] to give false information.

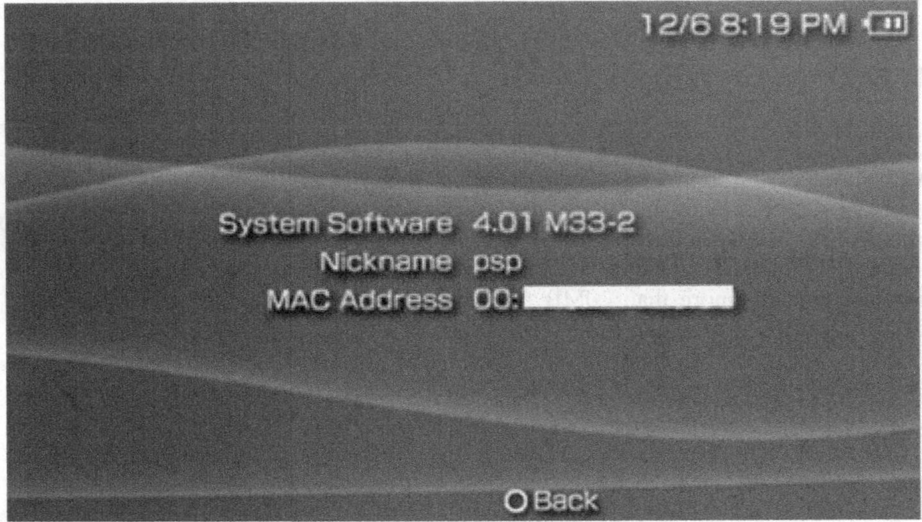

Fig. 1. System information (MAC address deliberately obscured)

3.2 Check If a Custom VSH Menu Is Enabled

If a custom VSH menu [10] such as the M33 VSH menu is enabled, each of the four FAT12 partitions in the LFlash area can be selected as "USB DEVICE" from the menu. Figure 2 shows a device with Flash 3 selected. Once the PSP system is connected to a PC via the USB connection, the selected flash partition appears as a USB connected memory stick and can be imaged using disk imaging tools such as FTK Imager [12], dd/dcfldd [13], or LinEn [14].

To check if the M33 VSH menu is enabled, one can just press the "SELECT" (or "HOME" in some cases) control to see if an extra menu appears on the screen as illustrated in figure 2.

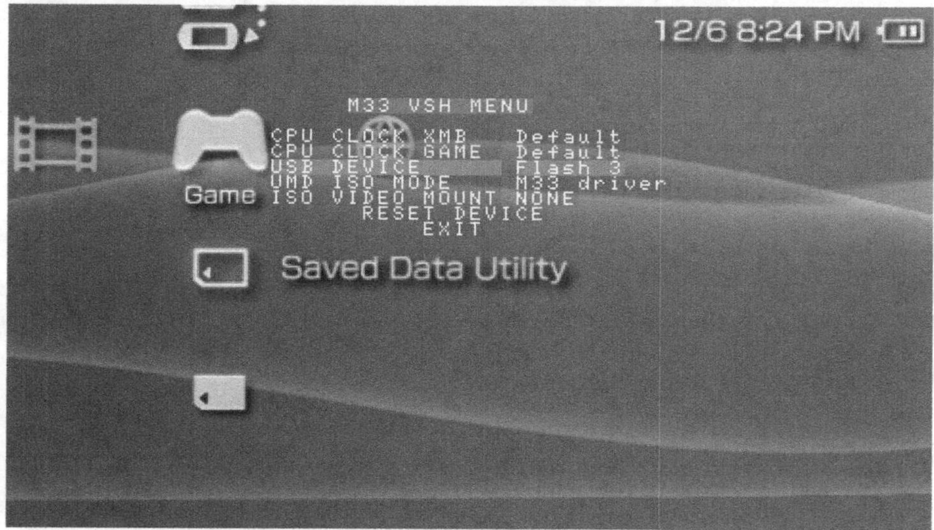

Fig. 2. M33 VSH menu with Flah3 partition selected for USB connection

If the M33 VSH menu is disabled, the flash partitions can be toggled from the M33 Recovery menu shown in figure 3 and accessed by a PC through the USB interface of the PSP. The M33 Recovery Menu can be accessed by switching off the system, then pressing the "R" control and keeping it pressed while powering on the system.

Fig. 3. M33 Recovery Menu

3.3 Imaging Issues

During the research, an interesting observation was made with regard to flash partition imaging. FTK Imager was found to perform better compared to Linux related imaging tools. FTK Imager only had difficulty in accessing the last sector of each partition during the imaging process while Linux related imaging tools such as dcfldd and LinEn have problems in accessing a number of sectors near the end of each partition. Figure 4 shows 18655 of 18656 sectors were copied successfully by FTK Imager and figure 5 shows only 18640 of them were copied by dcfldd.

```
[Physical Drive Information]
 Drive Model: SONY "PSP" MS USB Device
 Drive Interface Type: USB
 Source data size: 9 MB
 Sector count:     18656

ATTENTION:
The following sector(s) on the source drive could not be read:
        18655
The contents of these sectors were replaced with zeros in the image.

[Computed Hashes]
 MD5 checksum:     e1b3ff5d02ac1954f702d632ca914e8d
 SHA1 checksum:    a55704c52f98ab99b47848e071b5171d653663e0

Image Information:
 Acquisition started:   Mon Jun 15 13:32:19 2009
 Acquisition finished:  Mon Jun 15 13:32:22 2009
 Segment list:
  C:\Q\psp-forensics\psp-flash3-ftk.001

Image Verification Results:
 Verification started:  Mon Jun 15 13:32:22 2009
 Verification finished: Mon Jun 15 13:32:22 2009
 MD5 checksum:     e1b3ff5d02ac1954f702d632ca914e8d : verified
 SHA1 checksum:    a55704c52f98ab99b47848e071b5171d653663e0 : verified
```

Fig. 4. Log file created during imaging of Flash3 by the FTK Imager. It shows 18655 of 18656 sectors were copied successfully.

```
root@masterkey:/# dcfldd bs=512 if=/dev/sdb of=/root/psp/test.dd hash=md5
18432 blocks (9Mb) written.dcfldd:/dev/sdb: Input/output error
Total (md5): 0bd7ebcb31c0f7ad4b2cbb56b7135aeb

18640+0 records in
18640+0 records out
```

Fig. 5. Imaging of Flash3 by dcfldd. 18640 sectors out of 18656 were copied successfully.

The process of imaging the Flash0, Flash2 and Flash3 partitions is repeatable if a suitable write-blocking mechanism is in place. However the process of imaging Flash1 is not repeatable as the PSP's firmware accesses Flash1 on a regular basis to control settings and update logs.

3.4 NAND Flash Dumping

In addition to imaging individual partitions, it is possible to copy the raw data stored in the onboard flash memory to a removable memory stick in a modded PSP system for external analysis or later restoration. This is a valuable technique since it allows recovery from a number of system problems.

The utility Open Source NAND Dumper V.01for 3.xx [15] is an easy-to-use tool for backing up the raw content of the onboard flash memory. The procedure for executing the NAND dump is explained below:

a) Insert a Memory Stick Pro Duo card to the PSP system's card reader and use the system to format the card.
b) Connect the system to a PC through the USB interface, set the system to the USB mode, use the PC to create a folder \PSP\GAME on the memory stick's root directory and store a copy of the program, Open Source NAND Dumper V.01for 3.xx, in the newly created folder.
c) Exit from the USB mode and perform the NAND dump by navigating to Game → Memory Stick from the Home Menu and clicking the icon of the OPEN NAND DUMPER 3.xx to run the utility.
d) After the NAND dump completes, a file named "nand-dump.bin" can be found at the root directory of the memory stick. The file contains the raw content of the onboard flash memory.

3.5 Media Analysis

The easiest way to perform forensic media analysis of the PSP onboard memory is to examine the image files of its four plain logic FAT12 partitions acquired using the above method. Because three of the four logic partitions (Flash0, Flash2, Flash3) in the LFlash area of the flash memory have been encrypted and analysis of the raw NAND dump data proves to be difficult - it involves extracting the LFlash area, separating the four partitions and decrypting the three encrypted partitions.

4 Conclusions

The main data items of forensic interest within a PSP device reside in its internal flash memory or Memory Stick Pro Duo expansion memory. The memory Stick Pro Duo can be easily removed and attached to a separate PC equipped with a compatible card reader for analysis. The internal flash memory is not normally accessible for detailed analysis from devices running official firmware. Use of custom firmware will allow direct read and write access to this memory space if required. Areas within the flash memory would then become available for hiding sensitive data.

Techniques for identifying the presence of custom firmware on a PSP device, imaging its flash memory partitions and taking a raw dump of the memory have been presented. The underlying structure and function of the flash memory partitions has been described. Combined with conventional forensic analysis tools this enables a detailed examination of a device that potentially holds relevant evidence to be undertaken. Further work could usefully be directed to deducing the detailed structure of the flash memory partitions.

References

1. Matthews, M.: Opinion: What Will The PSP Do In 2009? Gamasutra, http://www.gamasutra.com/php-bin/news_index.php?story=21332
2. Cory1492, 64MB Nand, LAN.ST, http://www.lan.st/showthread.php?t=1435&page=3
3. Devilfish: Intro to Pandora, Custom Firmware & Homebrew Software for PSP. Digital Kaos, http://www.digital-kaos.co.uk/forums/f63/intro-pandora-custom-firmware-homebrew-software-psp-24168/
4. Miller, P.: Engadget & Joystiq live from Sony's E3 2009 keynote. Engadget, http://www.engadget.com/2009/06/02/engadget-and-joystiq-live-from-sonys-e3-2009-keynote/
5. PSP has evolved. Official PlayStation website, http://uk.playstation.com/games-media/news/articles/detail/item160412/PSP-has-evolved/
6. Cory1492, 64MB Nand, LAN.ST, http://www.lan.st/showthread.php?t=1435&page=3
7. Dax Hordes: [TUT]Nand Dumps and Nand Basics[/3r14nd]. Dark-Alex.org, http://www.dark-alex.org/forum/viewtopic.php?f=80&t=1327
8. Softmod. Wikipedia, http://en.wikipedia.org/wiki/Softmod
9. Larrylje: GUIDE: Create Pandora Battery + Magic Memory Stick Using Official/1.50/CFW PSP. Afterdawn.com, http://forums.afterdawn.com/thread_view.cfm/708959
10. Homebrew Jargon Buster. PSP Homebrew, http://www.psp-homebrew.eu/faq/jargon.php#XMB
11. Davee: Unlimited Character Version and Mac Address Spoofer. Davee's DavSite, http://davee.x-fusion.co.uk/
12. FTK Imager, AccessData, http://www.accessdata.com/
13. dcfldd, http://dcfldd.sourceforge.net/
14. LinEn, Guidance Software, http://www.digitalintelligence.com/software/guidancesoftware/encase/
15. Open Source PSP NAND Dumper v0.1, http://www.psp-hacks.com/file/1313

Smart Logic - Preventing Packet Loss in High Speed Network Intrusion Detection Systems

Ahsan Subhan, Monis Akhlaq, Faeiz Alserhani, Irfan U. Awan, John Mellor, Andrea J. Cullen, and *Pravin Mirchandani

Informatics Research Institute, University of Bradford,
Bradford BD7 1DP, United Kingdom and
*Syphan Technologies (www.Syphan.com)
{s.a.subhan,m.akhlaq2,f.m.f.alserhani,i.u.awan,j.e.mellor,
a.j.cullen}@Bradford.ac.uk, pmirchandani@Syphan.com

Abstract. Network Intrusion Detection Systems (NIDS) have gained substantial importance in today's network security infrastructure. The performance of these devices in modern day traffic conditions is however found limited. It has been observed that the systems could hardly stand effective for the bandwidth of few hundred mega bits per second. Packet drop has been considered as the major bottleneck in the performance. We have identified a strong performance limitation of an open source Intrusion Detection System (IDS), Snort in [1, 2]. Snort was found dependent on host machine configuration. The response of Snort under heavy traffic conditions has opened a debate on its implementation and usage. We have developed the Smart Logic component to reduce the impact of packet drop in NIDS when subjected to heavy traffic volume. The proposed architecture utilizes packet capturing techniques applied at various processing stages shared between NIDS and packet handling applications. The designed architecture regains the lost traffic by a comparison between the analysed packets and the input stream using Smart Logic. The recaptured packets are then re-evaluated by a serialized IDS mechanism thus reducing impact of packet loss incurred in the routine implementation. The designed architecture has been implemented and tested on a scalable and sophisticated test bench replicating modern day network traffic. Our effort has shown noticeable improvement in the performance of Snort and has significantly improved its detection capacity.

Keywords: Network intrusion detection systems, network performance, packet drop, Snort, serialization.

1 Introduction

Intrusion detection in the realm of information security is the technique of identifying any hostile attempt into the network. The concept has gained acceptance at all levels on account of increasing threats for users/ networks. It has also been complemented by various mechanisms to fulfill security requirements. Broadly Intrusion Detection systems (IDS) are categorized into two types. Signature based – these are designed to

D. Weerasinghe (Ed.): ISDF 2009, LNICST 41, pp. 57–65, 2010.

detect attacks on basis of well defined threats, these are accounted into system policies to prevent any future intrusion. Anomaly based - These base their logic on pre defined behavioral patterns where any violations from the defined routine generate an alert [4]. Both the techniques have inherent advantages and disadvantages. The anomaly based systems can detect undiscovered attacks; however they are suffered by large number of false positive. On the other hand signature based mechanisms cannot detect new attacks thus need continuous updates. We have based our research on signature based detection techniques on basis of low false positive, better performance and a greater acceptance in the domain of network security.

In modern day network traffic, the performance of these systems has been found debatable. It has been observed that the optimal potential of these systems has not been explored. A wide gap still exists between the capability of these systems and recent developments in hardware/peripheral devices. For example the systems still fails to maximize performance by using multi-core architecture. It also suffers from heavy packet loss once used in Giga-bit Ethernet environment.

Numerous efforts have been made to address the issues related to packet loss in high speed networks. Quite few techniques focus on securing a balance between the detection capacity of system and input traffic. Few substantially competent techniques make use of load balancing concepts. These involve the use of traffic splitting mechanism where input traffic is distributed across the set of detection engines for evaluation and filtering to block the traffic destined to unpublished ports.

Krugel et al in [5] explored a parallel architecture to increase the system capacity by splitting traffic into manageable sized slices; these are then fed to the set of detection sensor. Each sensor has been made intelligent to respond to set of particular threats and has no intercommunication. Unfortunately, this technique is strongly dependent on few parameters. Firstly, the sliced traffic must be fed to the detection engine capable of responding to the particular threat which in some cases is violated and may result in sensor overloading; thus resulting in packet loss. Secondly, it may fail to partition complex stateful signatures since correct partitioning of the traffic is known only at runtime. Thus any approach that uses a static partitioning algorithm needs to over-approximate the event space associated with the signature resulting in improper partitioning [6].

The parallel architecture for stateful detection described in [6] also based its logics on splitting the traffic and distributing it to detection sensors in a round robin fashion. It differs from [5] on grounds that sensors are able to communicate each other via control node on a high-speed, low-latency, dedicated control plane and all have the similar rule matching directory. The feedback allows the sensors to synchronize their scanning process. The stateful detection is ensured by replicating the matcher state which is same for all sensors at any time. Unfortunately, the concept too suffers from performance limitations. Storing already scanned packets in the buffer for a possibly pending evaluation in another sensor creates overhead. Response to slow attacks would also be an issue where every sensor would be maintaining the state and would keep on occupying buffer space. The use of a centralized node for synchronization creates overhead and consumes processing power.

The concept of Early Filtering (EF) applies to the filtering of incoming traffic before evaluation to handle heavy input as described in [7] is also found limited in performance. The technique uses filtering as a part of sensor functionality. The input is first evaluated through EF rule-set. If matched, the packets are discarded; otherwise analyzed. The EF rule-set belongs to the main rule directory and has comparatively a less complex analysis, for example, inspection of the header only. This could be easily evaded by the attempts, concealing payload in initial packets and bypassing the evaluation stage. Using locality buffers in the second stage creates performance bottleneck once subjected to heavy input traffic when packets awaiting session completions cross the buffer limit.

Our effort adopts a different approach. We base our mechanism on the serialization concept where input traffic is being analyzed by normal sensors and later the dropped traffic is recovered by our Smart Logic. The technique is distinguished in a way that limitation observed in the traffic splitting approaches and drawbacks in early filtering are avoided to improve the performance. The Smart Logic takes an approach using capture, identify and evaluate cycle with an RDBMS [8] acting as a common data repository. Periodic data cleansing has also been applied to ensure optimal performance of the database. We have implemented our logic on Snort [9], an open source NIDS analyzing real world traffic.

The paper is organized into sections. Section 2 describes the architecture and algorithm of Smart Logic. Section 3 & 4 gives the test-bench and results. Finally in the conclusion we analyze our contribution.

2 Smart Logic

2.1 Architecture

The architecture is based on Serialization Concept [1]. This incorporates two instances of IDS evaluation. The instances are separated by Smart Logic which is implemented to recover dropped packets by active comparison as shown in Figure 1. The first instance deals with the traffic directly fed from Ethernet interface and carries out evaluation. The output of first instance is fed to the data-store where it gets compared with the duplicated input using Smart Logic. The comparison of these two identifies the lost packets. These lost packets are then fed to the second stage serialized evaluation process.

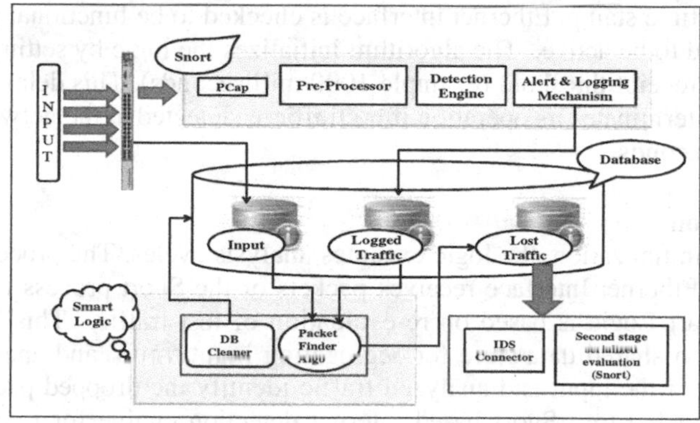

Fig. 1. System Architecture

The system is composed of two components Snort and Smart Logic. Snort, an open source NIDS has been selected because of its popularity and status as a de facto IDS standard. Snort relies on the packet capturing libraries. The libraries act as packet capturing interfaces to the underlying operating system [10].

Snort is an open signature based IDS; it uses rules to detect hostile attempts into a network. The rules are the set of requirements created to generate an alert and have a particular syntax. On successful detection of a hostile intrusion, the detection engine sends an alert to a log file/storage resource. The Smart Logic operates by collection of network traffic through multiple channels (Snort alert logging mechanism and Ethernet span port) and executes comparison logic to identify the lost packets. The lost packets are then re-evaluated by Snort based internal detection engine as shown in Figure 1. Shared data-store has been employed to act as a bridge between Snort and Smart Logic. We have also utilized Sharp PCap [11] wrapper around libpcap [10] for managed languages like C# [12], VB.NET [13] and Boo [14] on various frameworks such as Microsoft .NET [15] and MONO [16]. Sharp PCap has been installed on server and shall ensure the Smart Logic to respond to both open source and proprietary operating systems environments.

2.2 Operation

Packet capturing and handling is a vital requirement for a NIDS. A good packet capturing response by the system towards variant traffic reduces the probability of a system becoming compromised. Factors that affect the packet capturing performance of an NIDS in a Gigabit Ethernet environment include host configuration parameters (hardware and software) and application-specific parameters (NIDS). We have developed comparison logic - Smart Logic to address the issue of packet loss in high speed gigabit ethernet environment.

The designed algorithm – Smart Logic recovers the lost traffic by active comparison of input traffic with analyzed packets in the first stage. The operation unfolds in two steps, initialization and execution.

2.2.1 Initialization

Sharp PCap requires to be present on the server, Smart Logic extracts the current operating system time stamp. Ethernet interface is checked to be functional and status of Snort is verified to be active. The algorithm initializes the logic by setting parameters such as packet receipt threshold (example 1000 milliseconds). This delay ensures that the component terminates its operation if no traffic is detected at the network interface for 1000 milliseconds.

2.2.2 Execution

On successful initialization, the logic executes analysis cycles. The procedure iterates as long as the Ethernet Interface receives packets or the Snort process is active. The concept of Smart Logic is based on re-evaluation of lost traffic. This has been ensured by using a shared data-store for segregating input traffic and analyzed traffic. The difference of the input and analyzed traffic identify the dropped packets. These packets are then fed to a Snort based internal detection engine for re-evaluation as shown in Figure 2. The execution cycle terminates automatically once Snort process made inactive or once the variable packet receiving time out expires.

A periodic operational cycle is implemented to perform data purging on the data-store connected to the system. The data-store plays a vital role in the comparative analysis of network traffic. Smart Logic reads the current system time stamp and after every selected time period (example 15 minutes) it filters the lost traffic and purges the data-store.

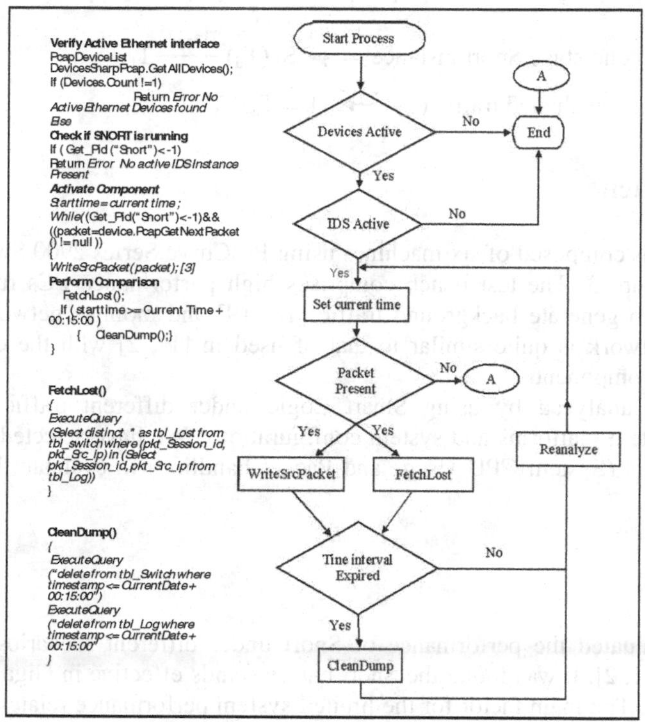

Fig. 2. Smart Logic Process Flow

Our algorithm executes a loop that iterates until one or more exit conditions met (termination of Snort process or packet receive threshold reached). In each iteration, the algorithm stores the input traffic and checks for the expiry of execution interval (15 minutes). On expiry of the interval, traffic filtering and purging are executed within the iteration.

The purging facility executes in parallel with the lost packet fetch routine (in a producer-consumer paradigm). The multiple delete operations remove the consumed input and analyzed packets from their respective tables *(Input traffic - tbl_Switch and analysed traffic – tbl_Log)* at fixed time intervals.

The traffic filtering component of Smart Logic classifies lost packets on the basis of session ID, source and destination IP addresses. The lost packets are identified by comparing incoming traffic captured by Sharp PCap to the packets analyzed by Snort available in the data-store. Difference of these shall give the dropped packets. Mathematically the Smart Logic has implemented as follows:

Let $D_T = T$ (D_T is the Traffic logged in the database from the network interface

Let x be the input traffic fed to first stage Snort instance S1 where $x = T$

$$\text{First stage evaluation} \longrightarrow S_1(x) \xrightarrow{\text{yields}} T_a \quad \text{where } T_a \in T \tag{1}$$

$$\text{Smart Logic} \longrightarrow T_d = D_T / T_a \quad \text{where } T_d \text{ is the dropped traffic} \tag{2}$$

$$\text{Second stage Snort instance} \longrightarrow S_2(T_d) \xrightarrow{\text{yields}} T_f \tag{3}$$

$$\text{Total evaluated traffic (T)} \longrightarrow T = T_a + T_f \tag{4}$$

3 Test Bench

The network is composed of six machines using ProCurve Series 2900 Switch [17] as shown in Figure 3. The test bench comprises high performance PCs running open source tools to generate background traffic [18, 19] and monitor network performance. The network is quite similar to that of used in [1 , 2] with the exception of Smart Logic component.

Snort was analyzed by using Smart Logic under different traffic conditions, operating system platforms and system configurations. We have selected two important parameters (System CPU Usage and Packet handling) to evaluate the proposed mechanism.

4 Results

We have evaluated the performance of Snort under different scenarios and traffic condition in [1, 2]. It was found the Snort barely stands effective in Giga bit Ethernet environments. The main factor for the limited system performance relates to the large number of packet drop. In order to identify the efficacy of our concept we have compared our results with ones' obtained in [1, 2]. Performance of the system in context of CPU usage and packet handling capability is described in following paragraphs.

Due to paucity of space we have included the results from Linux 2.6 platform only, we have also identified in the previous efforts that performance of Snort is better in Linux in comparison to others.

4.1 CPU Usage

Application performance largely depends upon CPU usage, higher the usage compromised would be the performance. In [1, 2] we have identified that a single instance of Snort consumes 20 – 40 % of the CPU once subjected to input traffic volume ranging from 200 Mbps – 2.0 Gbps as shown in Figure 4.

Implementation of Smart Logic and executing second stage serialized Snort increased the CPU usage upto 70 % for traffic volume of upto 1.2 Gbps as shown in Figure 4. Above 1.2 Gbps, CPU usage increased to 100% (2.0 Gbps input traffic) as shown in Figure 4. The increase in CPU usage affects the performance of system and cause packet drop.

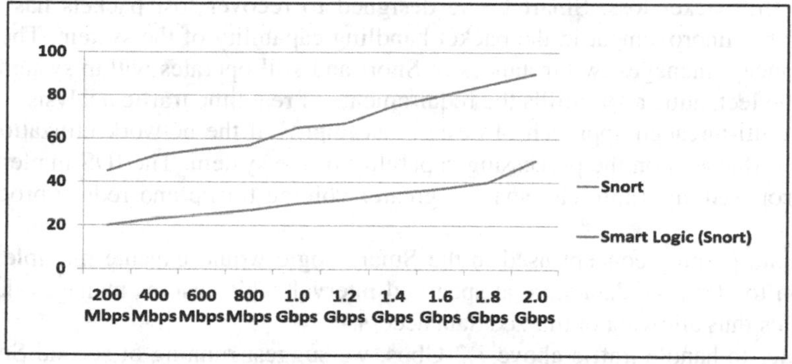

Fig. 4. Comparison – CPU Usage

4.2 Packet Handling

We have achieved a 100% processing response with no packet drop using Smart Logic. This is a significant improvement from a standard Snort which can barely handle input traffic reaching 500 Mbps as shown in Figure 5. Snort start dropping packets once bandwidth increased from 200 Mbps and at 2.0 Gbps it dropped more than 70% of the input traffic.

Our serialized implementation of evaluation process runs two instances of Snort. This has improved the overall evaluation process and successfully able to analyse traffic upto 1.2 Gbps as shown in Figure 5. The system start dropping packets above 1.2 Gbps, the basic cause of packet loss incurred in the evaluation is the bottleneck caused by a low disk data transfer rate.

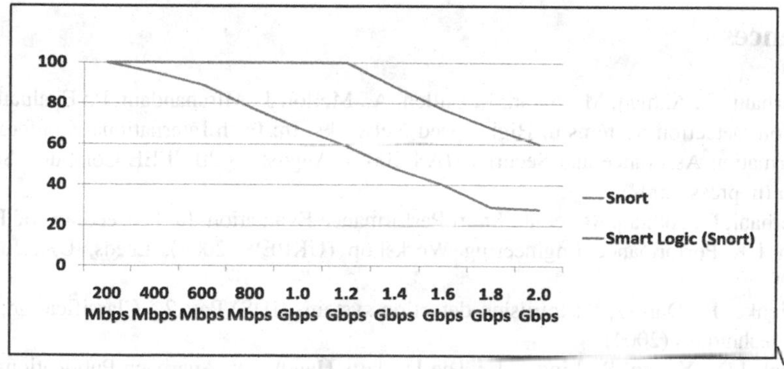

Fig. 5. Comparison – Packets Analyzed

5 Conclusion

We have proposed a serialized IDS evaluation concept to utilize system resource and mitigate the packet loss. Smart Logic designed to recover lost packets has shown considerable improvement in the packet handling capability of the system. The introduced concept manages two instances of Snort and still operates within system capability. The technique also fulfills the requirements of real time traffic analysis.

The multi-threaded approach of design has improved the network utilization, this has also influenced on the processing capability of the system. The IDS implemented in the proposed algorithm can analyze greater volume traffic and reduce processing delays.

The data purging concept used in the Smart Logic would execute multiple delete operation to clean the data-store at specified interval. This ensures managed depth of data-tables thus allowing optimized data access.

In order to handle traffic above 1.2 Gbps, we suggest running of second Snort instance on a different machine. We have performed few tests on this configuration and have found system responsive for input traffic volume up to 5.0 Gbps.

We have managed to eliminate the performance limitations relative to the use of load balancing concepts in traffic splitting mechanisms. This has been achieved by monitored duplication and multistage analysis of network traffic. The use of a shared data repository ensures minimal packet loss and detection efficiency while simultaneously reducing performance overhead.

Acknowledgment

We would like to thank Dr. D. R. W. Holton and Dr. R. J. Fretwell of University of Bradford for their guidance and support during the course of this research. We would also appreciate Syphan Technologies for providing us the opportunity to work on the SINBIN Test Lab and their assistance throughout.

References

1. Alserhani, F., Akhlaq, M., Awan, I., Cullen, A., Mellor, J., Mirchandani, P.: Evaluating Intrusion Detection Systems in High Speed Networks. In: Fifth International Conference of Information Assurance and Security (IAS 2009), August 18-20. IEEE Computer Society, Xian (in press, 2009)
2. Alserhani, F., Akhlaq, M., et al.: Snort Performance Evaluation. In: Proceedings of Twenty Fifth UK Performance Engineering Workshop (UKPEW 2009), Leeds, UK, July 6-7 (2009)
3. Kazienko, P., Dorosz, P.: Intrusion detection systems (IDS) Part 2 - Classification; methods; techniques (2004)
4. Tessel, J.D., Young, S., Linder, F.: The Hackers Handbook. Auerbach Publications, New York (2004)
5. Krugel, C., Valeur, F., vigna, G., Kemmerer, R.: Stateful Intrusion Detection for High Speed Networks. In: Proceedings of IEEE Symposium on Security and Privacy, Oakland, CA, May 2002, pp. 285–293 (2002)

6. Fischini, L., Thapial, A.V., Cavallaro, L., Kruegel, C., Vigna, G.: A Parallel Architecture for Stateful, High-Speed Intrusion Detection. In: Proceedings of fourth International Conference on Information system security, Hyderabad, India, pp. 203–220 (2008)
7. Xinidis, K., Charitakis, I., Antonatos, S., Anagnostakis, K.G., Markatos, E.P.: An Active Splitter Architecture for Intrusion Detection and Prevention. IEEE Trans. Dependable Sec. Computer 3(1), 31–44 (2006)
8. RDBMS, `http://www.databasedir.com/what-is-rdbms`
9. Snort, `http://www.Snort.org`
10. Baker, A.R., Esler, J.: Snort IDS and IPS Toolkit, Syngress, Canada (2007)
11. Sharp PCap, `http://www.chrishowie.com/pcap-sharp`
12. C Sharp, `http://en.wikipedia.org/wiki/C_Sharp`
13. VB.net, `http://vb.net`
14. Boo, `http://boo.codehaus.org`
15. Microsoft.Net, `http://www.microsoft.com/NET`
16. MONO, `http://mono-project.com/Main_Page`
17. VMware Server, `http://www.vmware.com/products/server`
18. LAN Traffic V 2, `http://www.topshareware.com/lan-traffic-v2/downloads/1.html`
19. D-ITG V 2.6, `http://www.grid.unina.it/Traffic/index.php`

Parameter Based Access Control Model for Mobile Handsets

Dasun Weerasinghe, Raj Muttukrishnan, and Veselin Rakocevic

Mobile Networks Research Group
School of Engineering and Mathematical Sciences
City University London,
Northampton Square, London, EC1V 0HB, UK.
dasun.weerasinghe@city.ac.uk

Abstract. The concept of mobile services is to provide the access to online content and services from anywhere, anytime and on any device. The mobile user is the consumer for the mobile services and the access to the services are enabled according to the user identification. Meanwhile, mobile device identity, SIM identity and location identity are some of the other identification parameters can be used by mobile service providers. The data and the services are delivered to the mobile device in encrypted format and the cryptographic key for the data decryption is derived using the identity parameters and key materials at the mobile. Therefore, the decryption key is not transmitted over the network and it is generated in the device before the service access. The generation of the decryption key in the mobile using the identity and attribute parameters will enable parameter based access control for mobile content. The data access rules are defined by service providers based on the availability of attributes and identities at the mobile handset.

Keywords: Parameter based Access Control, Security, Privacy, Mobile Devices.

1 Introduction

The security capsule [1] was introduced as a novel component to implement the security mechanisms in a mobile device and it enables secure consumption of mobile services in a mobile device. The security capsule is developed, deployed and distributed by the identity provider and it is assumed the identity provider is a trusted entity [2]. Therefore, the security capsule is considered as a trusted component in the mobile device. The Identity provider framework for mobile devices is presented in one of our previous publications [2]. The data and services in the mobile service environment are vulnerable to various security attacks during the distribution, consumption and storage phases. The security capsule is implemented to protect the data and services at the mobile handset and security protection for data distribution.

The security capsule establishes the mobile device communication with the identity provider and service providers. The service providers uniquely identify the mobile device for authentication and authorization to services. The unique identity is derived in the security capsule using the logical and physical identity parameters at the mobile

D. Weerasinghe (Ed.): ISDF 2009, LNICST 41, pp. 66–75, 2010.

device. The data and services are transmitted to the mobile device in encrypted format from the service providers. Meanwhile, a token is generated by the service provider and it is sent to the mobile device with the encrypted content. This token presents the mobile user's authorization to decrypt the encrypted content.

The service provider generates a unique token for each encrypted data item sent to the mobile device and each token is identified by its unique identity. Meanwhile, the token consists of a symmetric cryptographic key to derive the decryption key for the encrypted data. This decryption key is named as the data key and the key is generated in the mobile device with a number of static and dynamic input parameters. The parameter based key generation function enables the parameters based access control in a mobile handset. Meanwhile, the service provider controls the data access mechanism in real-time basis as the mobile handset requires a real-time cryptographic key for the data key generation process. The real-time key is sent to the mobile device during the decryption process.

The data key is generated in the mobile device rather than transmitting over the network from an external party. The key is generated using the mobile user dependent, the device dependent, the USIM dependent, the security capsule dependent, the service provider dependent and the token dependent parameters. The security capsule permanently deletes the decrypted data, cryptographic keys and tokens after the data access session by the mobile user. However, still encrypted keys and tokens are in the mobile device and only the real-time key has to be requested for data decryption process. The following are the identities are identified in the mobile device for the key generation process.

- IMPI (IP Multimedia Private Identity): The mobile operator assigned identity for the mobile user. This identity is stored in the USIM of the mobile device.
- IMEI (International Mobile Equipment Identity): The unique identity for the mobile device and this is issued by the mobile device manufacturer.
- UID: The Identity provider issued unique identity for the security capsule.

2 Related Work

Online mobile applications for mobile devices have introduced new security and privacy risks beyond those that are found in online desktop systems. The articles [3] [4] discuss the security and privacy vulnerabilities on personalized data in mobile devices. The technical report from Perelson S. et al [5] investigates the data access control on mobile devices. They claimed that mobile manufacturers have spent most of their efforts designing security routines for the communication protocols rather than for the data and applications in mobile devices. Therefore, data security on mobile devices should have high priority in the future. An author [6] from IBM Global services presented the same view about security mechanisms in mobile devices. He emphasised that today's challenge is to implement resource intensive security measures on mobile devices.

The security key management in a mobile device has been a top research topic due to the requirements of end-to-end security infrastructure for the mobile service environment. The key exchange schema in [7] allows mobile devices to dynamically agree on session keys with a server. Meanwhile the mobile device is able to perform public key computations in this schema. However, Dodis et al. [8] highlighted threats to cryptography when installing a private key in a device and especially when a user carries the mobile device which allows remote access from public or foreign domains. It recommended having a key as an output from a combination of different types of physical and logical cryptographic inputs. In public key infrastructure, the private key has to be distributed to the mobile device to use asymmetric key encryption technology. However, the publication [9] emphasized the drawbacks in transmitting the private key to a remote device even though the key is encrypted before transmission. However, the mobile device is able to validate public key certificates of service providers before starting any sensitive communication. The publications [10] [11] proposed light weight public key certificate evaluation techniques for mobile devices.

The article [12] emphasized the importance of mobile user authentication without exposing passwords on the network as a future approach. The authors of that article also suggested generating secret encryption keys in mobile devices and then sharing them with the mutually trusted parties. Storing the cryptographic keys in mobile devices is an open research question. Dodis Y. et al [13] proposed a key insulated security approach to protect cryptographic keys in mobile devices. Transmitting long term secrets between entities is vulnerable to the credential sniffing attacks and replay attacks [14].

3 Security Design

This section discusses the functional design of the security capsule to enable the parameter based access control in a mobile device. The design is categorized into the registration process, data transmission and the data access processes. During the registration, the security capsule registers with the identity provider and the service providers. The security capsule consists of identities and credentials for the secure communication with external parties. A secret key is generated at the service provider for the data encryption and then the encrypted data is transmitted to the service provider. The same secret key is generated at the mobile device for the data decryption and it is an output from the identity parameters and the attributes at the mobile device. The successful secret key generation enables the mobile user to access data from the service provider.

As a pre-requisite to the security capsule installation at the mobile device, the identity provider and service providers should agree to a publicly available hash function and a symmetric key encryption algorithm.

3.1 Registration Process

The registration process categorizes into two phases such as registration with the identity provider and the registration with the service provider.

Phase 1: Registration with the Identity Provider
This phase starts when the mobile device requests to download the security capsule from the identity provider. The security capsule will be downloaded using the over-the-air or the wired techniques. The following are the main steps in the registration process.

(1) The mobile device requests to download security capsule from the identity provider.
(2) The security capsule is downloaded to the mobile device.
(3) The mobile user verifies the authentication of the identity provider and the integrity of the downloaded security capsule using the following steps;
   - The public key certificate of the identity provider is used to authenticate the identity provider.
   - The calculated hash value of the security capsule binary installation is compared with the hash value at the identity provider for the security capsule integrity.
(4) The security capsule is installed in to the mobile device as a mobile application. The downloaded security capsule is uniquely identified using the UID. The UID is saved in the security capsule compilation and it will be used to present the security capsule identification to the identity provider during the future communications. The UID is an alphanumeric value in the security capsule and it is un-accessible to the device users.
(5) The security capsule accesses the IMPI and IMEI values from the mobile device and it generates the K_{IMPI} and K_{IMEI} using the inbuilt hash function.

$$HASH (IMPI) = K_{IMPI}$$
$$HASH (IMEI) = K_{IMEI}$$

(6) The K_{IMPI} and the K_{IMEI} are transmitted to the identity provider by encrypting them using the identity provider's public key.
(7) The identity provider records the $_{KIMPI}$ and $_{KIMEI}$ values with the UID of the security capsule.

Phase 2: Registration with the Service provider

The security capsule registers with the service provider for services during this phase and the following are the pre-requisites for the registration.

(1) The mobile user should have a unique identification with the service provider.
(2) The mobile device authenticates with the identity provider and both parties share a secret key (Ks) for the communication.
(3) The identity provider and the service provider share a secure communication channel and Service Provider has a Public Key Infrastructure.

Let's assume that SPUID is the mobile user identity at the service provider.

The following are the steps in the registration process with the service provider.

(1) The security capsule sends the registration request to the identity provider with the service provider identity and the SPUID.
(2) The identity provider calculates the key values: K_{IMPI_SPUID}, K_{IMEI_SPUID} and K_{APP_SPUID} using the hash function. Then the key values are sent to the service provider with the SPUID and these key values are distinct to each service provider. These key values will be used to establish a secure communication between the mobile device and the service provider.

$$HASH (K_{IMPI}, SPUID) = K_{IMPI\_SPUID}$$
$$HASH (K_{IMEI}, SPUID) = K_{IMEI\_SPUID}$$
$$HASH (HASH(UID), SPUID) = K_{APP\_SPUID}$$

(3) The service provider saves the key values with the SPUID. Then it acknowledges the identity provider by sending a User PIN derivation request to the mobile device. The request consists of the public key certificate of the service provider.
(4) The User PIN derivation request is transmitted from the identity provider to the mobile device.
(5) Finally the mobile device and service provider share a User PIN (4 digits).The User PIN is transmitted from the mobile device to the service provider over a secure channel using the service provider public key. The User PIN is obtained from the mobile user and it is obtained over the device keypad. The derivation of the User PIN is an optional step for extra security at the security capsule.

During the registration phase the mobile device shares unique key values (K_{IMPI_SPUID}, K_{IMEI_SPUID} and K_{APP_SPUID}) with the service provider for the future secure communication. The service provider and the mobile device generate the secret key for the communication using these key values and the User PIN. The key values are generated using the hardware (mobile device) dependent, SIM dependent and the capsule dependent parameters. However, these parameters are not sent outside the mobile device and the parameters cannot be derived using the key values due to the irreversible property of the hash function. The key values are transmitted in a secure communication link between the identity provider and the service provider and the attackers are unable to access them. Meanwhile, these values are only transmitted once in the network to the service provider and then these key values are utilized many times for the data key generation process.

3.2 Data Transmission

The data is transmitted to the mobile device in an encrypted format from the service providers to preserve the data confidentiality and the data is encrypted using the data key at the service provider. The service providers generate and send Data token to the mobile device before the data transmission and the data token presents the mobile device's authorization to access the data. The transmitted tokens consist of secret cryptographic key and this key will be used to generate the data key to decrypt the data from service providers. This key is named as 'Token key' and a unique token is generated for each encrypted data element. The tokens are uniquely identified by the service provider with the token ID. The service provider maintains a link between the token ID and the encrypted data in its domain.

The data transmission phase starts with generating the shared secret key for the data encryption at the service provider. The security capsule and the service provider share the symmetric key algorithm for the data encryption and the data decryption as a pre-request to the data transmission process.

Phase 1: Key Generation at Service provider
The Data key is generated at the service provider using the hash function and the Data key is a 192 bit (64 bit X 3) cryptographic key. The service provider generates a Real-Time key before the data key generation and this key will be an input to the Data key generation function. This Real-Time key enables the real-time security/authentication

protection at the security capsule and it is linked with the Token ID at the service provider. The security capsule has to send the Token ID to retrieve the correct Real-Time key from the service provider. Depending on the required security level for the data, the service provider will be able to configure the Real-Time key as a single key at the service provider or a unique key for each encrypted data segment. The generated Real-Time key is saved at the service provider with the Token ID. The following is the Data key generation hash function with the input parameters.

Function (Real-Time Key, Token Key, K_{IMPI_SPUID}, K_{IMEI_SPUID}, K_{APP_SPUID}) = Data Key

Phase 2: Data encryption at the service provider
The generated Data key is used to encrypt the requested data. The symmetric encryption algorithm is used for the data encryption functionality. Finally, the encrypted data is transmitted to the mobile device. The data will be sent to the security capsule. Meanwhile, the related Data Token for the encrypted data should be at the security capsule; otherwise the security capsule requests the token from the service provider.

3.3 Data Access at the Security Capsule

The security capsule obtains the request for the data decryption from the mobile user and it retrieves relevant Data Token from the memory. The Data key is generated as the initial step for accessing data at the mobile device. Then the encrypted data will be decrypted using the decryption algorithm.

Phase 1: Key generation at the Security Capsule
The following are the key generation steps at the security capsule.

(1) Validates the Data Token integrity and the Data Token freshness. If the token is not valid then it is deleted from the capsule and a new token is requested from the service provider.
  - The XML signature of the token is verified with the token issuer's public key for the token integrity
  - The timestamp of the token and the token lifetime are compared with the present timestamp from the identity provider for the token freshness.

(2) The Token ID and the Token key are extracted from the token.
(3) The security capsule sends the Real-Time key request message to the service provider while specifying the Token ID
(4) The service provider replies with a challenge request. The communication between the service provider and the mobile device is secured using a shared session key generated during the authentication process.
(5) The challenge response is generated by the security capsule as follows;

$F_{challenge}$ (User PIN, Challenge Request) = Challenge Response

(6) The challenge response is sent to the service provider
(7) The service provider executes the same function ($F_{challenge}$) and generates the Challenge Response. Then it compares the generated Challenge Response with the response sent by the security capsule. The service provider sends the Real-Time key to the mobile device if both challenge responses are the same.
(8) The security capsule obtains the IMPI and IMEI from the mobile device and the UID from the internal data storage.

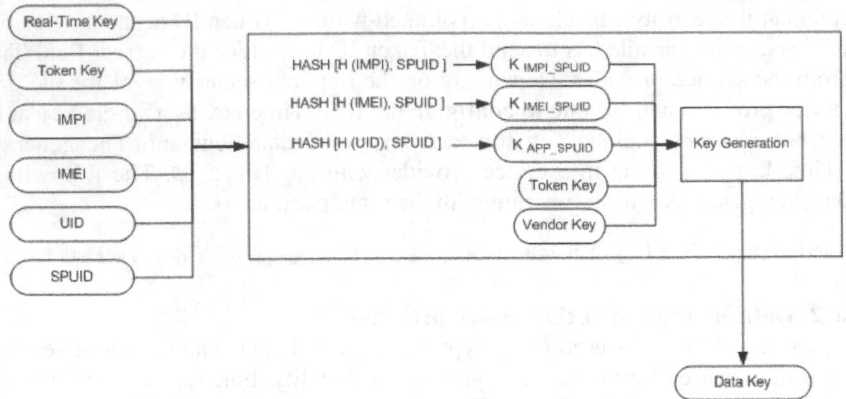

Fig. 2. Key generation at the Security Capsule

(9) The data key for the decryption is generated using the key generation algorithm as shown in Figure 2. The key generation algorithm is designed using the hash functions.

(10) Real-Time key, Token key, IMPI, IMEI, UID, K_{IMPI_SPUID}, K_{IMEI_SPUID} and K_{APP_SPUID} values are in the phone memory after the Data Key generation process. These values should be removed from the memory after the key is generated to prevent security attacks. Therefore, the security capsule discards those values for the memory location.

(11) The security capsule decrypts the data using the data key and symmetric decryption algorithm in the capsule. Then Data key is permanently deleted from the device memory.

Phase 3: Data access and data deletion

The security capsule presents the data in a viewable format to the mobile user and the data content or the data memory location details are not accessible to the mobile users. Therefore, the mobile user will not be able to save the data in a different memory location or send it to another mobile device. The security capsule controls the user interaction with the decrypted data during the utilization. The user will only be able to view the data and other functionalities such as save, edit, copy, delete, etc are disabled from the user interface. Once the data utilization session is completed, the capsule permanently deletes the decrypted data from the memory.

The key generation, data decryption, data access and data deletion functionalities of the security capsule are summarized in the Figure 3. The hash function for the key generation is implemented using the SHA-1 algorithm and it generates a 192 bit cryptographic key as the Data key. The Token key and Real-Time key are 64 bit cryptographic keys. The symmetric key encryption and decryption functionalities are implemented using the Triple DES / Electric Code Book / No Padding algorithm. The hash function and the encryption/decryption algorithms are publicly available. The operational data from the capsule is saved on the Random Access Memory of the mobile device. These memory locations are accessed from the security capsule to delete the memory contents permanently by making data bits to zero.

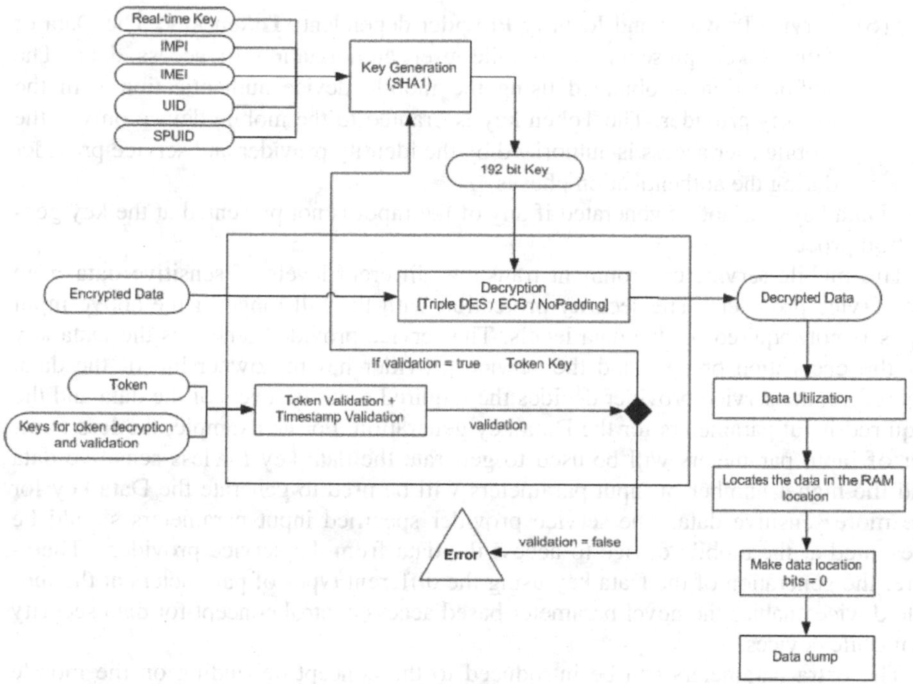

Fig. 3. Security Capsule Functionality

4 Parameter Based Access Control

The generation of the Data key at the mobile device enables the mobile user to access data from the service provider. The Data key is distinct to each encrypted data set and it is generated using the following types of inputs.

(1) Mobile User dependent: **User PIN;** the data cannot be access without the presence of the user

(2) Mobile device (Hardware) dependent: **IMEI;** the data can only be accessed in the specified mobile device. The mobile device identification is specified to the service provider during the registration.

(3) Mobile SIM dependent: **IMPI;** the data can only be accessed if the specified SIM card is in the mobile device. The SIM card identification is specified to the service provider during the registration.

(4) Security Capsule dependent: **UID;** the data can only be accessed in the specified security capsule. The security capsule identification is specified to the service provider during the registration.

(5) Service Provider dependent: **Real-Time key;** the data can only be accessed if the real-time authorization is granted by the service provider. The Real-Time key presents the real time access rights to the sensitive data.

(6) Service Provider and Identity Provider dependent: **Token key;** The Data or Trust token presents the mobile user authorization to access data. The authorization is obtained using the mobile device authentication with the identity provider. The Token key is granted to the mobile device only if the mobile user access is authorized by the identity provider and service provider during the authentication phases.

The Data key will not be generated if any of the input is not presented at the key generation process.

The mobile service environment transmits different levels of sensitive data from the service providers. The security protection with the full range of the above input types is not required for the data levels. The service provider generates the Data key for the encryption process and the service provider has the ownership of the data. Therefore, the service provider decides the required security levels of the data and the required input parameters for the Data key generation. For an example, the less number of input parameters will be used to generate the data key for less sensitive data and the higher number of input parameters will be used to generate the Data key for the more sensitive data. The service provider specified input parameters should be presented at the mobile device to access the data from the service provider. Therefore, the generation of the Data key using the different types of parameters at the mobile device enables the novel parameter based access control concept for data security in mobile devices.

The extra parameters can be introduced to the concept depending on the mobile service environment such as location ID verifies the user location before the data decryption. The service provider defines the access control level for the data based on the parameters. Then the required parameters should be available at the mobile device for the data access. The Data token is enhanced as follows with an extra XML element to present the parameter based access control level for the encrypted data.

XML element:

<p_access>User PIN, IMEI, IMPI, UID, Real-Time key, Token Key </p_access>

Explanation:

If the parameter is required then it is presented with '1' and else '0'

Example:

<p_access>1, 1, 1, 1, 1, 1 </p_access>: Highest access level and all the parameters are required for the data access

<p_access>0,0,0,0,0,0 </p_access>: lowest access level and the data access is allowed without verifying the presence of the parameters at the mobile device.

5 Conclusion

This paper presents the functionality and the architectural implementation of the security capsule to protect the data and services at the mobile devices. The novel key generation approach is introduced using the different types of input parameters. The parameter based access control methodology is process to configure the security for the mobile data.

References

1. Weerasinghe, D., Rajarajan, M., Rakocevic, V.: Device Data Protection in Mobile Healthcare Applications. In: The First International Conference on Electronic Healthcare in the 21st century, London, September 8 (2008)
2. Weerasinghe, D., Rajarajan, M., Rakocevic, V.: Federated Trust Negotiation for Mobile Services. In: International Conference on Security and Identity Management (SIM), Ahmedabad, India, May 10-11 (2009)
3. Villate, Y., Illarramendi, A., Pitoura, E.: Data Lockers: Mobile-Agent Based Middleware for the Security and Availability of Roaming Users Data. In: Scheuermann, P., Etzion, O. (eds.) CoopIS 2000. LNCS, vol. 1901, Springer, Heidelberg (2000)
4. Lankhorst, M.M., van Kranenburg, H., Salden, A., Peddemors, A.J.H.: Enabling technology for personalizing mobile services. In: Proceedings of the 35th Annual Hawaii International Conference on System Sciences, HICSS, January 7-10, pp. 1107–1114 (2002)
5. Perelson, S., Botha, R.: An investigation into access control for mobile devices. Departmentof Business Information Systems, Port Elizabeth Technikon, South Africa (July 2004)
6. Keely, D.: A Security Strategy for Mobile E-business. Tech. Rep. GSOEE213, IBM Global Services (2001)
7. Bresson, E., Chevassut, O., Essiari, A., Pointcheval, D.: Mutual Athentication and Group Key Agreement for Low-Power Mobile Devices. In: 5th IEEE International Conference on Mobile and Wireless Communications Networks (2003)
8. Dodis, Y., Katz, J., Xu, S., Yung, M.: Key-insulated public key cryptosystems. In: Knudsen, L.R. (ed.) EUROCRYPT 2002. LNCS, vol. 2332, pp. 65–82. Springer, Heidelberg (2002)
9. Sander, T., Tschudin, C.: Towards mobile cryptography. In: Proceedings of the IEEE Symposium on Security and Privacy, Oakland, CA, pp. 215–224. IEEE Computer Society Press, Los Alamitos (1998)
10. Berbecaru, D., Lioy, A., Marian, M.: On the complexity of public-key certificate validation. In: Davida, G.I., Frankel, Y. (eds.) ISC 2001. LNCS, vol. 2200, p. 183. Springer, Heidelberg (2001)
11. Umezawa, K., Susaki, S., Tezuka, S., Hirasawa, S.: Development and Evaluation of a Certificate Validation System in Mobile Environments. IEEJ Transactions on Electrical and Electronic Engineering 1, 84–93 (2007)
12. Forman, G.H., Zahorjan, J.: The Challenges of Mobile Computing. IEEE Computer 27(4), 38–47 (1994)
13. Dodis, Y., Katz, J., Xu, S., Yung, M.: Key-insulated public key cryptosystems. In: Knudsen, L.R. (ed.) EUROCRYPT 2002. LNCS, vol. 2332, pp. 65–82. Springer, Heidelberg (2002)
14. Oprea, A., Balfanz, D., Durfee, G., Smetters, D.: Securing a remote terminal application with a mobile trusted device. In: ACSAC (2004)

Ethical Dilemmas in Teaching Computer and Internet Security

Brian Tompsett

Department of Computer Science, University of Hull
b.c.tompsett@hull.ac.uk

Abstract. This paper could be subtitled "Are we teaching the next generation of computer criminals and internet terrorists"? This issue was raised by the Security Services as part of the collaborative network meeting in the area of IT Forensics and Data Analysis hosted by City University. These are valid concerns about the nature of material taught to computer science students in the area of security.

The questions are also important ethical dilemmas for any professional working in the computer and internet security field. These are also applicable when discussing such security risks with the media, members of the public and even legislators. Information on vulnerabilities has to be presented so that it informs programmers and computer users about the areas of risk, but without providing recipes for them to use to conduct criminal activities or mischief themselves.

The paper will look at several case studies from the curriculum at the University of Hull at both undergraduate and postgraduate level. Some specific problem areas of email forgery, security of the Windows operating system and exploitation of buffer overflows, and deception in online auctions, will be explored.

Keywords: Security, Teaching, Ethics.

1 Introduction

Students at Hull perform an assessed practical where they evaluate the security of existing laboratory computers, which allows them to put the security theory into a practical context. The response of system managers to this exercise is interesting; although they cannot influence the taught component of a course, they express their discomfort with the practical aspects. Despite this, the students find the practical aspect valuable, and each year a new set of vulnerabilities in our laboratory computers in exposed. This enables the configuration of laboratory computers to be improved on an ongoing basis. The experience does show that organisations often prefer to believe that their computers are secure, and find any information to the contrary painful. Security by obscurity seems to be the desire of management within organisations, which in the security business in known to be no security at all.

It is an interesting question, "what do computer science students know about computer security and vulnerabilities?" Discussions in the media resulting from recent

D. Weerasinghe (Ed.): ISDF 2009, LNICST 41, pp. 76–81, 2010.

computer hacking and attacks [1], [2] have shown that there is a general view that those attacking computers have a special form of arcane knowledge which is not taught. In fact, this material is taught; since we need to improve the knowledge base of all computer graduates to enable them to construct better and more reliable systems. Such systems are crucial since computer users, on the other hand, are not supplied with knowledge that would enable them to protect themselves from being compromised. Furthermore, the knowledge necessary to protect against such attacks on existing systems is rarely included in a standard computer curriculum, or anywhere else in a standard educational programme. In short, we tend to tell computer science students much about building new systems but little about protecting existing ones, which we tell computer users virtually nothing about either.

This paper results from meetings and discussions which were part of the EPSRC research network in IT Forensics and Data Analysis hosted by City University in London from 2008 to 2009. The research network is composed of academics from around the UK research community and also involves the security services. Meetings of the research network examined research topics of mutual interest which included visual or audio analysis, data mining, forensic analysis, computer and network security and so on. Although the group was constituted primarily to facilitate research networking, the topic that appeared to be of most concern to the security services was not research into new criminal detection techniques, but a concern over the curriculum taught to computer science students.

The paper does not attempt to thoroughly explore this wide and contentious topic, but rather to highlight certain issues by way of a quick tour of the subject and to focus on a couple of specific areas by way of example from the topics in programming, e-business, networking, and security.

2 The Issues in Computer Teaching

Software development is a key part of the computer science where the issues of vulnerabilities due to software flaws arise. Students need to be aware of these from the programming and engineering perspectives in that students need to be taught what are common mistakes to make and which ones have been made in the past. The mechanism of the flaws needs to be explained so the students can understand why it is an issue, and also how it can be solved.

In initial teaching of computing and software engineering, the focus is more on the correct implementation of a specification, the crafting of data structures, algorithms, the design user interfaces and databases. These subjects do not expose many ethical dilemmas where students could be taught inappropriate material.

When teaching internet and distributed computing however, the ethical issues begin to appear. The interconnection of computers with the internet exposes the smallest flaws in computer software to a severe test, since each application is itself another vulnerable portal to the computer system as whole. Every networked application or interactive web page made by a student could potentially compromise a whole computer system. This is much more of a security vulnerability than the problems of software development in unconnected systems.

When the topic becomes the operation and implementation of network protocols and internet applications the ethical questions become more acute, and it is these topics that the paper will examine by way of some examples from current curricula.

3 Teaching Network Programming

The basic tenets of good practice and software engineering are taught to students at the beginning of most computer courses in the selected initial teaching language and, later, often in their second year, they learn to build applications that use the network, by initially programming a simple client and server application. The next stage is to develop an understanding of multithreading and concurrency and the associated issues of deadlock, as well as connection timeouts, in order to make a robust and functional server. They will also learn, as a side effect, about resource starvation and denial of service attacks. These become evident when a student is shown how to properly test their client and server implementations for multiple connections and responsiveness. Along with this they also need to understand the issues regarding interoperability and portability of solutions, since a server that only talks to a single client and *vice versa* is not a realistic solution.

This might seem to be uncontentious in terms of the ethical issues it raises, but can lead to knowledge of how to attack systems since knowledge about constructing a robust system often leads to an understanding of the vulnerabilities. It is not far from the teaching laboratory experience to discover that a denial of service attack or resource starvation is not detected or prevented by the computer system or network infrastructure and that, further, they can easily either by accident or deliberately attack servers run for the class, those operated by other students, those run operationally by the university (such as the main web server) and any server of any kind elsewhere on the network. We can only explain that it is wrong to do so!

4 Teaching e-Business

Many computer science (and business) courses include material on e-Business. In teaching the material issues of trust need to be covered, particularly when explaining online identities and money transfer systems. The ease with which fraud can be conducted online becomes apparent to the students, and may become a temptation to them. Further, when teaching aspects of online marketing, the ability to reach a large number of people is also evident, and the students may also see an attraction in undesirable technical-based marketing, such as spam and ad-ware.

5 Teaching Internet Protocols

Network protocols are considered in a layered manner using the OSI 7 layer notation. In the following subsections a few sample problem areas in the teaching of each layer are examined.

5.1 Datalink Layer

The main elements at the datalink layer that students become familiar with in a basic computer networking course on internet protocols are the dynamic address assignment protocols such as ARP, RARP, dhcp and perhaps bootp. This does expose the students to the notion that they could implement servers to answer these requests or monitor this traffic and the information it contains.

5.2 Network Layer

The IP layer is fairly straightforward and its teaching does not expose too many ethical issues, but to understand the operation of IP the rôle of ICMP needs to be explained. The use of the TTL field, the ICMP echo and error responses and their application in programs such as Ping and Traceroute are essential for a student to understand. Understanding of these mechanisms can allow a student to probe network topologies or conduct denial of service attacks [3]. The students may also discover that most computer systems and network infrastructure will not interfere with these activities, however, coverage of these topics is essential to a proper computer networking course. When considering IP addressing students may also be exposed to the concepts of IP address spoofing, as it becomes clear when the mechanisms of routing are covered that the relationship between datalink address and IP address is not fixed.

5.3 Transport Layer

TCP contains several features that, when explained, expose security issues with the protocol [4]. To understand the operation of the protocol students need to understand the acknowledgement system, which includes the numbering of the bytes and the reasons for not starting the numbering at a known point. The connection orientation and the open and close protocols also expose mechanisms of resource starvation and denial of service attacks, particularly when combined with an explanation of the state diagram of the protocol. The state change mechanism for the protocol is flawed and this becomes obvious as that aspect of the protocol is taught.

5.4 Application Layer

It is essential in a networking course to explain the operation of basic internet application protocols. Those often taught include telnet, ftp, smtp (for email) and http (for the web). In explaining the operation of the protocol for technically oriented computing students some exploitable flaws in these applications will become self-evident. For example, when covering telnet and ftp the unencrypted nature of user names and passwords is exposed. The http protocol is fairly straight forward, and its use as the backbone of the web means that many potential weak areas have all been closed and made unavailable to experimenting students; it therefore does not present so many ethical issues in teaching. Smtp, conversely, is full of flaws that stand out and whose symptoms are evident to any user of email. When covering the protocol it is necessary to explain that the sender and the host details are not authenticated and can be forged, and that the entire email headers and body can be user-supplied. Students can then see how spam can easily be generated, but by implication they can also see how easy it is to send. It also is clearly visible to the student how denial of service attacks using email (mail bombs) can be generated.

6 Teaching Trustworthiness and Security

At higher levels in computer science teaching, usually at the master's level, students need to know how to build systems that are trustworthy and secure. At the undergraduate level the students will have a full education in software engineering and computer networking protocols this is not sufficient for them to understand how to engineer fully secure and trustworthy systems. Students need to understand mechanisms of cryptographic security including public key encryption. They then look at the use of encryption in networking such as the secure socket layer (SSL) and possible flaws in key exchange. This exposes students to possible weaknesses in standard encryption and key exchange systems in common usage. Similar weaknesses in encryption in wireless protocols make students aware of mechanisms to attack WEP and WPA.

In software trustworthiness students need to be aware of the rôle of buffer overflow in system compromise, as well as how attack vectors for buffer overflows are constructed and exploited so they can protect against them. Other prominent flaws covered are ones that can be found commonly in operating systems such as timing race conditions, and poor input validation in internet tools. One often overlooked area is the mathematics of randomness that affects the security of operations such as online gambling. Students also consider fully trustworthy systems mechanisms such as a TPM chip [5] which provide onboard encryption and key escrow to authenticate booting software chains. Knowledge of these areas allows students to have the potential to fully exploit all the weaknesses of computer systems, but also allows them to construct systems that are resistant to such vulnerabilities, which is the pedagogic goal of the material.

7 Conclusions

There has been recent discussion of these matters in the professional press [6], [7] which shows that the dilemmas are still omnipresent. When the House of Lords Science and Technology Committee considered Personal Internet Security [8], [9] they also exposed aspects of the problem.

The law enforcement and security community seems to be unaware that knowledge of computer insecurity is widespread and the frequently used with inappropriately. As suggested by the House of Lords, the environment for reporting, detecting and prosecuting these offences needs improvement in order to make the chances being caught greater.

It is clear that it is a necessity to retain within our curricula coverage of technical flaws within computer systems and to educate future developers on how to avoid them. I would go further and say that we should also explain how to protect users and developers from flaws in existing systems. Above all, we need to educate students on their ethical responsibilities in how they use their knowledge.

References

1. Boyd, C.: Profile: Gary McKinnon, BBC News Online (30 July 2008), http://news.bbc.co.uk/1/hi/technology/4715612.stm
2. BBC News: Estonia fines man for 'cyber war', BBC News Online (25 January 2008), http://news.bbc.co.uk/1/hi/technology/7208511.stm
3. Gont, F.: Security Assessment of the Internet Protocol, CPNI (July 2008), http://www.cpni.gov.uk/Docs/InternetProtocol.pdf
4. CPNI: Security Assessment of the Transmission Control Protocol, CPNI Technical Note 3/2009 (2009), http://www.cpni.gov.uk/Docs/tn-03-09-security-assessment-TCP.pdf
5. Trusted Computing Group: Trusted Platform Module (2009), http://www.trustedcomputinggroup.org/developers/trusted_platform_module
6. Li, H.K.: Security Ethics, Letter to the Editor, IT Now, British Computer Society, p. 32 (May 2009)
7. Wanigaratne, S.: Teaching Security, Letter to the Editor, IT Now, British Computer Society, p. 32 (July 2009)
8. House of Lords Science and Technology Committee: Personal Internet Security, 5th Report of Session 2006-07, HL Paper 165, TSO (2007)
9. House of Lords Science and Technology Committee: Personal Internet Security: Follow-up, 4th Report of Session 2007-2008, HL Paper 131, TSO (2008)

Overview of SIP Attacks and Countermeasures

Fadi El-moussa[1], Parmindher Mudhar[2], and Andy Jones[1,3]

[1] Centre for Information & Security Research
[2] Security Design and Operate
[3] Edith Cowan University
BT
Adastral Park, Ipswich IP5 3RE
Fadiali.el-moussa@bt.com,
parminder.mudhar@bt.com,
Andrew.28.jones@bt.com

Abstract. The Security threats to current circuit switched networks dedicated to a single voice application such as the Public Switched Telephone Network (PSTN) are considered minimal. However, in open environments such as the Internet, conducting an attack on voice applications such as Voice over IP (VoIP) is much simpler. This is because VoIP services such as Session Initiation Protocol (SIP) are using servers that are reachable through the Internet. The aim of SIP is to provide the same functionality as traditional PSTN over the Internet. SIP service is implemented in either software or hardware and can suffer similar security threats as HTTP or any publicly available service on the Internet such as buffer overflow, injection attack, hijacking, etc. These attacks are simple to mount, with minimal charges or no cost to the attacker. This paper describes various possible security threats that a VoIP provider could encounter and the impact of these threats on the VoIP infrastructure. In addition, this paper investigates current solutions and mitigation techniques for VoIP attacks in order to provide more reliable VoIP services. The SIP taxonomy presented in the paper can be used as a baseline model to evaluate a SIP product against current and future vulnerabilities and gives a number of possible countermeasures that can be used to mitigate the threats.

Keywords: SIP, Denial of Service, Authentication, Buffer overflow, SIP Injection, SPIT, Internet Telephony.

1 Introduction

Session Initiation Protocol (SIP) [11] is an application layer control protocol that is used for creating, modifying and terminating sessions with one or more participants. The SIP protocol is a signalling protocol used for establishing sessions in an IP network. A session could be a simple two-way telephone call, the distribution of multi-media, multi-media conference sessions, the distributed computer games, etc. The aim of SIP is to provide the same functionality as a traditional PSTN over the Internet.

D. Weerasinghe (Ed.): ISDF 2009, LNICST 41, pp. 82–91, 2010.

The SIP network infrastructure consists of the following:

- The SIP end-point device: a user agent that is responsible for generating and terminating SIP requests. This could be a soft-phone, an instant messenger, an IP phone or even a cellular phone.
- SIP Proxy: an application that enables SIP devices to locate and communicate with one another.
- SIP Registrar: an application with which the SIP devices need to register in order to make and receive calls.
- SIP Redirect Server: an application that receives a request from another SIP device or proxy and returns a redirection response indicating where the request should be directed.
- Usually the SIP proxy, SIP registrar and SIP redirect server are implemented on one system.

Figure 1 illustrates a typical SIP call between two user agents [4]. In the SIP infrastructure the user is defined as a SIP Uniform Resource Identifier (URI) in the form of sip:user@domain. The SIP agent needs to register the URI and the corresponding IP address with the SIP registrar responsible for the domain in order to identify the SIP device location. In order for the SIP agent to register it needs to send a SIP REGISTER message request which informs the SIP registrar that a SIP device is available to place or receive calls and associate a device's IP address with the SIP URI. Registration is performed via UDP protocol.

2 SIP Security Measures

This Section discusses possible attacks on the SIP infrastructure [1] [2] [8]. The SIP infrastructure consists of a number of components dealing with signalling messages, user management, address resolution, packet transfer and services. It is crucial that each component of the SIP infrastructure is secured in order to secure the SIP environment.

2.1 Denial of Service Attack

Flooding attacks occur when an attacker sends a high volume of traffic that causes the target system to consume all of its resources and renders it unable to serve legitimate customers. Flooding in the SIP network infrastructure can easily occur since there is no separation of the channels for signalling and data transfer. It is difficult to trace the source call and a single device can simultaneously generate a high number of calls.

In the following sub-sections the different types of flooding attacks are discussed.

2.1.1 SIP Register Flooding

SIP devices need to send REGISTER requests in order to register with the SIP registrar as they start up. The SIP Register flooding attack occurs when an attacking source sends a stream of SIP REGISTER messages to the SIP registrar to deplete its

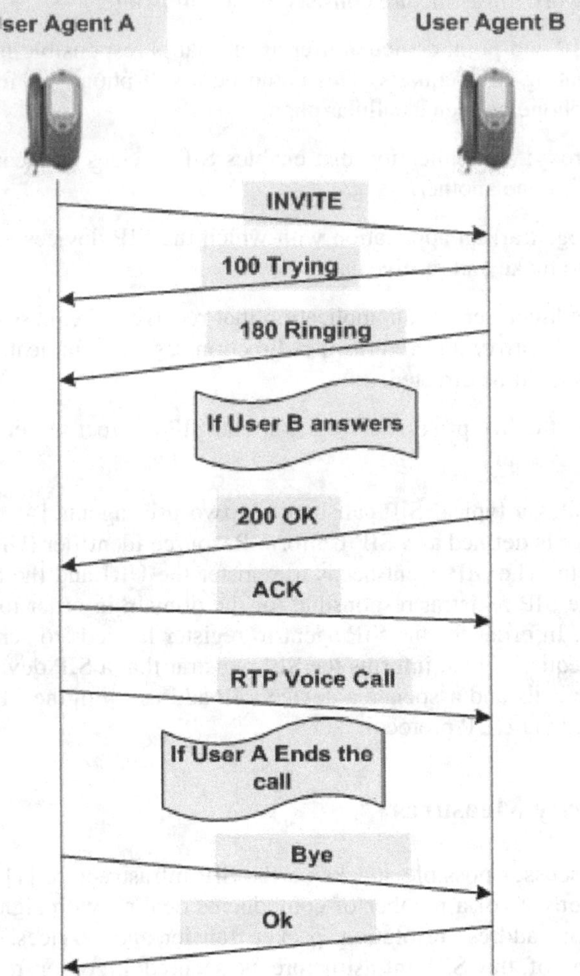

Fig. 1. SIP Signalling Protocol

resources and force it to a point where it cannot handle legitimate new calls. The attacker can use a tool to craft a REGISTER request with multiple user names in order to create a unique spoofed request and flood the application server. The SIP registrar will spend time looking into the database and sending back "Not Found" error messages which will be ignored by the attacker.

2.1.2 Call Flooding Attack

This type of attack occurs when a malicious attacker sends a stream of SIP INVITE requests to an end SIP device. The attacker keeps sending SIP INVITE requests and hangs up once it receives the Ringing or 100 OK messages from the end-device. As a result, the end device will not be able to make any calls or receive any legitimate calls.

There are several ways of defending against the attacks mentioned above if an organization adopts the following countermeasures:

- The use of ingress filtering at the network border: Implementing ingress filtering at the network border will allow spoofed IP packets to be dropped. However, an attacker can still perform DDoS attack by spoofing addresses within the network.
- Deploying a VoIP rate limiting device that can monitor and limit the number of SIP messages accepted at the border gateway.
- The use of a separate VLAN for VoIP signaling and data.
- Enabling authentication for various type of requests.

2.2 SIP Injection Attack

SIP is a complex protocol with many different messages. Attackers may exploit the SIP application layer or network layer by injecting malicious code [5] or traffic to either trigger a failure in the SIP server, leave it in unstable state or to gain full control over the system. There are several different types of SIP injection attacks and two of these are described below.

2.2.1 Buffer Overflow Attack

A buffer overflow attack [13] exploits a vulnerability in the SIP implementation which allows an attacker to inject malicious code into the victim's machine and gain full control. For example, Cisco Unified IP Phone series [3] was vulnerable to buffer overflow that allow an attacker to execute a malicious code at the system. Keeping in mind that VoIP software will inherit any vulnerability from the operating system or firmware that it is running at. The consequences of buffer overflow can be serious given that the attacker can run malicious code and gain control of the target system.

2.2.2 RTP Injection Attack

SIP is a call management protocol that carries voice or video data in its payload. The voice or video data is carried via the Real-Time Transport Protocol (RTP) protocol. The RTP runs on top of the UDP or TCP protocol in order to transmit media such as audio or video via the Internet. The RTP protocol does not provide an encryption or authentication mechanism to the transmitted media. Therefore, an attacker would be able to monitor the INVITE message request between the two end SIP devices to determine the IP address and the port number that the RTP call stream is being sent to. Once these details are known, the attacker can start sending streams of RTP packets to the appropriate IP address and port number. This results in one of the callers receiving the injected RTP stream rather than the actual conversation.

Possible countermeasures to SIP injection attacks are:

- Enforcing audio encryption to prevent RTP injection/mixing.
- Adopting authentication where possible.
- Keeping operating system and application patches up-to-date.
- Deploying a VoIP Intruder Detection Systems (IDS)/Intrusion Prevention Systems (IPS) system for detecting malicious code and vulnerabilities

targeting the VoIP devices. The IDS should be able to learn the SIP message grammar of the deployed SIP devices within the network in order to detect any SIP traffic that deviates from the stored ones.

2.3 SIP Spoofing Attack

As SIP control messages are text based and in most cases are sent in clear text, they are prone to spoofing, modification or interception. Basically, SIP allows any request to be processed without authentication and does not enforce SIP source message validation mechanisms. The SIP authentication service is optional and the system allows a SIP request to be processed without authentication. Most of the attacks in this section can be easily mitigated by the use of a SIP authentication mechanism.

2.3.1 De-registration Attack

This type of attack is based on an attacker sending a REGISTER message with the *Expire* field set to zero. This type of message is normally sent by a soft phone to indicate that it is shutting down and that no more calls can be sent. An attacker can generate a crafted REGISTER request message that spoofs a user identity with an *Expire* field set to zero as shown in Figure 2. The illustration shows the attacker spoofing the identity of user 100 by sending a SIP REGISTER request message with the *Expire* field set to zero. As a result, user 100 will not be able to receive any calls, will not have a dial-tone and will not be able to make outbound calls.

Implementing a strong authentication mechanism before processing the REGISTER request can mitigate such attacks. Both the SIP device and SIP registrar should use a strong authentication mechanism for registration in order to prevent this type of attack.

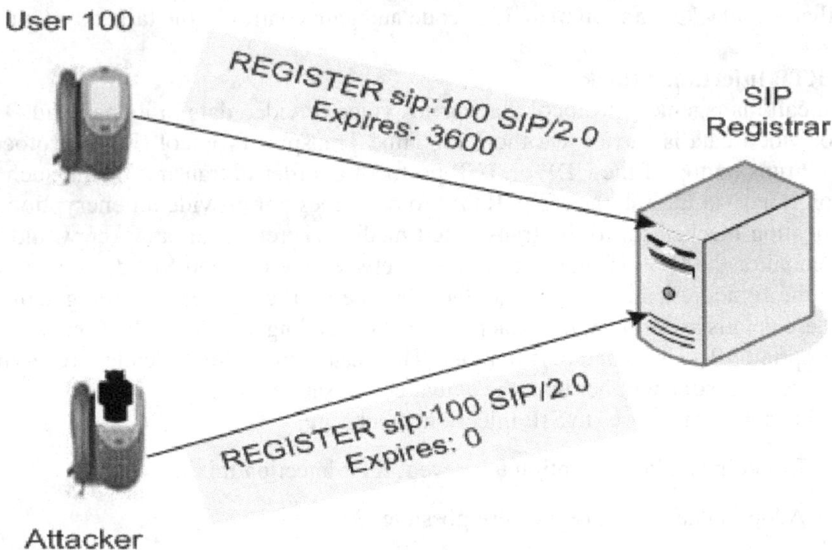

Fig. 2. De-Registration Attack

2.3.2 SIP Spoofing BYE Attack (Call Tear Down Attack)

The BYE request is used to terminate a SIP connection. An attacker can construct a BYE request and send it to the end device to terminate calls between participants. An attacker has to be able to intercept the calls between the participants and spoof a BYE request message with the Call-ID, To and From tag number fields and user SIP URI in order to achieve his attack.

If an attacker manages to listen to an organizations call centre and capture all the required fields then the attacker could launch a devastating attack and close down all the established calls.

2.3.3 SIP Re-Send Attack

An attacker can resend a SIP request message to an already established session in order to modify one or more of the parameters of the existing dialog session. For example, an attacker can resend a spoofed INVITE message to modify dialog parameters such as the To or From fields and this can cause a DoS attack to occur against the end system.

2.3.4 SIP Call Hijacking

SIP call hijacking is based on the attacker hijacking a call and re-directing it to his device. A call hijack attack is a combination of a de-registration attack and a registration attack. In order for an attacker to perform a call hijacking attack, the attacker needs to de-register one of the end SIP devices and then register the attacker's own device, masquerading as the user's identity in order to redirect the calls to the attacker's phone. A stealthier call hijacking might involve skipping the de-registration attack phase and simply sending a spoofed INVITE message with the victims identity to another SIP proxy. Depending on the SIP device, some systems will direct calls to both the original device and to the attacker's device. As a result the attacker may be able to passively listen and record any confidential conversation.

In order to reduce the likelihood of successful SIP spoofing attacks, the following measured should be enforced:

- A strong authentication mechanism to authenticate SIP request messages.
- The SIP proxy should ignore any SIP CANCEL request that follows any other message type than INVITE request.
- The challenge/response mechanism should be used to protect against replay attack. This method can be adopted by a SIP gateway solution to challenge SIP terminals before passing their SIP request.
- To prevent spoofing, an organization can modify the soft phone client software to embed the user's information into the application, thus making it unique to that user.
- Encrypt the SIP communications. By encrypting SIP messages, an attacker will not be able to gather information about the call itself in order to determine how to inject the attacker's control messages.
- Enable ingress filtering at the edges to drop packets that have a spoofed IP source address.

2.4 SIP Authentication Attack

SIP authentication [12] [7] does not provide a high level of security as it is based on the MD5 digest algorithm rather than using a public key algorithm. In addition, SIP authentication is based on a challenge/response where a trust is built based on a server sending a challenge to the client and then the client responding to the server. The challenge/response is based on MD5 hash (where the server needs to check the client response by repeating the MD5 calculation using a stored value of the username and password. Calculating the response is a computationally expensive task for the server, since it has to look for the username and password stored in the server database and combine it with the original challenge to compute the MD5 hash. The following subsections describes some of the SIP authentication attacks.

2.4.1 SIP DoS Authentication Attack

An attacker can exploit the SIP authentication mechanisms by generating a large number of requests and response messages to each challenge with a randomized or fixed response. The attack does not need to go through the expensive MD5 calculation and can just send a random response. All responses will fail but that will still keep the server busy checking the bogus requests and it will therefore have less time/resource to serve or handle legitimate calls.

2.4.2 Dictionary and Enumeration Attack

The SIP authentication mechanism is only as strong as the user password and as a result, a user's password could be vulnerable to a dictionary attack. An attacker might use a dictionary attack to discover a weak password of an end user. A dictionary attack can be detected as the result of multiple authentication failures. However, a much stealthier attack can be executed by monitoring the challenge and response session, which is sent in clear text, in order to predict the user's password.

In order to mitigate SIP authentication attacks:

- The SIP proxy should verify the client identity before going through the expensive SIP message verifications.
- Users should use a strong password to protect against dictionary attacks.

2.5 SIP Traffic Capturing

The SIP protocol does not provide encryption or authentication to the transmitted media. Therefore, an attacker can simply capture and record the SIP traffic using tool such as Wireshark [14]. SIP traffic capturing is the basic method for recording a conversation without the consent of the participants. For example, an attacker can eavesdrop on the current call, extract the RTP stream from the traffic and then convert the stream to a WAV file for unauthorized recording or to listen to it. By capturing and recording the media stream, an attacker may gain access to unauthorized material such as user's confidential information, passwords or personal information.

2.6 SIP Messages Modification Attack

As mentioned earlier, SIP consists of an envelope and a payload which are sent in clear text. The SIP envelope and payload contain various parameters that can be read and modified by an attacker. If an attacker intercepts a call message between the participants then he may be able to manipulate those parameters and affect the whole communication. For example an attacker can simply alter the Content-Length field from 450 to 200 in the SIP envelope. This would result of loss of 250 bytes and as a result the content would be truncated and the full contents will not be interpreted by the server. An attacker could also alter any other fields such as Content-Encoding, Content-Type field to disrupt the conversation.

Possible countermeasures for call eavesdropping are:

- Encrypt the SIP header and payload using the Secure Real-Time Transport Protocol (SRTP). Both media and signalling should be encrypted. If the signalling protocols contain encryption keys or if the identity of call participants is sensitive then it should be encrypted. Encrypting the media content prevents eavesdropping.
- Send the SIP messages over a secure channel such as Transport Layer Security (TLS)[4].

2.7 VoIP SPAM (SPIT)

Spam over Internet Telephony (SPIT) [6] is similar in nature to email SPAM where hundreds or thousands of unsolicited voice mail messages arrive at the end device. However, it would be very disruptive and time consuming to listen to and delete every voice mail message. When the VoIP service is free or cheap, users will be tempted to use it for spamming. Therefore, VoIP SPAM can be much more disruptive to a VoIP system than e-mail SPAM. A simple attack is to create a script that initiates calls to a range of numbers or IP addresses with a recorded voice message.

Countermeasures for voice SPAM include the deployment of a SPAM controller such as the White List/Blacklist technique, speech segmentation, speaker classification, automated verification, and content/header filtering [9]. Other solutions including voice prompts, for example "press 45 if you are real person" can be used [1].

3 Conclusions

Most organizations today are deploying VoIP in their infrastructure or providing VoIP as a service to their customers. While it has become increasingly attractive to deploy VoIP, many organizations still need to understand how VoIP can be deployed without placing their information and the continuity of their business at risk. Determining VoIP security threats and mitigation techniques is the first step in securing an organization's information from the increasing number of threats in this area. Once the security threats and mitigation processes are understood and identified an organization can then map out the type of features a vendor product must have in order to secure the VoIP network.

The vendor product should implement as many mitigation features as possible and make it easy for an organization to manage those features. Defence-in-depth is essential as there are no single mechanism that can ensure total security and as a result, multiple layers of security are recommended. For example, besides the security mitigation mechanisms proposed, a virtual separation of data and control information is essential. Virtual separation, for example by using VLANs, makes managing the security of the network easier and isolates different services into different network zones.

Most of the VoIP threats can be mitigated by having strong authentication, authorization and encryption in place. Implementing these security measures in the VoIP infrastructure will make spoofing, impersonation, and eavesdropping difficult to carry out. In order to prevent buffer overflow and application level exploitation, each device needs to be updated, patched and all unnecessary services and applications must be disabled.

In general, adopting best practice in the design and deployment of VoIP will ensure that the existing effectiveness of network security for an organization is not negatively impacted.

References

[1] Amber Group, VoIP Security Considerations for Service Providers, Centre for the protection of national Infrastructure (2007), `http://209.85.229.132/search?q=cache:fDKtkHCdsUoJ:csrc.nist.gov/publications/nistpubs/800-58/SP800-58-final.pdf+Amber+Group+%2B+VoIP+Security+Considerations&cd=1&hl=en&ct=clnk&client=firefox-a`

[2] Collier, M.: Basic Vulnerability Issues for SIP Security, SecureLogix Corporation (2005)

[3] Cisco, Cisco Security Advisory: Cisco Unified IP Phone Overflow and Denial of Service Vulnerabilities (2008), `http://www.cisco.com/warp/public/707/cisco-sa-20080213-phone.shtml`

[4] Dierks, T., Rescorla, E.: The Transport layer Security (TLS) Protocol, RFC 4346 (2006)

[5] Endler, D., Collier, M.: Hacking VoIP Exposed: Voice Over IP Security Secrets & Solutions. McGraw-Hill, London (2007)

[6] Kaplan, H., Packet, A., Wing, D.: The SIP Identity Baiting Attack. Cisco Systems, Internet Draft paper (2008), `https://datatracker.ietf.org/drafts/draft-kaplan-sip-baiting-attack`

[7] Kent, S., Atkinson, R.: Security Architecture for the Internet Protocol, RFC 2401 (1998)

[8] META Group, IP Telephony Security: Deploying Secure IP Telephony in the Enterprise network, META Group White Paper (2005), `http://seclab.cs.ucdavis.edu/seminars/ReynoldsSeminar.ppt`

[9] Pantridge, M.: VoIP SPAM Counter Measure. MSc Thesis, Informatics and Mathematical Modelling department, Technical University of Denmark (2006)

[10] Rivest, R.: The MD Message-digest Algorithm, RFC 1321 (1992)
[11] Rosenberg, J., Schulzrinne, H.: SIP: Session Initiation Protocol, RFC3261 (2002)
[12] Stefano, S., Luca, V., Donald, P.: SIP security issues: the SIP authentication procedure and its processing load. IEEE Network 16(6), 38–44 (2002)
[13] Thermos, P., Takanen, A.: Securing VoIP Networks: Threats, Vulnerabilities, and Countermeasures. Addison Wesley, London (2008)
[14] Wireshark (2008), `http://www.wireshark.org/`

Security Challenges in Multihop Wireless Mesh Networks–A Survey

Divya* and Sanjeev Kumar**

Computer Science & Engineering
Punjab Engineering College,
Chandigarh. India
{divya,sanjeevsofat}@pec.edu.in

Abstract. Security is a paramount concern in Wireless Mesh Networks (WMN) and also one of the core components in making WMNs successful and an enabler into different markets. A core challenge in securing the WMN is the large number of communication links over the air; as each mesh device may be mobile and deployed outdoors, each mesh link presents an exposure and vulnerability into the mesh network. These vulnerabilities are partially due to the structure of WMNs and cannot be removed easily. Security procedures present in 802.11s only take care of the potential security attacks in network association and secure link establishment. Ensuring that the routing protocol is secure is also not specified in the standard. In this paper we analyze the security problems in WMN and present few promising open research challenges which need immediate attention.

Keywords: Vulnerabilities, Attack prevention, IEEE 802.11s, Key Management, Secure routing.

1 Introduction

Original mesh architectures emerged from mobile ad hoc networks (MANETs) for military networks. The IETF MANET Work Group has been developing various MANET protocols for almost a decade [1]. MANETs were envisioned to be military and tactical networks where peer nodes could gain mutual trust between them. Mesh networks are different from MANETs in that there is more infrastructure communication rather than direct, peer-to-peer communication with mesh networks becoming a popular deployment in public spaces. IEEE 802.11s inherits security framework from 802.11i with certain extensions. Thus, whatever security problems exist in 802.11i will also occur in 802.11s. Moreover, due to the multihop mesh network architecture, security becomes a more challenging issue. It is thus evident that especially in the metropolitan space, existing IEEE networks' security standards 802.1X and 802.11i-2007 [2] based security mechanisms lack the specificity for securing the WMN. Even though

---

* Lecturer and Associate Coordinator, Cyber Security Research Centre.

** Professor and Coordinator, Cyber Security Research Centre.

D. Weerasinghe (Ed.): ISDF 2009, LNICST 41, pp. 92–101, 2010.

many vendors are using strong 128-bit encryption to relay client and infrastructure traffic over the air, as previous wireless LAN attacks have shown, a hacker may not necessarily need to crack the key to get user information or damage the network.

2 Potential Attacks on WMN Protocols

As mentioned earlier, WMNs face a range of security challenges that emerge due its multi-hop nature. To achieve availability, routing protocols should be robust against both dynamically changing topology and malicious attacks. Several routing protocols for WMNs have been proposed. A majority of these protocols assume a trustworthy collaboration among participating devices that are expected to abide by a "code-of-conduct". But there lie several security threats [3], some arising from shortcomings in the protocols, and others from the lack of conventional identification and authentication mechanisms. We classify the attacks into two categories namely external attacks and internal attacks. The attacks that are designed to exploit the vulnerabilities of WMN are called external attacks. In such attacks the attacker is in the close proximity but not a trusted node. In contrast, in internal attacks the attackers are actually willing to participate in the mesh network.

2.1 External Attacks

By injecting erroneous routing information, replaying old routing information, or distorting routing information, an attacker can successfully partition a network or introduce excessive traffic load into the network by causing retransmission and inefficient routing. External attacks are usually prevented with conventional security mechanisms such as member authentication.

2.2 Internal Attacks

These are more severe kind of threats which come from compromised nodes advertising incorrect routing information to other nodes. Detection of such incorrect information is difficult as merely requiring routing information to be signed by each node would not work, because compromised nodes are able to generate valid signatures using their private keys. External attacks are usually used as stepping stones leading to internal attacks. To defend against the first kind of threats, nodes can protect routing information in the same way as they protect data traffic. However, this defense is ineffective against attacks from compromised servers. Detection of compromised nodes through routing information is also very difficult in a WMN because of its dynamic topology changes.

Attacks on routing layer can be classified into two categories, attacks on routing protocols & attacks on packet forwarding/delivery. Attacks on routing prevent a victim from finding the path from source to destination even if routes exist and attack on packet forwarding disrupt packet delivery even if the path is known.

Attacks on routing can create various undesirable affects. On the other hand, certain properties of WMNs can be exploited to achieve secure routing which are discussed in the end of the paper. Routing protocols for WMNs must also be able to handle outdated routing information to accommodate the dynamically changing topology.

False routing information generated by compromised nodes could, to some extent, be considered outdated information. As long as there are sufficiently many correct nodes, the routing protocol should be able to find routes without involving these compromised nodes. Such capability of the routing protocols usually relies on the inherent redundancies in WMNs.

3 Secure Routing Protocols

The mechanisms discussed in this section prevent internal attacks by preventing misbehaving nodes from attacking the routing information. To address the security attacks on routing mechanism, several secure routing protocols have been proposed: such as SAODV, Ariadne, SEAD, CSER, SRP, SAAR, BSAR, and SBRP [4]. The default routing protocol in 802.11s TGs is Hybrid Wireless Mesh Protocol (HWMP) [5], which provides the ability for a mesh node to learn routes to another mesh node using a broadcast route discovery mechanism. Broadcast-based route discovery mechanisms are traditionally susceptible to DoS attacks as they use exhaustive rebroadcasting methods.

3.1 Use of Cryptographic Approaches

In [6] the use of asymmetric cryptography to secure on-demand ad hoc network routing protocols has been proposed. However, as above, when the nodes in an ad hoc network are generally unable to verify asymmetric signatures quickly enough, or when network bandwidth is insufficient, these protocols may not be suitable. In [7] *symmetric*-key approaches to implement the authentication of link-state updates have been described, but they do not discuss mechanisms for detecting the status of these links. Furthermore, these protocols assume the use of periodic routing protocols, which are not always suitable in ad hoc networks. In [8] cryptographic mechanisms similar to those used in Ariadne with TESLA have been used but this approach optimistically integrates routing data before it is authenticated adversely affecting security. A number of other researchers have also proposed the use of symmetric schemes for authenticating routing control packets. In [9, 10] a mechanism requiring shared keys between all communicating routers is proposed. This scheme may not scale to large mesh networks and may be vulnerable to single-node compromise. In [10] use of symmetric primitives to secure routing between nodes and a trusted base station has been proposed. In [11] use a network-wide symmetric key to secure routing communication is proposed which is vulnerable to a single node compromise, although the use of secure hardware to limit the damage that can be done by a compromised node is also specified.

There is yet another kind of routing protocols which use one-way hash chains. SEAD is one such routing protocol which builds on the DSDV-SQ version of the DSDV (Destination Sequenced Distance Vector) protocol. However SEAD does not cope with wormhole attacks. SEAD [12] uses hash chains to authenticate routing updates sent by a distance-vector protocol; however, this approach builds on a periodic protocol, and such protocols tend to have higher overhead than on-demand protocols and may not be suitable in highly mobile networks.

IETF's AODV and DSR are efficient in terms of network performance, but they allow attackers to easily advertise falsified route information, to redirect routes, and to launch DoS attacks. In case these protocols are applied to WMNs, an attacker may easily snoop frames over a WLAN mesh backhaul and learn about MAC addresses or various mesh nodes in the network. Although the network infrastructure of 802.11 WMNs tends to have less mobility and most of the traffic is to and from the Internet, however, some nodes such as handset devices, laptops, etc. can be an MP and may need mobility support.

In a routing protocol, nodes usually need to exchange routing messages for the purpose of finding link status, collecting neighbor information, requesting routing path, and so on. Thus, many control messages are involved. In order to meet diverse requirements by making the routing protocol be efficient for different scenarios, HWMP is being specified in 802.11s. In 802.11s, such messages are sent in various mesh action frames as information elements. Before draft 1.06 of 802.11s, one mandatory routing protocol and one optional routing protocol have been specified. The mandatory routing protocol is called hybrid wireless mesh protocol (HWMP), which is a hybrid routing protocol of on-demand routing and proactive tree-based routing. The optional routing protocol is based on link state routing and is called radio aware optimized link state routing (RA-OLSR).

The basic features of on-demand routing protocol based on radio-metric ad hoc on-demand distance vector (AODV) routing are adopted in HWMP with certain extensions 802.11s. The proactive tree-based routing is applied when a root node is configured in the mesh network. With this root, a distance vector tree can be built and maintained for other nodes, which can avoid unnecessary routing overhead for routing path discovery and recovery. It should be noted that the on-demand routing and tree-based routing can run simultaneously. Wireless Mesh Network (WMN) has emerged as a key technology and found a great deal of interest for the researchers in the recent past. Hybrid Wireless Mesh Protocol (HWMP) is the default path selection (i.e., routing) protocol fully specified in the current draft D.1.06 of 802.11s for WMN. However, security in routing or forwarding functionality is not specified in the standard. As a consequence, HWMP in its current from is vulnerable to various types of routing attacks. Since HWMP is based on the AODV [13], an open-source AODV software stack can be used to continually generate route request (RREQ) frames keeping all mesh nodes in the network busy re-broadcasting those. This may cause one or more mesh nodes to melt down, reboot, or stop servicing the network.

Further, most of the fields used in routing related information in AODV such as RRER, RREP, and RERR, are vulnerable to modification and forgery. Example of such mutable fields is: ID, Hop Count, Metric, Sequence Number, etc. Most damaging is the vulnerability of an MAC address, as an adversary can impersonate an MP by simply using its MAC address; an adversary can simply form part of mesh forwarding paths and launch any attack from there. Similar attacks are also possible against RA-OLSR, which is the optional path selection protocol in IEEE 802.11s draft standard.

SAODV [13] is a secure version of the original AODV protocol, which combines these techniques and more (e.g., digital signature for static fields in headers and hash chains to protect Hop Count). While SAODV is appropriate for ad hoc networks, it comes with some costs for WMNs. Even though hash chains are efficient for Hop

Count authentication, a malicious node can still choose not to increase it. Other drawbacks of SAODV include PKI infrastructure usage and key distribution, too frequent signature computations, and extra overhead for exchanging signatures, which can be up to two signatures per message, makes SAODV computationally prohibitive. IEEE 802.11 TGs is evaluating these techniques and may incorporate some subset of SAODV for securing the default path selection protocol, HWMP. ARAN [14] and Ariadne [15] are two other techniques for securing AODV, which can be adapted for securing HWMP. ARAN provides authentication and non-repudiation services using pre-determined cryptographic certificates that guarantees end-to-end authentication. As a result, ARAN limits or prevents attacks that can badly affect other insecure protocols. ARIADNE is an on-demand secure ad-hoc routing protocol based on DSR that implements highly efficient symmetric cryptography. It provides point-to-point authentication of a routing message using a message authentication code (MAC) and a shared key between the two communicating parties. Although ARIADNE is free from a flood of route request packets and cache poisoning attack, but it is immune to the wormhole attack and rushing attack.

3.2 Internal Attacks in WMN

The internal attacks in WMN also pose a serious threat. If an attacker gains full control of a legitimate node, the cryptographic approaches will not be able to prevent the attacks launched from the node because the node has valid cryptographic keys and the messages sent by the node are also cryptographically valid. The compromised nodes could attack the routing mechanisms by generating false routing information, scheduling the data packets forwarding for their own benefits, selectively forwarding the packets, or not forwarding any packet at all.

If an attacking node lures all traffic around it by installing an attractive node using powerful transmitters and high-gain antennas to emerge as high-quality routes, it is termed as **sinkhole attacks**. Detection of sinkholes is difficult [18] without higher-layer protections such as asking for acknowledgments from the final destinations for all messages. Another kind of internal attack is the **black hole attack** which is performed in two steps. At first step, the malicious node exploits the mobile ad hoc routing protocol such as AODV, to advertise itself as having a valid route to a destination node, even though the route is spurious, with the intention of intercepting the packets. In second step, the attacker consumes the packets and never forwards. In an advanced form, the attacker suppresses or modifies packets originating from some nodes, while leaving the data from the other nodes unaffected. In this way, the attacker falsified the neighboring nodes that monitor the ongoing packets. **Byzantine attack** [17] can be launched by a single malicious node or a group of nodes that work in cooperation. A compromised intermediate node works alone or set of compromised intermediate nodes work together to form attacks. The compromised nodes may create routing loops, forwarding packets in a long route instead of optimal one, even may drop packets. This attack degrades the routing performance and also disrupts the routing services. **Rushing attacks** [17] are yet another kind of serious attacks which subvert route discovery process to increase the likelihood that hostile station will be included in the given route. At present there are no integrated mechanisms in the routing protocols to defend against these kinds of attacks. An attacker may leverage multiple attacking nodes and create low-latency and high-speed route tunnels between them. This strategy will make attacker's tunnel appear attractive over a multi-hop path and cause a wide area of nodes to attempt to use the tunnel. Black hole/gray hole/sinkhole attacks might follow. Unfortunately, wormhole attacks are effective even if the protocol/system provides authenticity and confidentiality. Given the use of strong identification credentials, e.g., strong entropy keys and unique identities, IEEE 802.11 TGs may be able to address some of the above attacks, but may still be susceptible to insider attacks. The Packet Leash solution [16] is to add some extra information to each message at the sender side in order to allow the receiver to determine if the packet has traversed an unrealistic distance. The extra information could be a precise timestamp, which requires extremely precise clock synchronization, or the location information with a timestamp, which requires less precise clock synchronization.

4 Intrusion Detection Techniques

Because WMN has features such as an open medium, dynamic changing topology, and the lack of a centralized monitoring and management point, many of the intrusion detection techniques developed for a fixed wired network are not applicable in WMNs. In [22, 23] a specific design of intrusion detection and response mechanisms is proposed. In [24] two mechanisms: watchdog and pathrater are proposed, which improve throughput in the presence of nodes that agree to forward packets but fail to do so. In WMNs, cooperation is very important to support the basic functions of the network so the token-based mechanism, the credit-based mechanism, and the reputation-based mechanism can be used to enforce cooperation. In the case of WMN the Authentication becomes very critical issue to handle. However we have briefly studied the Central and Distributed Authentication mechanism that can be applied in case of WMNs but there is more to do with it. Although the need for a distributed authorization service is necessary to cope with the WMN necessities, the challenge still resides in the establishment of trust inside the network. As explained before, a totally centralized approach is unlikely to be an ultimate solution for trust establishment inside a WMN. However, a scheme based on transitive trust within the network can also create security breaches.

Thus from the above discussions it is clear that all security procedures present in 802.11s only take care of the potential security attacks in network association and secure link establishment. Ensuring that the routing protocol is secure is not specified in the standard. Routing security is usually considered as out-of-scope work for an IEEE 802.11 standard. However, for 802.11s [25], since the routing functionality is specified in the link layer, it becomes imperative to specify a security mechanism for routing protocols in 802.11s standard. WMNs are extremely vulnerable to attacks due to their dynamically changing topology, absence of conventional security infrastructures and open medium of communication, which, unlike their wired counterparts, cannot be secured. To secure a WMN, Secure routing and wireless Intrusion detection systems are considered to be the major attributes in context of the present paper to prevent internal and external attacks.

5 Mesh Security

The conventional WLAN security mechanisms (e.g., such as WPA2/802.11i) provide standardized methods for authentication, access control and encryption between a wireless client and an access point. Since most wide-area mesh solutions strive to retain compatibility with commercial off-the-shelf WLAN client adapters, existing standardized WPA2 mechanisms are commonly retained (e.g., the mesh network "looks like" an access point to the client). However, there are many different types of wireless mesh architectures, where each type of architecture may use a different approach for wireless security. Many approaches for mesh security may be derived from ad-hoc security research, but any future commercial mesh products will standardize security through 802.11s (e.g., will be based primarily on 802.11i security mechanisms).

5.1 Client Access Controls

Wireless mesh infrastructure networks provide access to wireless clients. In most 802.11-based wireless networks, clients are standard wireless LAN stations with no mesh networking capabilities. Some vendors, such as Motorola and PacketHop offer client mesh solutions, but all Metro-WiFi technologies are intended on providing access to non-mesh capable 802.11 stations. Client access security may vary depending on the type of network: a Metro-WiFi network may use open wireless authentication with a Layer 3 billing service access gateway, while an enterprise/private mesh network will typically use WPA2-compliant wireless access controls.

5.2 Inter-mesh Access Point Controls

While there are many progressive technologies available through ad-hoc security research, many commercially available mesh networks use a far more simple security model in advance of a mesh security standard. Most existing 802.11-based communication between mesh access points leverages a wireless-distribution system (WDS) mode-of-operation. A conventional (e.g., non-mesh) access point in WDS mode is simple wireless relay between wireless clients and wired access points. Many chipset vendors and mesh equipment providers offer communication protection between nodes using a static key to encrypt WDS links with WEP or AES. With the availability of fully compliant WPA2/802.11i chipsets, separate WPA2 security profiles can be defined for the WDS links (clients will be able to connect to the mesh APs with an alternate security profile – such as without encryption). Thus, there are two primary methods to protect inter-mesh AP communication in advance 802.11s standardization that are based mainly on WPA2/802.11i compliance levels for WDS mode:

- Static keys configured into the APs at both ends of the WDS link, providing WEP or AES encryptions between mesh nodes.
- WPA2/802.11i [22] specifies how key handshake works in ad-hoc mode, letting peers derive dynamic encryption keys. This makes it possible to apply the 802.11i four-way key handshake defined for ad-hoc mode to mesh APs connected by WDS. In other words, mesh traffic relayed using WDS modes for inter-mesh AP traffic is secured by WPA2. It is common for each mesh AP on the

network to be set with the same unique key, otherwise the mesh APs will not be able to communicate with one another. The number of session keys is directly proportional to the number of neighbors. Authentication is provided either through knowledge of a network-wide pre-shared key (e.g., in a similar manner as WPA-PSK), but some vendors already provide X.509v3-based authentication that derives unique pair-wise session keys per link. Challenges for mesh networks relate mainly to support for broadcast between mesh APs, which is an essential component of mesh routing protocols. Group session keys are used for broadcast messaging, while pair-wise keys are used for unicast routing messages. The 802.11s standardization efforts will provide authentication and communication protection in consideration of these factors, and the functional requirements of the mesh routing algorithms. The 802.11i security mechanisms and the associated WiFi-Protect Access (WPA2) profiles provide the basic building blocks for 802.11-based security (e.g., either in mesh networking or typical client access). The 802.11 security framework uses the 802.1X port-based access control mechanisms to prevent unauthorized wireless access. The client is the supplicant that requests authentication from an authentication server such as RADIUS where the authenticator gates access until the client is authenticated. The authentication exchange occurs between the client and the authentication server using the EAP protocol, which encapsulates the specific type of authentication. The Extensible Authentication Protocol (EAP) is a flexible protocol used to carry arbitrary authentication information, and rides on top of 802.1X and RADIUS to protocols to transfer data between the wireless client and an authentication server. EAP does not specify an authentication method. Commonly used methods are based on TLS/SSL technologies, where a secure tunnel and network-to-client authentication can be performed using a digital certificate, and clients can authenticate using either their own client certificate (e.g., EAP-TLS) or provide a username and password authentication exchange inside the secure TLS tunnel (e.g., EAPPEAP or EAP-TTLS). Upon success authentication, keying material is generated and distributed to enable encryption and integrity checking. The integrity checking prevents both message tampering and ensures an authenticated client cannot be impersonated. The WPA2 profile adds AES encryption and key management. The wireless security schemes for mesh networks are based on these fundamental capabilities.

5.3 Standardization

The IEEE is presently working on a standard for mesh networking through the 802.11s working group. The standard will use the WPA2/802.11i security methods to protect the wireless links, where the key principles in 802.11s security is summarized below:

- Standardization activities for security will focus on inter-AP security controls, where client access uses standard WPA2/802.11i authentication and encryption.
- Standardization on security between mesh access points is still being finalized within the standard. However, link-by-link security mechanism will be based on 802.11i, with a security architecture based on 802.1X authentication.

- Mesh APs may have supplicant, authentication and authentication server roles.
- All mesh routing must be authenticated using 4-way handshakes which can be attained using centralized 802.1X authentication. However, means of communicating between authentication server and remote mesh AP is presently not within the scope of the standard.

6 Conclusion

WMN has the several research challenges which need immediate attention. Study of WMN's specifics led to many critical security challenges which have been discussed in detailed in the paper. While the techniques and standardization considerations discussed in this paper can deter certain attacks in WMN, there is a limitation to the effects of prevention attacks. There is no single efficient and reliable security solution suitable for WLAN mesh as many of those solutions may be compromised due to vulnerabilities of channels and nodes in shared media, absence of reliable links to infrastructure, and dynamic topology changes. Use of cryptographic extensions in HWMP is also desirable to provide authenticity and integrity of routing messages and prevents unauthorized manipulation of mutable fields in the routing information elements. It therefore becomes evident that much work remains in developing integrated framework which can collectively battle multi-protocol attacks as well as detect and prevent intrusion in WMNs. Furthermore, an integrated, cross-layer security solution is more desirable.

References

1. `http://www.ietf.org/html.charters/manet-charter.html`
2. IEEE STD 802.11-2007. Wireless Local Area Networks, IEEE, WLAN Standard (2002)
3. Xuyang, D., Mingyu, F., Xiaojun, L., Dayong, Z., Jiahao, W.: Multi-path based secure communication in wireless mesh networks. Journal of Systems Engineering and Electronics 18(4), 818–824 (2007)
4. Zhang, W., Rao, R., Cao, G., Kesidis, G.: Secure Routing in Ad Hoc Networks and a Related Intrusion Detection Problem. In: Proceedings of IEEE Military Communications Conference, October 2003, vol. 2, pp. 735–740 (2003)
5. Bahr, M.: Update on the Hybrid Wireless Mesh Protocol of IEEE 802.11s. In: Proc. in IEEE International Conference on Mobile Adhoc and Sensor Systems, October 8-11, pp. 1–6 (2007)
6. Wu, B., Chen, J., Wu, J., Cardei, M.: A Survey of Attacks and Countermeasures in Mobile Ad Hoc Networks. In: Wireless Network Security. Network Theory and Applications, vol. 17. Springer, Heidelberg (2006)
7. Cheung, S.: An Efficient Message Authentication Scheme for Link State Routing. In: 13th Annual Computer Security Applications Conference, pp. 90–98 (1997)
8. Blunk, L., Vollbrecht, J., Aboba, B., Carlson, J., Levkowetz, H.: Extensible Authentication Protocol (EAP). Internet Draft draft-ietf-eap-rfc2284bis-06.txt (September 29, 2003)
9. Heffernan, A.: Protection of BGP Sessions via the TCP MD5 Signature Option. RFC 2385 (August 1998)

10. Batina, L., Mentens, N., Sakiyama, K., Preneel, B., Verbauwhede, I.: Low-cost Elliptic Curve Cryptography for Wireless Sensor Networks. In: 3rd European Workshop on Security and Privacy in Ad hoc and Sensor Networks, pp. 6–17 (2006)
11. Basagni, S., Herrin, K., Rosti, E., Bruschi, D.: Secure Pebblenets. In: Proceedings of the Second Symposium on Mobile Ad Hoc Networking and Computing, October 2001, pp. 156–163 (2001)
12. Hu, Y.-C., Johnson, D.B., Perrig, A.: Secure Efficient Distance Vector Routing in Mobile Wireless Ad Hoc Networks. In: Fourth IEEE Workshop on Mobile Computing Systems and Applications (WMCSA 2002), June 2002, pp. 3–13 (2002)
13. Zapata, M., Asokan, N.: Securing Ad hoc Routing Protocols. In: ACM Workshop on Wireless Secuirty (WiSe) (September 2002)
14. Sanzgiri, K., Dahill, B., Levine, B.N., Shields, C., Belding-Royer, E.M.: A Secure Protocol for Adhoc Networks. In: IEEE International Conference on Network Protocols, ICNP (2002)
15. Hu, Y., Perrig, A., Johnson, D.: Ariadne: A Secure On-demand Routing Protocol for Ad hoc Networks. In: ACM Annual International Conference on Mobile Computing and Networking (MOBICOM) (September 2002)
16. Hu, Y.C., Johnson, D.B., Perrig, A.: Packet leashes: A defense against wormhole attacks in wireless networks. In: Proc. IEEE INFOCOM 2003, March/April 2003, vol. 3, pp. 1976–1986 (2003)
17. Glass, S., Portmann, M., villipuram: Securing Wireless Mesh Networks, pp. 1089–7801. IEEE Computer Society, Los Alamitos (2008)
18. IEEE Std 802.11i/D4.1, Wireless Medium Access Control (MAC) and Physical Layer (PHY) Specifications: Medium Access Control (MAC) Security Enhancements (2003)
19. Joint SEE-Mesh/Wi-Mesh Proposal to 802.11 TGs (2006)
20. Luo, H., Zerfos, P., Kong, J., Lu, S., Zhang, L.: Self-securing ad hoc wireless networks. In: Proc. IEEE ISCC 2002, July 2002, pp. 567–574 (2002)
21. Zhang, W., Das, S., Liu, Y.: A trust based framework for secure data aggregation in wireless sensor networks. In: Proc. IEEE SECON 2006, September 2006, pp. 60–69 (2006)
22. Tsakountakis, A., Kambourak, g., Gritzalis, S.: Towards effective Wireless Intrusion Detection in IEEE 802.11i. In: Proc. of Third International Workshop on Security Privacy and Trust in Pervasive and Uniquitous Computing, IEEE SecPerU (2007)
23. Zhang, Y., Lee, W., Huang, Y.: Intrusion Detection Techniques for Mobile Wireless Networks. ACM/Kluwer Wireless Networks Journal (ACM WINET) 9(5) (September 2003)
24. Marti, S., Giuli, T., Lai, K., Baker, M.: Mitigating Routing Misbehavior in Mobile Ad Hoc Networks. In: Proceeding of the Sixth Annual International Conference on Mobile Computing and Networking (MOBICOM), Boston, pp. 255–265 (2000)
25. Wua, T.-W., Hsieh, H.-Y.: Interworking wireless mesh networks: Problems, performance characterization, and perspectives. National Taiwan University, Journal Parallel Distributed Computing 68, 348–360 (2008)
26. Gerkis: A Survey of Wireless Mesh Networking Security Technology and Threats, SANS Institute InfoSec Reading Room (September 2006)

A Security Architecture to Protect Against Data Loss

Clive Blackwell

Information Security Group, Royal Holloway, University of London,
Egham, Surrey. TW20 0EX. UK
C.Blackwell@rhul.ac.uk

Abstract. Data loss poses a significant and increasing problem for organisations. This is shown by the regular stories of data loss reported daily in the media, such as the mailing of 2 CDs containing 25 million personal records by the Revenue and Customs in the UK. There is a need to provide systematic protection to data in all its forms and locations however it is accessed. We have developed Searchlight, a three-layer security architecture containing the physical, logical and social levels, which we use to analyse data loss holistically to prevent, detect and recover from exposure. We examine deliberate and accidental data loss by employees, but the same analysis can be straightforwardly applied to external attacks. Our practical security model appears to have widespread application to other problem domains such as critical infrastructure, the insider threat and financial systems, as it allows the analysis of systems in their entirety including human and physical factors, not just as technical systems.

Keywords: Data loss, security architecture, Searchlight model, attack and data loss classification.

System Modelling

Data Loss and Its Causes

We define data loss as the disclosure of sensitive confidential or private data held about an organisation or person, or metadata about systems and their means of access such as passwords. The effects of data disclosure on an organisation may be financial loss, interference with business activities, loss of trust and reputation, and stronger regulatory controls and fines. The ultimate victim may be a third party data subject whose information is held by the organisation, who may suffer financial and identity fraud, or loss of privacy or reputation, that may take time and effort to recover, and cause psychological distress.

We investigate data loss incidents caused by employees and other insiders with legitimate access, but the same analysis can be straightforwardly applied to external theft. Insiders can cause great damage to organisations because of their privileged access, knowledge of weaknesses and the location of valuable data that can be misused for their own purposes or inadvertently revealed. The insider threat is the biggest threat to organisations' intellectual property and other sensitive data according to 68% of respondents in a recent McAfee report [1]. The disclosure of the personal records of third

D. Weerasinghe (Ed.): ISDF 2009, LNICST 41, pp. 102–110, 2010.

parties is also serious, as the cost of recovery averages $202 per record, according to the Ponemon Institute [2]. Some new books cover data loss in more detail [3], [4].

Accidental Data Loss by Her Majesty's Revenue and Customs

We show how to use our systematic model to analyse data loss, by applying it to the loss of 25 million personal records by HMRC. The goal of the employee in the HMRC fiasco was helping the organisation satisfy its regulatory responsibilities. HMRC was required to reveal a specific subset of Child Benefit data to the National Audit Office for auditing. This lead to the employee sending out all 25 million personal records by mail on 2 CDs that was an unacceptable breach of policy and lack of commonsense, which lead to him losing his job, and the head of HMRC resigning. We use our model to analyse weaknesses in the data handling procedures that led to the incident, and determine the security measures that could have avoided it and minimise the likelihood of a reoccurrence.

The Searchlight Model

Multilevel Security Model

We believe that data loss is a complex multifaceted problem that requires systematic analysis to mitigate. We have designed a three-layer architectural security model called Searchlight to investigate and evaluate system security, which we apply to data loss. The use of layers is a common structuring method used to decompose and analyse systems. We are influenced by Neumann's practical classification system for attacks with eight layers [5], [6], which are, in descending order: the external environment, user, application, middleware, networking, operating system, hardware and internal environment.

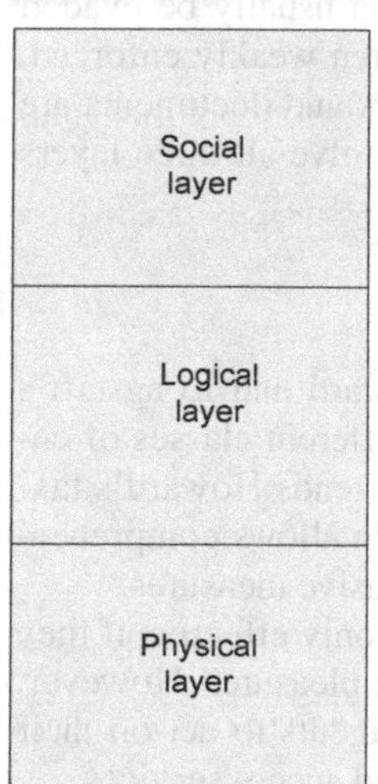

Fig. 1. The Searchlight model

The Searchlight model is a three-layer model, which includes the social layer (people and organisations) and physical layer along with the middle logical layer containing computers and networks. This allows a holistic representation and analysis of complex systems such as organisations in their entirety, including human and physical factors, rather than as technical systems alone.

Data has a separate spatial scope at each layer. For example, the number of people that know some information is its scope at the social level; the extent of logical data is its availability to computers and applications that may extend worldwide over the Internet; whereas physically stored data may be restricted to paper documents on a desk or in a filing cabinet.

The social or organisational layer contains the abstract representation of organisations by their attributes including their goals, policies and procedures. It also includes people and their characteristics such as their goals, knowledge and beliefs. Business and personal information exists at the social level, because it does not have meaning at lower levels. Data may be stored, processed and transmitted on computers and paper at lower levels but this representation is not understood semantically. This is similar to Searle's argument with his Chinese room [7], where a program that simply transforms inputs of Chinese characters to corresponding outputs of Chinese outputs could possibly pass the Turing test without demonstrating any intelligence.

The logical layer is the intermediate layer that contains intangible computational entities including computers, networks, software and data. Logical data is a representation of information at the social level, where it is more amenable for processing, distribution and storage. It also includes data used to supply logical services to social level entities such as authentication information like passwords that link people to their accounts. The logical layer is incorrectly the focus of most attention in security, because all layers need protection to provide comprehensive security.

The physical layer is the bottom layer that contains tangible objects including buildings, equipment, paper documents, and the physical aspects of computers and associated devices. In addition, it contains electromagnetic radiation such as radio waves, electricity and magnetism that are used to transmit and store data. All higher layer entities, including people and information, have a physical existence as well as a higher layer representation that must be considered when analysing data security.

Examples of data loss from physical objects include insecure laptops, USB sticks and paper documents. Data can also be leaked in transmission over various physical communication channels with differing spatial scopes: overheard during face-to-face and phone conversations, and over computer communication channels such as the Internet, local networks, and from keyboard inputs.

Technical data protection measures alone are incomplete and cannot stop attacks that occur partially or totally at other layers. The comment that Butler Lampson and Roger Needham attributed to each other: "Whoever thinks his problems can be solved using cryptography, doesn't understand his problem and doesn't understand cryptography", can be extended to the inadequacy of technical controls in general. In addition, the social level controls such as policies and procedures can usually be evaded by employees, as they cannot cover every eventuality and are often weakly enforced. Physical attacks to steal, damage or misuse equipment, computers and documents are also common. We conclude that organisational security must involve all three layers to provide comprehensive defence against data loss.

An Attack Classification Scheme

We investigate the stages of data loss with an extension of Howard and Longstaff's taxonomy [5], [6] for network security incidents that show the different classes of entity involved and their relationships. Our classification scheme extends Howard's taxonomy to include the social and physical aspects of systems, which allows comprehensive modelling of organisations, including the corresponding defensive measures.

All incidents are initiated by people at the social layer and are only effective if they meet a social goal such as obtaining money, power, reputation or pleasure. However, people cannot operate directly at the logical layer, so they use agents to act on their behalf such as user accounts to issue commands, run programs and access services.

In the active stage of an incident, the *perpetrator* or their *agent* employs a *method* to perform an *action* that executes a *threat* to exploit a *vulnerability* with an *immediate effect* on a *target*. This ultimately achieves the perpetrator's social layer goal, which could be benign and have an unintentional effect on the victim. We distinguish between the *immediate effect* at the lower layer on the confidentiality, integrity and availability of data loss, and the *ultimate effect* on the victim at the social layer of financial, privacy and reputational loss.

In addition, we have corresponding concepts to describe and classify defensive mechanisms, where there is a matching defensive category for each incident concept described above. For example, there are different defensive controls to stop the immediate effect of loss of data confidentiality using data loss prevention (DLP) tools, and to minimise the ultimate social level financial impact on a victim when their compromised credit card details are used in a fake transaction.

Possible incidents can be plotted in a table showing the active elements of our classification as columns in a grid with a row for each level. Incidents' progression through the various stages are shown as paths through the grid from left to right starting with access to the target before moving on to demonstrate the subsequent damaging effects on the organisation. We can then create an analogous table with the corresponding defensive measures, to provide a complete and consistent defence at all layers to prevent or constrain incidents, as we demonstrated elsewhere [10], [11].

Data Loss Classification

We need a clear understanding of the functions and weaknesses of data along with the powers of users that may be abused. We consider that sensitive organisational and personal information, and account access data such as passwords constitute the main targets for data disclosure. Impacts on reputation, recovery costs and psychological wellbeing may also be the primary motive of the data breach, but are generally side effects of the incident.

We can classify data loss incidents according to their effect on the victim or the benefit to the perpetrator. We can focus on the purpose of the perpetrator to classify their intent into financial gain, business advantage, psychological pleasure and accidental disclosure. Incidents can also be classified by their effects on the victim from damage, fraud and theft, which have an undesirable impact indirectly by first breaching the fundamental security service of confidentiality, usually at lower layers.

The effects on the organisation from the three classes of data loss are:

- Damage – Caused by reducing organisational reputation and business abilities. Indirect effects arise from interfering with its ability to perform its normal business activities by greater competition resulting from the disclosure of information about its business activities and products. Loss of reputation and trust arise from the release of sensitive third party information
- Fraud – Causes financial losses to the organisation or their customers by allowing unauthorised transactions, illegitimate access to resources, and impersonation to gain financial, business or personal services. An indirect attack caused by the loss of authentication or authorisation data
- Theft – Includes logical resources that give access to computer-held data, and physical assets such as computers, storage devices and paper documents

The impact to third party data subjects arising from an organisational breach includes:

- The loss of privacy from personal information lost, and possible interference with activities subsequently such as caused by identity fraud
- The time, effort and money to carry out recovery measures
- Psychological distress.

Attack Surface

Michael Howard, a Microsoft employee, invented the idea of the attack surface [1], which is the set of available channels to access and use computer systems. For example, it is the set of commands offered by an application or the available links on a Web page. We extend the idea of attack surface to all three layers, which allows a complete determination and analysis of exploitable access paths.

In addition, we extend the attack surface to include boundaries that the attacker can move through to gain local access to the target, rather than operating at a distance over a channel. Higher layers entities have a conceptual location that can describe their position, proximity and relationship to other entities at the same level. For example, every file has a logical position within a directory, and processes execute in virtual memory. People have a conceptual social-level position such as a role within an organisation, or a personal position that can be taken over by an identity thief.

A complete attack surface can provide systematic defence by constraining movement to and remote access of the target at every layer. Insiders are not limited by external system boundaries such as building entrances and firewalls that protect the organisation from external attack. An employee may instead be constrained by internal attack surfaces that partition the system with defensive controls, such as role-based access controls that must be breached to gain unauthorised access to sensitive data. Many insider incidents, however, use authorised access, such as accessing the target data using their own accounts, so there is no interposed attack surface. For example, finance or sales employees may use their permitted access to steal money from accounts.

Impact Zone

We also need to limit the scope and impact of data breaches, which includes limiting undesirable effects on the organisation and third parties. The impact zone is the set of resources affected that are unavailable, modified or disclosed illegitimately. TJ Maxx [13] allowed at least 45.7 million credit and debit card details to be revealed because of inadequate protection. Data disclosure can be limited by data minimisation as far as possible to reduce the impact of incidents.

The impact zone from disclosed data extends past the organisational or system boundary, so that access is no longer under its control. This is a dual notion to the attack surface that constrains the inward movement and access to organisational resources. The impact zone is already used informally in data protection at all three layers to limit the effects of disclosure. Employees are trained not to reveal sensitive information about the organisation to third parties on the phone. Data loss prevention (DLP) refers to controlling the disclosure of sensitive information by searching documents and messages for confidential information before release. Paper documents naturally have a restricted scope compared to digital data, as they are more difficult to distribute physically. Finally, it applies to the rule of least privilege that limits employees' privileges to the minimum required for the job, which limits the impact of data incidents using authorised access.

The impact must have an ultimate effect at the social layer, as lower-level resources only have value to the extent that they support organisational goals. Data disclosure can only has an effect from its subsequent misuse. For example, the loss of sensitive business data, such as intellectual property and business plans, may lead to business disadvantage from stronger competition when it is used by their competitors.

The impact zone is fundamental to data disclosure, which must have an external scope to be effective. For example, fraudulent use of third party credit card details causes losses to third-party victims. To affect the organisation, however, the effects must boomerang back to the organisation by the actions of the victims who seek compensation or the authorities who levy fines. The effect of data disclosure is thus an external release through the impact zone that returns to the organisation in a transformed form from a third party.

Protecting against Data Loss

Accidental Data Loss by Her Majesty's Revenue and Customs

We apply the Searchlight model to analyse the loss of 25 million personal records by HMRC, as described in detail in the Poynter report [14]. An employee mailed all 25 million Child Benefit records on 2 CDs to the National Audit Office to satisfy their regulatory responsibilities to audit Child Benefit cases, which never arrived. This incident did not have a direct effect on HMRC, as the data concerned third party data subjects, but there were indirect effects on their reputation and trustworthiness, so they needed to improve their security procedures to minimise the likelihood of a reoccurrence. We indicate some of the main security measures to protect organisations, illustrated by the weaknesses of HMRC's data handling procedures, and refer the reader to [3] for an in-depth discussion.

System Hardening

The aim is to stop the ultimate social level effect on the organisation, so we can consider protective measures at multiple stages before, during and after a data exposure incident, which equate to attack surface reduction, hardening the target, and limiting the impact zone. The access and use of a data target is part of both the attack surface and impact zone, but is considered separately for clarity.

Sensitive data should be difficult to misuse or disclose, which requires comprehensive protection at all layers. There should be a complete attack surface to limit movement and routes to data at all layers to restrict unauthorised access and constrain authorised use. For example, the perpetrator of the HMRC data disclosure should not have been allowed access to the complete Child Benefit database.

The potential impact may be limited to the target, organisation wide or have an external impact on third parties. Redundant protection measures can provide defence-in-depth to provide multiple independent impact zones. This includes initial controls on the use of data internally, and subsequent controls on its export to other computers, copying to storage devices such as CDs or USB sticks, or printing on paper. The HMRC disclosure would have been avoided had there been controls on copying data to CDs, or if the physical protection boundary was replaced with a logical boundary by encrypting the data before it left the organisation.

The impact may be limited to the lower physical and logical layers or cause an ultimate effect at the social layer. Additional protection measures may avoid interference with lower layer resources from harming an organisation's essential activities. For example, loss of credit card details can be overcome by spotting anomalous transactions or by compensating victims afterwards. Unfortunately, recovery from data exposure is very difficult, as data may take on a life of its own, especially on the Internet.

Targeting the Perpetrator

We showed in our attack taxonomy that all incidents are initiated at the social level by a person pursuing a goal. The actions may be well meaning if an employee accidentally reveals data when work tasks are incorrectly executed, as with the HMRC fiasco, or they may have dishonest motivation for personal gain. We use the perpetrator's goals to determine appropriate social-level protection measures to reduce attackers' motivation and increase honest employees' alertness.

Attacks are often prompted by the need to resolve or relieve personal and work problems. Personal issues include divorce, drug abuse, financial problems and emotional disturbance. Organisational issues include job dissatisfaction, workplace disputes and disciplinary sanctions. The organisation can reduce the threat by addressing employees' personal and financial issues, and encouraging greater loyalty by good work conditions, fair treatment and attending to grievances. They may deter attacks with strong defensive measures that make the cost/benefit equation less favourable by increasing the risk or reducing the benefits of stealing data.

We now indicate how to deal with accidental data exposure by employees. The perpetrator often lacks foresight of the possible consequences, as data is intangible and easy to undervalue. Employees' obligations should be made clear by the explicit allocation of duties and responsibilities, with well-publicised understandable policies enforced by disciplinary action for breaches, which increase their incentive to be careful because of the possible repercussions.

Accidental disclosure is often caused by employees trying to get their jobs done by solving problems and being helpful to others. Contributory factors include ignorance, poor morale, and a lack of loyalty or acceptance of organisational values and rules. There may be a lax corporate culture where data is inadequately valued with inconsistent procedures and inadequate policies, leading to a lack of care. Perverse incentives must be avoided, as in the failure of the financial system, where the reward structure pressures employees into risky behaviour. All of these factors were present in the HMRC data loss according to Poynter [14]. Accidental data disclosure by employees can be reduced by awareness and training to make them conscious of the possible risks, and there should be rewards for good behaviour.

System issues can be remediated by redesign to avoid so called 'accidents waiting to happen'. Organisations should make their systems easier to use correctly, and give visible indicators when sensitive data may be revealed. The complexity of the HMRC systems contributed to the data loss, because of their lack of integration and usability, which caused a social-level issue because required tasks could not be easily executed.

Conclusions

Data loss poses a significant and increasing problem for organisations, because of its increasing quantities, uses and access routes. Systematic defence is required as no single method can protect against employees with legitimate access. We proposed an architectural three-layer security model to analyse complex systems. We provided attack and data classification models, and extended the attack surface with the dual concept of impact zone that allowed investigation of the stages in data loss. This enables a systematic determination of protection measures within the classes of limiting access to sensitive data, constraining the use of the data and limiting the impact of successful breaches. We also considered how to reduce the insider's motivation and accidental errors.

Our model has been used to analyse data loss incidents caused by employees and external attackers [3], but we focussed on accidental disclosure by employees, as illustrated by the HMRC fiasco. The corresponding determination of defensive measures helps to provide comprehensive protection against data loss incidents at all three layers from any source. It aids the provision of multiple supporting controls offering defence-in-depth, including recovery methods that limit the impact of incidents that are difficult to avoid.

Our security model appears to have widespread application in other areas such as the insider threat, critical infrastructure and financial systems, as it allows the analysis of systems in their entirety including human and physical factors, not just as technical systems. We have applied to model to the insider threat [10], [11] and to investigate critical infrastructure with its widespread scope and weaknesses at all layers [15]. In addition, it has application to complex financial systems, such as banking networks where weak procedural and physical controls are usually exploited, rather than the technical controls such as cryptography [16].

References

[1] McAfee, Unsecured economies: protecting vital information (2009), `http://resources.mcafee.com/content/NAUnsecuredEconomiesReport`

[2] Ponemon Institute. 2008 Annual Survey: Cost of a Data Breach (February 2009), `http://www.encryptionreports.com/download/Ponemon_COB_2008_US_090201.pdf`

[3] Blackwell, C.: Data Loss: the Essentials (September 2009), IT Governance at `http://www.itgovernance.co.uk` or `http://www.27001.com`

[4] Bunker, G., Fraser-King, G.: Data Leaks for Dummies. Wiley, Chichester (2009)

[5] Neumann, P.G., Parker, D.: A Summary of Computer Misuse Techniques. In: Proceedings of the 12th National Computer Security Conference (1989)

[6] Neumann, P.G.: Practical Architectures for Survivable Systems and Networks. SRI International (2000), `http://www.csl.sri.com/neumann/survivability.pdf`

[7] Searle, J.R.: Minds, Brains, and Programs, from The Behavioral and Brain Sciences, vol. 3. Cambridge University Press, Cambridge (1980), http://web.archive.org/web/20071210043312/ http://members.aol.com/NeoNoetics/MindsBrainsPrograms.html
[8] Howard, J.D.: An analysis of security incidents on the Internet 1989-1995. Carnegie Mellon University (1997), http://www.cert.org/archive/pdf/JHThesis.pdf
[9] Howard, J.D., Longstaff, T.A.: A common language for computer security incidents. Sandia National Laboratories (1998), http://www.sandia.gov
[10] Blackwell, C.: The insider threat: Combating the enemy within (2009), IT Governance at http://www.itgovernance.co.uk or http://www.27001.com
[11] Blackwell, C.: A Security Architecture to Model Destructive Insider Attacks. In: 8th European conference on information warfare. Academic Publishing Ltd. (2009)
[12] Howard, M.: Attack surface: mitigate security risks by minimizing the code you expose to untrusted users. MSDN Magazine (November 2004), http://msdn.microsoft.com/en-us/magazine/cc163882.aspx
[13] MSNBC. T.J. Maxx data theft worse than first reported (29 March 2007) MSNBC at: http://www.msnbc.msn.com/id/17853440
[14] Poynter, K.: Review of information security at HM Revenue and Customs. HMSO (2008), http://www.hm-treasury.gov.uk/d/poynter_review250608.pdf
[15] Blackwell, C.: A Multi-layered Security Architecture for Modelling Complex Systems. In: 4th Cybersecurity Information Intelligence Research Workshop. ACM Press, New York (2008)
[16] Anderson, R.: Why cryptosystems fail. In: 1st ACM conference on computer and communications security. ACM Press, New York (1993)

A Simple Method for Improving Intrusion Detections in Corporate Networks

Joshua Ojo Nehinbe

School of Computer Science and Electronic Engineering System
University of Essex, Colchester, UK
jnehin@essex.ac.uk

Abstract. Intrusion redundancies are fundamental flaws of all intrusion detection systems. Over the years, these are frequently exploited by stealthy attackers to conceal network attacks because it is fundamentally difficult to discern false alerts from true positives in a massive dataset. Consequently, attacks that are concealed in massive datasets often go undetected. Accordingly, the jobs of system administrators and the return on investment on network intrusion detectors are often threatened. Therefore, this paper presents clustering method that we have designed to lessen these problems. We have broadly evaluated our method on six datasets that comprised of synthetic and realistic attacks. Alerts of each dataset were clustered into equivalent and unique alerts and a cluster of unique alerts was eventually synthesized from them. The results that we have obtained have indicated how system administrators could achieve substantial reduction of redundancies in corporate networks.

Keywords: Redundancy, probing attacks, correlation, aggregation, equivalent alerts and unique alerts.

1 Introduction

Intrusion redundancies that are classical flaws of [1], [17], [18], [15], [19] traditional intrusion detection systems often pose serious threats to both the system administrators and continuous usage of intrusion detection systems. In reality, there are three critical issues that are associated with intrusion redundancy. Firstly, how to achieve reasonable reduction in the proportion of redundancy that is present in a collection of alerts so that security breaches on the networks are not overestimated is a difficult task. The second problem is how to accurately discern true positives from unrealistic attacks that are erroneously reported together so that countermeasures are not implemented against legitimate events. Also, timeliness in responding to attacks is another critical issue that relates to intrusion redundancy.

Generally, the origin of these problems is traced to the point at which network detector decides which network packet is suspicious or which packet is a normal event. Basically, each network detectors has collections of rules that contain signatures, patterns or characteristics of what should be classified as security violations. These rules are used to validate incoming traffics by comparison to identify matches that indicate intrusions. Unfortunately a detector treats each event as a new occurrence and thus

D. Weerasinghe (Ed.): ISDF 2009, LNICST 41, pp. 111–122, 2010.

assigns a unique sequence identity to each of them irrespective of whether it is repeated within the same timestamp. Hence, the system administrators [9], [7], [11], [14], [3], [19] are overwhelmed with repeated notices whenever there are continuous migration of repeated packets across the networks. Now, the classification problems that could not be adequately tackled by the detector are invariably transferred to the system administrators. However, alerts that need urgent attentions are manually analyzed. Also more time and efforts are spent [9], [22] to ascertain the correctness of each alert and to ensure that preventive actions are not taken against legitimate network activities. Furthermore, this process becomes extremely cumbersome especially if there are very few novel attacks that are purposely buried in massive alerts.

One of the effective approaches to lessen these problems is to configure the detector and the detection rules to [16] suppress some proportions of alerts that will be reported at a specified frequency [9]. The implementation can also be directed towards specific addresses (source and destination), protocols, etc. Similarly, detection rules can also be prioritized to completely deactivate nuisance rules or rules with low priorities but then, these methods would only be feasible for a detector that has such functionalities.

Although alerts suppression techniques can significantly reduce some proportions of redundancies in some datasets [16] but their flaws often outnumber their benefits. For instance, they cannot significantly reduce redundancies that are caused by equivalent events that occur in different time windows. Also, suppression methods are vulnerable to high rate of false negatives especially when a target machine is attacked with probing attacks that are below the threshold that has been designed for suppressing alerts. For instance, a packet of ping attack is just enough to evade detections. For these reasons, alerts suppression methods frequently underestimate security breaches on the networks. Furthermore, alerts suppression methods have limited capacity to cluster long sequence of attributes. Hence, they cannot substantiate variability in redundancies using different alerts' attributes. Apart from the trouble in reconfiguring tons of detection rules to suppress alerts, fundamentally, the efficacies of alerts suppression methods are limited to a few selection criteria. Accordingly, these flaws have necessitated the implementation of intrusion detectors in default modes while reduction of the redundancies that are simultaneously generated are central research issues in a recent time [18].

Furthermore, the capability of adapting some methods such as [23] intrusion correlation and aggregation to solve these problems have been fully established [19] in recent publications. Intrusion correlation is the process of finding fundamental relationships that connect two or more alerts together through in-depth analysis of audit logs while intrusion aggregation is a correlation technique to succinctly reduce intrusion redundancy. Essentially, both techniques should enhance prompt post-intrusion reviews so that appropriate countermeasures that would foil computer attacks can be promptly achieved. Nevertheless, the existing methods have three inherent limitations. They are unable to substantiate the complexity in removing all redundancies in a set of evaluative datasets. Also, they were not objectively evaluated and they were not design to model system administrators that were saddled with these important responsibilities in realistic networks. Consequently, these three core issues were explored in this paper to solve the aforementioned problems. Our idea was that attacks on realistic and experimental networks could only be thoroughly investigated using offline analyses of synthetic and realistic trace files. We also premised that the results obtained could be used to preempt future attacks, establish root causes of most computer attacks and to demonstrate feasible countermeasures that would reduce the problems of intrusion redundancy and other related issues in realistic computer networks.

Therefore, we deployed Snort intrusion detector on a segment of our Local Area Network (LAN) that enabled it to sniff simulated and realistic attacks. The alerts produced in each case were processed with an automated clustering technique that was designed to model system administrators that were saddled with the aforementioned challenges in corporate networks.

One of the significant contributions of this paper was our ability to reduce redundancy with a simple clustering technique. Also, series of experiments that we have conducted with wide-range of selection criteria have been able to substantiate the variability of redundancies across realistic and synthetic datasets.

The remainder of this paper is organized as follows. Section 2 discusses related works that have been done to reduce redundancy. Section 3 gives fundamentals of intrusion detections with particular reference to Snort. Section 4 gives an overview of evaluative datasets and description of our method to reduce redundancy. Section 5 gives the results of various experimentations that we have conducted while section 6 gives conclusion of our work and future research direction.

2 Related Work

Extensive researches that have been conducted on log analysis [8], [13], [23] cannot be fully elaborated in this paper due to space limitation. However, these methods were not directly designed to solve the problems of intrusion redundancy. Instead, intrusion redundancies are solved with the problems of false positives.

Algorithm that uses [7] implicit rules is used to eliminate alerts that have the same consequence as redundant alerts and the rules generate a new attack thread each time a new attack is discovered in the audit log. Furthermore, this idea is further extended to design expert systems that transform attributes of alerts into expert rules [12], [14]. In this approach, each incoming alert is validated against the expert rules to detect similar patterns of attacks while a deviation is taken as a false positive. A substantial difference in the two approaches that we have reviewed was the mode of updating the rules. While a group adopted an automatic update of the expert rules [12], the second group manually updates its rule engine [14]. Nevertheless, the major problem with rule-based methods is that their performances depend on the ability of the rules to correctly identify attacks.

Furthermore, queue graph is implemented to [20] derive the patterns of multistep attacks that occur at different timestamp. The algorithm searches for the most recent alerts of each type that prepare for future alerts and correlates them on the basis of timestamp. To the best of our knowledge, this model will mismatch multistep attacks that do not feasibly prepare for future attacks. Also interpretation of queue graphs become complex as the quantity of novel attacks in a dataset increases.

Besides, the outcome of earlier attacks (consequences) and the conditions that enable them to succeed (prerequisites) [4] on a network have been aggregated to reduce redundancy. Similarly, we have noticed that this method usually mismatches probing attacks such as version and operating system attacks that have roughly the same consequence and prerequisites.

Bayes probabilistic [2] theorem is adapted to aggregate log entries using a correlation algorithm that takes synthetic alert as input data and returns series of values from 0 to 1. Another statistical method that [22] has a statistical-based correlation algorithm is implemented on the premise of Granger Causality Test. Similar alerts are aggregated using their corresponding pre-conditions and the impacts they have on the networking infrastructure[22]. However, statistical methods are unable to aggregate alerts that do [23] not form statistical relationships and they are unable to process complex alerts [14].

Clustering technique that analyzes [8] audit log and construct attack scenarios to show attack graphs has been implemented to lessen the proportion of redundant false positives in an audit log. In this method, causality matrix is introduced to automatically extract attack scenarios using small number of rules and the model clusters alerts on the bases of attack, addresses and time of occurrence. Apart from its low ability to reduce redundancy, the model was not extensively evaluated.

Similar alerts that are commonly reported by all the detectors in a network have been adopted [21] to isolate redundancy. Alerts are prioritized and the impact of each attack on the network is determined. Thus, redundancy is expunged as alerts with low priority while non-redundant alerts are converted to Intrusion Detection Message Exchange Format (IDMEF) for further processing. However, high false positives and manual evaluation are some of the major flaws of this technique.

A formalized approach [13] is proposed to eliminate redundancy and some fundamentals challenges of intrusion detection technology based on a detailed understanding of the resources on the networks. Basically, inconsistency in the alerts of any of the detectors whenever they are clustered together [21] is presumably taken as redundancy. However, this method often underestimates the topological effects, the locations of the detectors on the networks and the detection capabilities of each detector on the discrepancies of their results. Practically, a formalized method is unable to handle attacks that elude detections. We have also noticed that formalized approach is complex and it was not implemented. Hence it was not objectively evaluated to ascertain its efficacy.

The performances of [3] three different classifiers in reducing redundancies have been substantiated in a model that uses Naive Bayesian (NB), k-nearest neighbors (K-NN) and Neural Network (NN) classification methods to process alerts from multiple intrusion detectors. All alerts are classified on the basis of their severity and each classifier eliminates redundancy with alerts that have low severity details. Nonetheless, ability to correctly determine interesting alerts, eliminate the problems of discrepancy that are associated with multiple detectors and capability to correctly map heterogeneous alerts together are some of the factors that militate against the efficacy of this method.

3 Network Intrusion Detections

Snort is a rule-base expert system that uses precedence rules to process network packets during intrusion detections. We have observed that the rules can monitor specified addresses, protocols and intrusive signatures or characteristics in every network packet and report any suspicious pattern as a security violation.

Hence, Snort validates each network packet that migrates across its sensor against its rules and coded actions are invoked upon detection of event that matches any of the rules. Routinely, each suspicious event is further validated against the alert rules and if it is successful, it is subsequently (fig 1 below) validated against the log rules. At this point, an alert would be raised to notify the system administrators of the presence of such suspicious event on the network and simultaneously, the event will be logged into two audit repositories (log and database). These repositories are used as contingency approach and further for post-intrusive review. However, if a packet fails alert rules, Snort subsequently reject the event by invoking its pass rules. Logically, the more the detection rules are unable to differentiate repeated events from new activities on a network, the more the proportion of redundancy in the audit repositories.

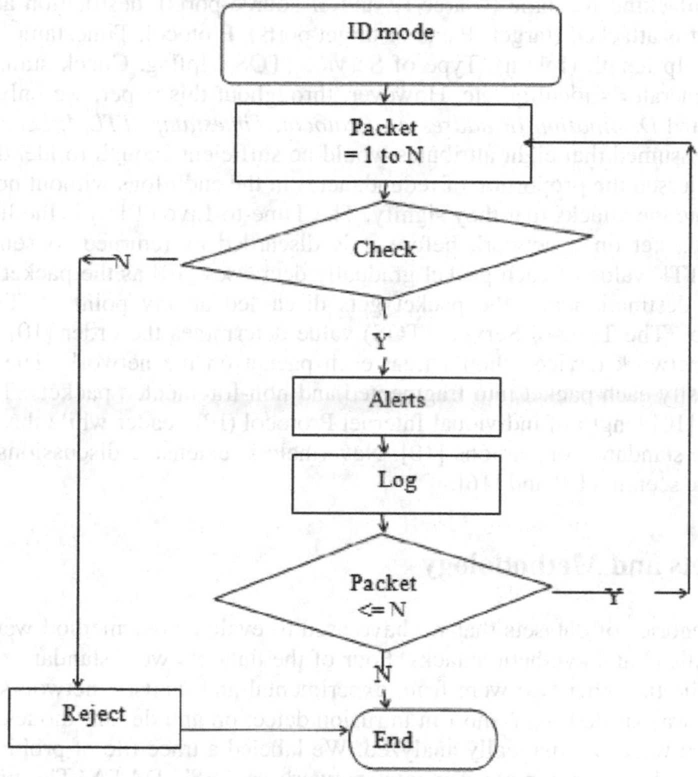

Fig. 1. Intrusion Detection (ID) mode

Selection criteria to reduce redundancy

The alerts of each audit repository are usually the same but in a different format. The alerts in the audit log are in printer text formats (prn) while those of the database are in relational formats.

```
[1] [**] [116:150:1] (snort decoder) Bad Traffic Loopback IP [**]
[2] [Priority: 3]
[3] 04/16-21:06:15.785691 127.93.72.86:23348 -> 131.84.1.31:4692
[4] TCP TTL:255 TOS:0x8 ID:14030 IpLen:20 DgmLen:40 DF
[5] ***A**** Seq: 0x7BE9C279 Ack: 0x0 Win: 0x4000 TcpLen: 20
[6] [**] [116:150:1] (snort decoder) Bad Traffic Loopback IP [**]
[7] [Priority: 3]
[8] 04/16-21:06:15.794429 127.192.221.148:23406 -> 131.84.1.31:21551
[9] TCP TTL: 255 TOS:0x8 ID:14088 IpLen:20 DgmLen:40 DF
[10] ***A**** Seq: 0x7BE9C2B3 Ack: 0x0 Win: 0x4000 TcpLen: 20
```

Fig. 2. Darpa-2 alerts from audit log

Basically, each alert is described by series of attributes (fig 2 above) such as source address or attacking machine (source-IP and or source-ports), destination address or machine that is attacked (target IP and or target ports), Protocol, Timestamp, Time To Live (TTL), Ip length (IpLen), Type of Service (TOS), Ipflag, Check sum, description, ID, Generator's identity, etc. However, throughout this paper, we only adopted the *Source* and *Destination IP addresses, Protocol, Timestamp, TTL, IpLen, TOS and Ipflag*. We assumed that eight attributes would be sufficient enough to identify possible ways to lessen the proportion of redundancies in the audit logs without necessarily underestimate the attacks that they signify. The Time-to-Live (TTL) is the lifetime of a network packet on a network before it is discarded or returned to sender [10]. Hence, the TTL value of each packet gradually decreases [10] as the packet migrates towards its destination and the packet gets discarded at any point its TTL value reaches zero. The Type-of-Service (TOS) value determines the order [10] of precedence that network devices should treat each packet on the network. The Ipflag is used to classify each packet into fragmented and non-fragmented packets. The IpLen denotes the [10] length of individual Internet Protocol (IP) header while the protocols are message standard conventions [10]. Nevertheless, extensive discussions of these attributes are seen in [10] and [16].

4 Datasets and Methodology

The six categories of datasets that we have used to evaluate our method were chosen to cover realistic and synthetic attacks. Four of the datasets were standard evaluative datasets while the other two were from experimental and realistic networks. Each of the datasets was sniffed with Snort in intrusion detection and default modes to generate alerts that were automatically analyzed. We labeled a trace file of probing attacks that were simulated on our experimental network as TEST-DATA. The probing attacks contained Ping of death (POD), port scan, UDP, Xmas tree, SYN stealth scan, versions and O/S attacks. The attacks started on 2009-04-28 at 12:45:45 hour and lasted for 2009-04-29 at 15:21:38 hour. We define probing attacks as attacks that seek for vulnerabilities in target machines while non-probing attacks exploit vulnerabilities that are present in target systems. The UNI-DATA dataset was a trace file that was extracted from real-time monitoring of a segment of the university's networks. The dataset contained truncated traffics that were launched between 2009-06-21 at

14:41:55 hour and 2009-06-22 at 15 11:38:05 hour. Additionally, we extracted DARPA2000 [6] datasets (LLDoS 1.0 or first scenario) and LLDOS 2.0.2 (second scenario) and labeled them as DARPA-1 and DARPA-2 respectively. Both datasets were examples of DDoS attacks only that attacks in DARPA-1 were launched by a novice attacker within 5s on 2000-03-07 at 16:27:51 hour of the same day and stopped at 16:27:56 hour while DARPA-2 was launched by experienced attackers on 2000-04-16 at 21:06:15 hour for about 8s.

The fifth and sixth datasets were traces of DEFCON-8 and DEFCON-10 datasets [5]. DEFCON-8 dataset was port scan and fragmented packets that initiated buffer overflow attacks. The attacks were launched on 2000-07-28 at 16:39:03 hour through 2000-07-30 at 02:11:15 hour while DEFCON-10 dataset was bad packet, attacks on administrative privilege, FTP attacks via telnet protocol, ports scan and port sweeps and they were launched from 2002-08-03 at 00:57:17 hour to 2002-08-04 at 20:56:00.

A new taxonomy of alerts

There are numerous classifications of computer attacks or alerts [1] in recent literatures but they were not adaptable to our method of reducing the aforementioned problems. Hence, we reclassified them on the premise that alerts of each dataset can be perfectly categorized into unique and equivalent groups. Hence, we defined alerts that have closely related attributes as equivalent alerts while an alert that occurred once in the audit repository was regarded as unique alert. We also noticed some variability in these classifications that are determined by the attributes that we have considered in each case. For example, 2 alerts that are shown in fig (2) above could be classified as equivalent and they could as well be classified as unique alerts. For instance, they could be aggregated into a cluster of 2 unique alerts if they are aggregated by source-ip, ID, timestamp or a sequence of <Source-ip, ID, Timestamp>. Contrarily, the alerts can be transformed to form 1 unique alert if they are aggregated by their destination-ip and or TTL, TOS, IpLen, or a sequence of < Destination-ip, TTL, TOS, IpLen>.

Clustering-based analysis Method

We designed a simple clustering technique that used selection criteria to automatically reclassify alerts and eventually reduced the proportion of redundancy in each of the datasets to substantial quantity. Our technique was divided into *alerts-filtering* and *alerts-aggregation* stages as shown in fig (3) below.

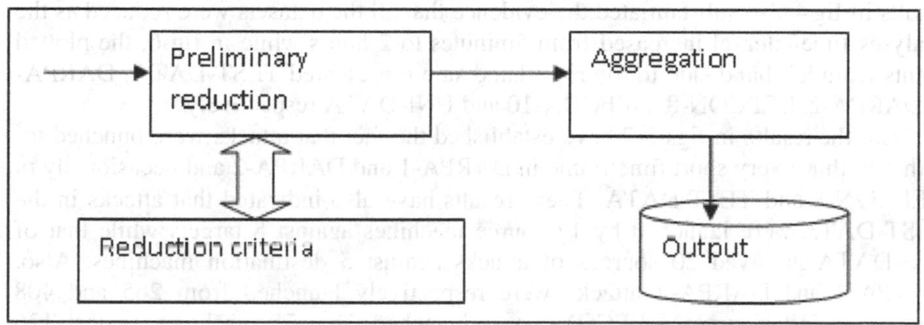

Fig. 3. Redundancy reduction process

Both processes were further implemented in C++ language to cluster alerts of the datasets. The reduction criteria were a collection of user-defined criteria with two flags. The first input flag only used Timestamp as selection criteria and at each of the time intervals of t=5mins, t=10mins, t=20mins, t=1hr and t=2hrs to cluster each group of the input data while the second input flag only used each of the selection criteria.

The input data to *alerts-filtering* stage was a sequence of audit alerts of each dataset together with an input flag while the final out of the entire model was sequence of unique alerts. For each dataset, *alerts-filtering* carried out preliminary reduction of the alerts using each of the user-defined reduction criteria and an input first flag. In this stage, all kinds of alerts in the dataset were identified and were clustered into sequences of unique and equivalent alerts. Also, the outputs were further passed to the next phase. In the second phase, a*lerts-aggregation* carried out intrusion aggregation. This phase processed all input data from previous phase and generated a cluster that contained sequences of unique alerts. This phase also totaled all unique alerts that were synthesized and the final output data were warehoused in an output repository. Hence, the system administrators then execute countermeasures to forestall attacks the alerts signify. In addition, the entire processes were repeated for all other datasets using the second flag and the results obtained in each experiment before and after we have applied our method are described in section (5) below.

To the best of our knowledge, our method was a simplified clustering method that automatically modeled system administrators that were saddled with the responsibilities of reducing intrusion redundancy in realistic world. Moreover, extensive investigations of the variability of these problems across six different datasets that represented realistic environment that we carried out were another uniqueness of our technique.

5 Results of Experiments

The experiments aimed to reduce redundancy and to substantiate the variations in the proportions of redundancies across several datasets. Also, Snort generated 67,469 alerts on TEST-DATA, 16,087 on UNI-DATA, 834 on DARPA-1, 816 on DARPA-2, 917,221 on DEFCON-8 and 5,372 alerts on DEFCON-10. In addition, fig 4 below indicates distributions of alerts when we clustered each dataset at respective time intervals while figures 5-8 indicate results that substantiated variability of redundancy reductions and clustering with the second flag (i.e. different selection criteria). The results in fig 4 also substantiated the evidence that all the datasets were reduced as the analyses time interval increased from 5minutes to 2 hours while in fig 6, the plotted points from left-hand side to the right-hand side represented TEST-DATA, DARPA-1, DARPA-2, DEFCON-8, DEFCON-10 and UNI-DATA respectively.

Also, the results in figs 5-7 have established the fact that attacks were bunched together within a very short time frame in DARPA-1 and DARPA-2 and occasionally in DEFCON-8 and TEST-DATA. These results have also indicated that attacks in the TEST-DATA were launched by 12 source machines against 8 targets while that of UNI-DATA involved 20 sources of attacks against 5 destination machines. Also, DARPA-1 and DARPA-2 attacks were respectively launched from 265 and 408 sources against a target. DEFCON-8 was launched from 75 machines against 126 destinations while DEFOCN-10 was launched from 21 sources against 27 targets.

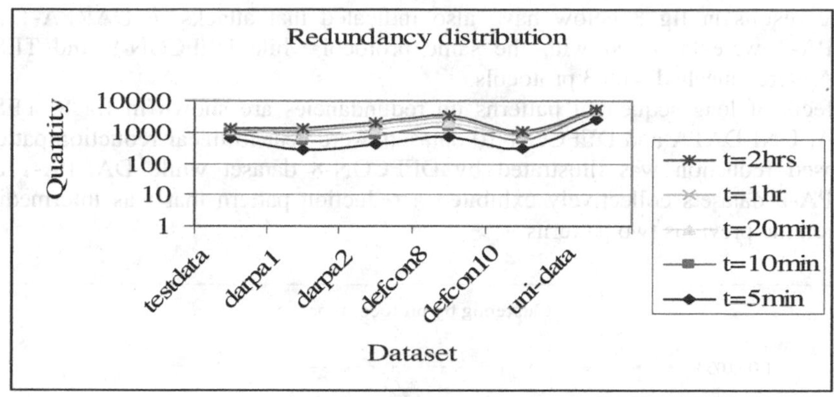

Fig. 4. <Time intervals>

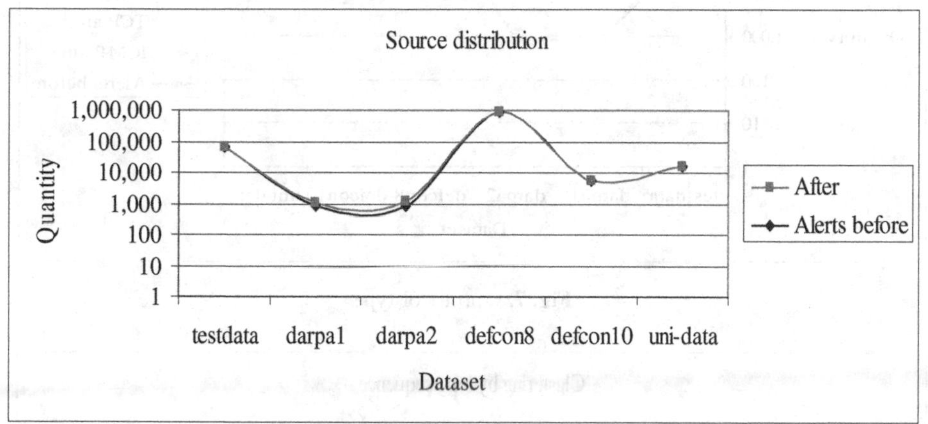

Fig. 5. <source-ip address>

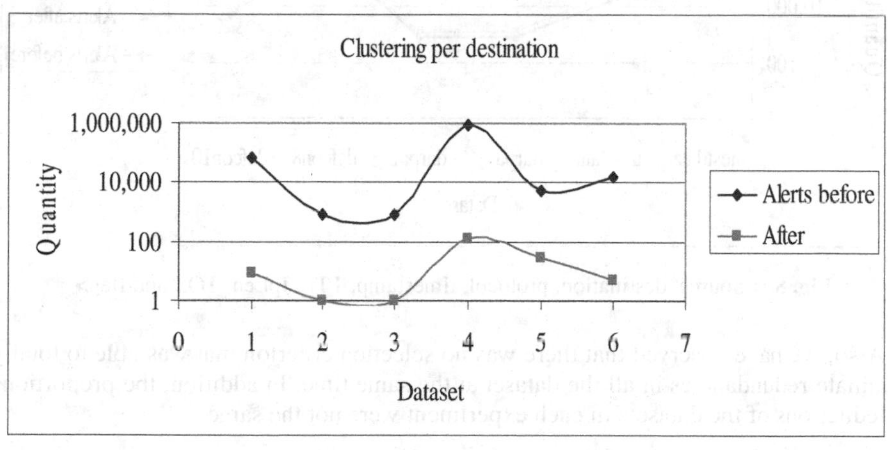

Fig. 6. < destination-ip address>

The results in fig 8 below have also indicated that attacks in DARPA-1 and DARPA-2 were launched with the same protocol while DEFCON-8 and TEST-DATA were launched with 3 protocols.

Effects of long sequential patterns on redundancies are shown in fig 8. TEST-DATA, UNI-DATA and DEFCON-10 datasets were near to linear reduction pattern, collapsed reduction was illustrated by DEFCON-8 dataset while DARPA-1 and DARPA-2 datasets collectively exhibited a reduction pattern that was intermediate between the previous two patterns.

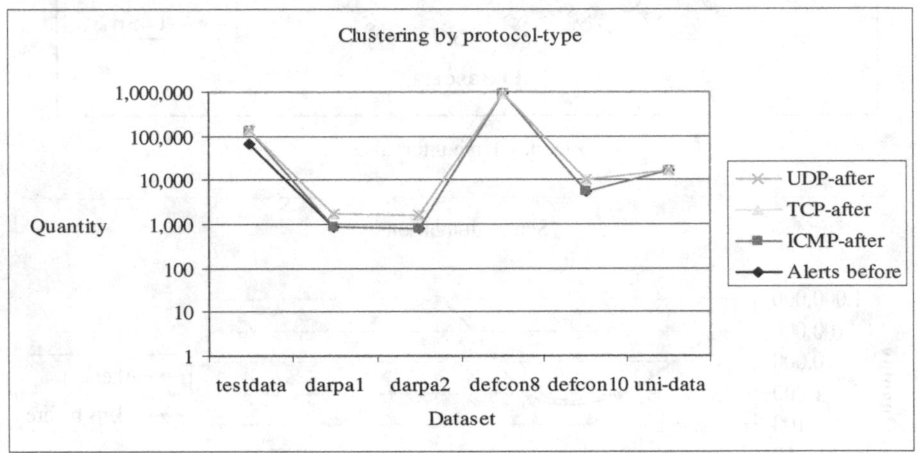

Fig. 7. < protocol-type>

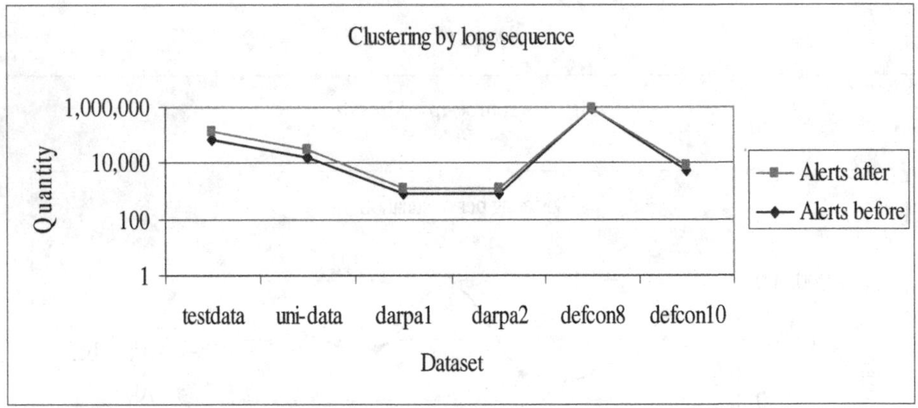

Fig. 8. < Source, destination, protocol, timestamp, TTL, IpLen, TOS and flag>

Also, we have observed that there was no selection criterion that was able to totally eliminate redundancies in all the dataset at the same time. In addition, the proportions of reductions of the datasets in each experiment were not the same.

6 Conclusion and Future Research Work

Intrusion redundancies are classical problems that are difficult to completely eradicate in corporate networks. As a result, some system administrators erroneously ignore them completely because of the complexity of separating true positives from tons of false positives. Since attackers often exploit these weaknesses to achieve malicious motives, we have critically investigated these problems across six kinds of datasets that covered probing and none-probing attacks that are commonly encountered on corporate networks. We have also demonstrated our automated clustering method that modeled system administrators that are saddled with the roles of logs analyses in realistic networks with the view to lessen these problems. Also substantiated was the difficulty in achieving total elimination of these problems in realistic networks using collection of filtering criteria. These experiments have also confirmed the variability of these problems across different categories of datasets and of course, our experiments have demonstrated that redundancies and attacks have some behavioural patterns.

Though our method has the tendency to have concurrently reduced some other fundamental problems of intrusion detection technology, however, we were unsure about the efficacy of such results. Also, we were not surely convinced that our results were not influenced by the kinds of attacks that were present in the datasets. Therefore, we plan to explore these issues in our future experiments.

References

1. Aleksandar, L., Vipin, K., Jaidep, S.: Intrusion detection: A survey. Computer Science Department, University of Minnesota (2005)
2. Alfonso, V., Keith, S.: Probabilistic alert correlation. In: Lee, W., Mé, L., Wespi, A. (eds.) RAID 2001. LNCS, vol. 2212, pp. 54–68. Springer, Heidelberg (2001)
3. Chyssler, T., Burschka, S., Semling, M., Lingvall, T., Burbeck, K.: Alarm Reduction and Correlation in Intrusion Detection Systems, Department of Computer Science, Linkoping University, Sweden (2004)
4. Cuppens, F., Miege, A.: Alert correlation in cooperative intrusion detection framework. In: Proceedings of IEEE symposium on security and privacy (2002)
5. Capture The Flag Contest-Defcon datasets (2009), http://cctf.shmoo.com/data/
6. DARPA.: Intrusion Detection Scenario Specific Data Sets (2009), http://www.ll.mit.edu/mission/communications/ist/corpora/ideval/data/2000data.html
7. Debar, H., Wespi, A.: Aggregation and correlation of intrusion detection alerts. In: Proceedings of international symposium on recent advances in intrusion detection, Davis, CA, pp. 85–103 (2001)
8. Fatima, L.S., Mezrioui, A.: Improving the quality of alerts with correlation in intrusion detection. International Journal of Computer Science and Network Security 7(12) (2007)
9. Hartsein, B.: Intrusion Detection Likelihood: A Risk-Based Approach SANS Institute (2008)
10. Internet Protocol: Internetworking Technology overview (1999), cisco.com/en/US/docs/../technology/handbook/Internet-Protocols.pdf (2009)

11. Jan, N.Y., Lin, S.C., Tseng, S.S., Lin, N.P.: A decision support system for constructing an alert classification model. Journals of Expert Systems with Applications (February 2009)
12. Kabiri, P., Ghorbani, A.A.: A Rule-Based Temporal Alert Correlation System. International Journal of Network Security 5(1), 66–72 (2007)
13. Morin, B., Me, L., Debar, H., Ducass, M.: M2D2: A formal data model for IDS alerts correlation. In: Wespi, A., Vigna, G., Deri, L. (eds.) RAID 2002. LNCS, vol. 2516, pp. 115–137. Springer, Heidelberg (2002)
14. Ning, P., Cui, Y., Reeves, D.S.: Constructing Attack Scenarios through correlation of alerts, department of computer science, NC state University, USA (2002)
15. Paxson, V.: Considerations and Pitfalls for Conducting Intrusion Detection Research, International Computer Science Institute and Lawrence Berkeley National Laboratory Berkeley, California USA (2007)
16. Roesch, M.: Introduction to Snort, A lightweight Intrusion-Detection-System (2009), http://www.seren.net/documentation/unix%20utilities/Snort.pdf
17. Sadoddin, R., Ghorbani, A.: Network Security Laboratory, University of New Brunswick, Fredericton, Canada (2006)
18. Scarfone, K., Mell, P.: Guide to Intrusion Detection and Prevention Systems (IDPS), Recommendations of the National Institute of Standards and Technology, Special Publication 800-94, Technology Administration, Department of Commerce, USA (2007)
19. Urko, Z., Roberto, U.: Intrusion Detection Alarm Correlation: A Survey, Computer Science Department, Mondragon University, Gipuzkoa Spain (2004)
20. Wang, L., Liu, A., Jajodia, S.: Using attack graph for correlating, hypothesizing, and predicting intrusion alerts. Science Direct, pp. 2917–2933. Elsevier, Amsterdam (2006)
21. Valeur, F., Vigna, G., Kruegel, C., Kemmerer, R.A.: A Comprehensive approach to Intrusion Detection Alert Correlation. IEEE Transactions on Dependable and Secure Computing 1(3) (2004)
22. Xinzhou, Q., Wenke, L.: Discovering Novel Attack Strategies from INFOSEC Alerts, College of Computing Georgia Institute of Technology, Atlanta, GA 30332, USA (2004)
23. Yusof, R., Sulamat, S.R., Sahib, S.: Intrusion Alert Correlation Technique Analysis for Heterogeneous Log. International Journal of Computer Science and Network Security 8(9) (September 2008)

Detecting Sybils in Peer-to-Peer File Replication Systems

K. Haribabu[1], Chittaranjan Hota[2], and Saravana[1]

[1] Computer Sc. & Information Systems Group, Birla Institute of Technology and Science Pilani, Rajasthan, India

[2] Computer Sc. & Information Syst. Group, Birla Institute of Technology and Science, Pilani Hyderabad Campus, Hyderabad, Andhra Pradesh, India

Khari@bits-pilani.ac.in, hota@bits-hyderabad.ac.in, saravana87@gmail.com

Abstract. The test of a peer-to-peer file sharing network is how efficiently the objects are discovered and retrieved. One of the most important factors that contribute towards this is optimal replication of the objects across the network. One of the security threats to replication model is Sybil attack. In this paper we propose an approach that aims at detecting sybil identities in peer-to-peer file sharing networks. The sybils can corrupt, hide or destroy the replicas in file sharing network. This approach makes use of the fact that sybil doesn't scale its storage to the factor of its identities. The approach safeguards the availability and accessibility of objects in a peer-to-peer network from sybil attack. Experimental evaluations have shown that our approach works very efficiently in detecting sybils. More than 50% of the sybils were detected in first few seconds of the simulation and loss or damage of objects is reduced to less than .0001%.

Keywords: Peer-to-Peer, Overlay Networks, Sybil Detection, Replication.

1 Introduction

P2P overlay networks are application-level logical networks built on top of the physical networks. These networks maintain separate addressing and routing mechanisms to enable efficient search and data exchange between peers. They don't require any special administrative or financial arrangement. They are self-organizing and adaptive, distributed and decentralized. P2P overlay networks are categorized as unstructured and structured. An unstructured P2P system is composed of peers joining the network with some loose rules, without any prior knowledge of the topology. Gnutella [1], and KaZaA [2] are examples of unstructured P2P overlay networks. In structured P2P overlay networks, network topology is tightly controlled and content is placed not at random peers but at specified locations that will make subsequent queries more efficient. Most of the structured P2P overlays are Distributed Hash Table (DHT) based. Content Addressable Network (CAN) [3], Chord [4], and Pastry [5] are some examples of structured P2P overlay networks.

When compared to P2P model, client/server model has smaller security risks due to the presence of centralized authority which can authenticate requesting nodes. P2P model, due to its decentralized model thus lacking centralized authority to authenticate nodes, faces security challenges such as masquerading, denial of service (DOS),

D. Weerasinghe (Ed.): ISDF 2009, LNICST 41, pp. 123–134, 2010.

and tampering [6]. By masquerading or acting as another node, a node can give misinformation to other nodes. This can lead to partitioning the network, DOS attack, and illegal actions on the network. A malicious node can repeatedly send requests for content from a particular node and thus preventing it from fulfilling legitimate requests. Another challenge is to protect content that is replicated on different nodes from alterations. Powerful attacks such as Sybil [7], Byzantine agreement disruption [8], and DOS [8] attacks make the large part of the network fail. Routing in P2P networks involves passing messages to intermediate nodes which can be malicious. Secure routing deals with malicious nodes actively trying to disrupt communication. Since there is no central authority to verify the one to one mapping between identity and node, a node can masquerade as multiple identities. This way it can control large part of the network. This is called Sybil Attack [7]. Although this kind of attack is possible in P2P networks, ad-hoc networks and sensor networks, it can do major damage in P2P networks because of their large global size and lack of physical constraints as in ad hoc and sensor networks [9]. It is not very difficult to set up this attack because it requires one node and many different identities or abstractions.

This attack can disrupt the network message routing for look up process and overlay maintenance by controlling large portion of the network. It is necessary to ensure that a message will be delivered to the intended node despite malicious node activity such as message corruption or misrouting [10]. A Sybil has the power to actively monitor and control the ongoing unicast communications or collaborative agreement tasks. The specific attacks that can be mounted are impersonating different routes and controlling them, dividing or segmenting a part of the overlay by positioning itself conveniently, mounting a denial of service attack on a particular node, or disrupting a Byzantine agreement.

Sybil attack is the attack against identity where an entity in a network can masquerade itself as multiple simultaneous identities in the network. This problem is pervasive in all distributed systems. In real world election scenario, people can rig the elections or in other words they represent themselves forcefully on behalf of many people. Using this attack, companies increase the rank of the web pages in Google search results[11] and some people associate certain search terms with popular personalities out of fun[12]. The peer-to-peer systems are used for many purposes; computational [13-14], messaging [15], file sharing [1]; most popularly used in file sharing networks. Sybil attack has its affect on file sharing systems especially in replication of copies of files. By knowing the mechanism of replication which is used in a particular P2P network, a malicious user (Sybil attacker) can create fake identities in the network so that the file replication of a particular file happens entirely or partially happens on the Sybil identities created by this particular user. Once the replica is in the hands of Sybil identity, it can corrupt, hide or destroy the copy what to speak of when all copies are replicated on Sybil identities only. Sybil attack goes against maintaining quality and accessibility of content, and robustness of the network. In this paper, we address this problem by developing a protocol that is capable of detecting Sybil identities.

The simulation results show that this approach can detect Sybil identities to the degree that loss of file replicas are reduced to less than .0001%. However, this approach is less efficient when the number of replicas being maintained is less. Having very few replicas of the objects, which is of course an unlike scenario in today's peer-to-peer file sharing systems.

2 Related Work

Douceur [7] describes puzzle methods that exploit communication, storage or computational resource constraints. He proves that computational puzzle methods are not viable. In these puzzles, the verifier sends a large random value to every other identity it wants to verify. These identities must then compute the solution within a constrained amount of time. If an entity has more than one identity it will fail to compute the solution within the time. The paper says that this can be circumvented by taking help of other powerful nodes. Thus he advocates the existence of a central authority to prevent Sybil attacks. Castro, et al. [10] argue that in a P2P overlay network, if a central authority distributes uniform node identifiers (IDs) then it is difficult for attackers to have any control over this process. They allow multiple node IDs per IP address. Dinger and Hartenstein [9] proposed an identity registration procedure called self-registration that is a natural extension of P2P mechanism to safeguard against Sybil attacks. Their approach clearly distinguishes network nodes from participants. The results of their self-registration process show that it is able to regulate number of nodes per participant. It has open-ended questions like within what duration the network becomes free from dominance. Danezis, et al. [16] present a modified DHT routing using a bootstrap tree for Chord to resist the impact of Sybil attacks. In the bootstrap tree, two nodes share an edge if one introduced the other into the DHT. These relationships are established outside the tree off-line. With this logic Sybil nodes will attach to the tree at limited nodes. Also, a trust metric is used to minimize the probability of a malicious node being on the routing path of the Chord. Fiat, et al. [17] proposed S-Chord which is a variant of Chord where a node uses a set of nodes called Swarm which randomly selects an ID using which the node positions itself at a critical position in the Chord ring. In Sybilguard [19], the authors have proposed a distributed algorithm for limiting entry of Sybil identities into a social network. They have used the principle that in a social network, the trusted edges between honest group and a Sybil group will be very few. They have designed a protocol in which the verification of new entry into the network is done by intersection of random routes.

Our approach is based on challenging resources of the Sybil identities. The approaches [20-21] also fall into the same category. Unlike the other challenge-resource approaches, this approach is more reliable because the storage is persistent. Here it is not difficult to simultaneously test the storage capacity of most identities because it can be done over a period of time.

3 Sybil Detection

In this section we discuss design of our approach.

3.1 Scope

File replication in P2P has many advantages such as reducing traffic congestion; increasing object availability and aiding in fault tolerance. Single node failures, like crashes of nodes, can be tolerated as faults within the system as a whole facilitated with the help of the redundancy introduced by replicas. If a host of a replica fails, requestors may access another host with a replica. Data replicated at more than one site facilitate to minimize the number of hops before the data are found. But, large scale Peer to Peer systems face security threats from faulty or hostile remote computing elements [7]. Peer-to-Peer (P2P) based file sharing applications have become highly popular in today's Internet due to the spread of platforms such as Napster, Gnutella, KaZaa, eDonkey, BitTorrent, and others. The Sybil attack in which a single user can pose as multiple identities is a serious threat to P2P File Sharing Systems because the malicious entity can sabotage the P2P file sharing system in whatever way he likes. The various ways in which a Sybil Node can attack or disrupt the functioning of the file sharing networks are given below:

Content Pollution: The Sybil identities can behave in various ways such as replacing all or part of the content with white noise, cutting the duration, shuffling blocks of bytes within the digital recording, inserting warnings of the illegality of file sharing in the recording, and inserting advertisements; the main aim being to render the file unusable and thereby reducing its popularity [18]. Now, this polluted content can be replicated on a large number of honest or Sybil nodes in the P2P Network. A normal user who is oblivious to all these, downloads these content and thus the polluted content spreads throughout the file sharing network eventually exceeding the number of original copies. As the users download more and more polluted copies, it might lead to frustration among users and subsequently leading them to abandon the file sharing itself. A situation can happen is that when a recording company is on the verge of releasing a song that will likely be popular; the rival record company might pay a pollution company to spread bogus copies of the song through one or more P2P network thereby reducing the popularity of the file.

Content Deletion: Consider the other side of file replication on multiple nodes; it introduces a new set of challenges. The Sybil identities on which the files are replicated might delete the files that were replicated and be detrimental towards to the file sharing system. For example, a person X may store his audio or video at a remote node Y located elsewhere so that persons near that can download the files from that particular node. If that node was a Sybil node, the file might be deleted and the basic purpose of replication in file sharing systems is defeated.

Content Concealment: The Sybil node can possess the file and not send it to the requesting node. By this way, again the motives of the P2P file sharing network reduces because of congestion etc. In this case, the Sybil Identity might still possess the data (so that if the owner node verifies, it would be able to resend the data and confirm it) and thus conceal it from other requesting nodes.

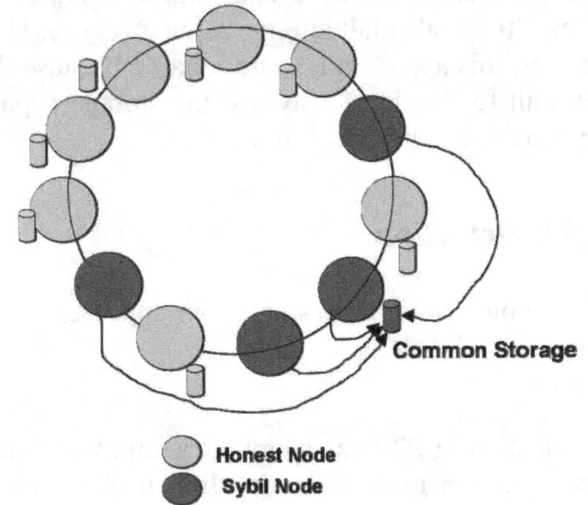

Fig. 1. Sybil identities having common storage in Chord network

Therefore, the effects of Sybil Identities can be devastating to a P2P file sharing network. So, it is advisable that files are not replicated wholly on Sybil Identities. Towards this SybilGuard [19] mentions that maintain g+1 replicas in case there are g Sybil groups is wasteful and instead propose a mechanism which bounds the number of nodes in each Sybil Group. Whereas, in our work we don't present any restrictions on the minimum number of replicas that need to be maintained as our theory works even if all the files are replicated wholly or partially on the Sybil Identities.

In this paper, we attempt to solve this problem, by a two phase method. 1. Detecting Sybil identities in the process of replication 2. Adapting replication process so that the replicas will not go to already detected Sybil identities

3.2 Algorithm Overview

As we have seen that Sybil attack creates multiple simultaneous virtual identities in the network. Virtual identities mean that although these identities created by the user appear to be normal, they don't have their own computational, memory and storage resources. But for the nodes in the network, these identities appear to be no different than normal nodes. Literature describes various ways to detect Sybils. One of the ways is to detect whether the node is a virtual or just a normal node.

The network is a structured network where the nodes are placed in pre-determined positions according to the node id. The data is placed in the node whose id is the closest to the key of the object. In most structured networks, the objects are replicated in r number of successors, r being dependent on individual system. The node where the object is originally stored is called 'owner' of the object. The owner replicates the copies of the object. The owner of the file has details about to which all nodes the file has been replicated. For all the Sybil identities created by one particular malicious user the storage would be done in one particular place i.e., the malicious user's storage system. So, the data that has been replicated in Sybil identities created by that malicious user will be stored in the storage area of the malicious user. The malicious user has a limited storage capacity. As the number of Sybil Identities on which file replication takes place increases, the storage capacity needs to be increased and the cost involved in increasing storage compared to the benefit in doing that proves ineffective for the malicious user as the data which is replicated is not a highly confidential data in normal P2P networks.

The owner of the object replicates a file on a set of nodes. The owner needs to keep track of the node identities where it has replicated the files. It is assumed that for a normal node, there will not be a situation where it doesn't have space to store the file. This is because the replication placement is done by the consistent hashing [22]. This will ensure equal distribution of load.

Every owner of the object verifies the existence of the files at regular intervals. The owner sends a message to each node where the replica is placed asking for a randomly chosen byte range within the file. The receiver is supposed to send the reply with those few bytes extracted from the object. When the verifier receives a reply, it verifies the reply. If either the reply is not received or the reply is not correct then, the owner notes the node identifier of the node. If the same situation occurs for a more than threshold number of times, the owner detects the node to be a Sybil identity. Then it will not replicate the objects anymore on this node.

The verification message consists of {fileId, fromByteOffset, toByteOffset}. The verification reply message consists of {fileId, fromByteOffset, toByteOffset, bytes}. After sending the verification request, the owner waits for the reply. If the reply is not received in an expected amount of time, the owner takes it to be a no reply. The replication and verification procedures are outlined in Fig2 and Fig3.

```
Replicate(File:f)
{
   Successors: S
   SybilDetected: D
   Int: noOfReplica=0
   ReplicaList: L
   for each successor s  ∈ S
     if (s  ∈ D) = false then
        putIntoNetwork(s, f)
       add(L, s, f)
     noOfReplica = noOfReplica+1
     if noOfReplica>REPLICA_LIMIT then
   exit for
}
```

Fig. 2. Algorithm for replicating a file f

```
VerifyReplications(ReplicaList:L)
{
   SybilDetected: S
   ReplicaList: L
   VerificationMessage: v
   VerificationReplyMessage: vr

   for each replica r  ∈ L
      v= makeVerificationMessage(r)
      sendVerificationMessage(r.s, v)
      vr = waitForReply()
  if verifyReply(r, v, vr)==false or
vr==null then
       L.noReplyCount =     L.noReplyCount
+ 1;
  If L.noReplyCount > THRESHOLD then
      S.add(r.s)
}
```

Fig. 3. Algorithm for verification of a copy of file f

```
VerificationMessage
makeVerificationMessage(Replica: r)
{
    Int: fromByte
    Int: toByte
   VerificationMessage: v

  fromByte=getRandomNo() Mod sizeof(r.f)
  toByte= getRandomNo() Mod sizeof(r.f)
 if fromByte>toByte then
    swap(fromByte,toByte)

  v.f = r.f
  v.fromByte = fromByte;
  v.toByte = toByte;
   return v
}
```

Fig. 4. Procedure for making a verification message

```
verifyReply(Replica: r,
VerificationMessage: v,
VerificationReplyMessage: vr)
{
  If byterange(r.f, v.fromByte, v.toByte)
== vr.data  then
       return true
  else
      return false;

}
```

Fig. 5. Procedure for verifying a reply sent from a node

4 Simulation Results

Simulation was carried out on a 1000-node Chord network. We used PlanetSim [23] overlay network simulator. Necessary changes were made in the Node classes to represent the current purpose of simulation. New procedures were written for replication and verification. The simulator was a step based simulator. Every step, the messages are transferred from current node to next node. The simulation was carried out for 45000 steps. The files are replicated in the system throughout the simulation using a Poisson process with average as 4. The threshold value for terming a node as

Sybil is 4. The waiting time for a verification reply is set to 10 seconds. The topology of the Chord network is shown in Fig 6.

In the beginning of the simulation, all the honest and Sybil nodes are created. The honest nodes are 1000 in number. The Sybil nodes are varied from 50 to 850 i.e. 4.7% to 46%. We see in graph Fig 7 that all the graphs follow the same pattern. Initially all the curves are steeply falling, indicating that there is high probability that the objects are distributed to Sybil identities but since there is no storage space, they could not hold all the replicas. As the number of Sybil identities reduce in the network, the probability that a object is replicated in a Sybil node also reduces. That is why the steepness of the curves reduces. Also we can observe that as the Sybil identities percent in the network is increased, the time taken to detect Sybil identities also increases. In Fig 8, we can observe that, as the percent of Sybil identities increase in the system, the total number of Sybil identities detected in 45000 steps is reduced. In Fig 9, we see that reducing the number of Sybil identities has direct effect on file losses incurred in the network. We can see from the Sybil CDF that when it has reached a slow progress state, accordingly the file losses also have reduced. Normally the file losses are due to the Sybil identities, since they don't have the storage space to store replicas of all the Sybil identities. When they are detected, the files are replicated on a different set of nodes probably honest nodes. That way the file replicas are safer. In Fig 10 we can see how the Sybil detection procedure is dependent on the number of files being replicated in the network. The whole algorithm is dependent on the replicas of files. More the number of files replicated, more will be the detection of the Sybil identities. In Fig 11, it can be observed that, the waiting time for a verification reply from a node has no drastic influence of the detection of Sybil identities. This is because several nodes replicate their objects on a Sybil node. The increase in waiting time doesn't delay the detection because there are several other nodes which are verifying meanwhile.

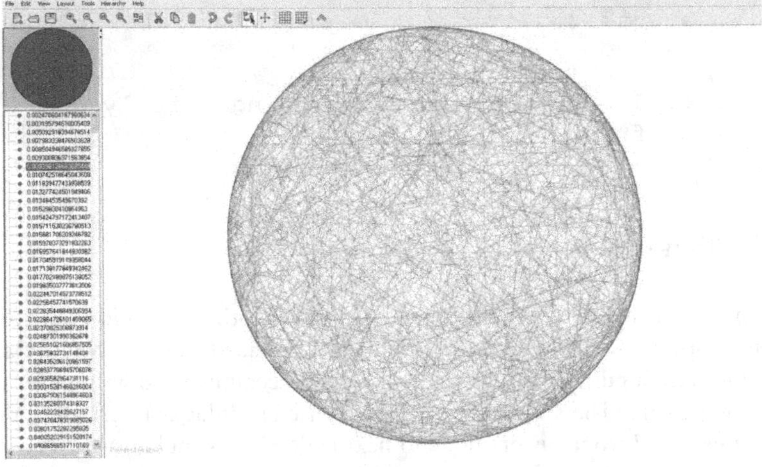

Fig. 6. Chord network topology for 1000 node network

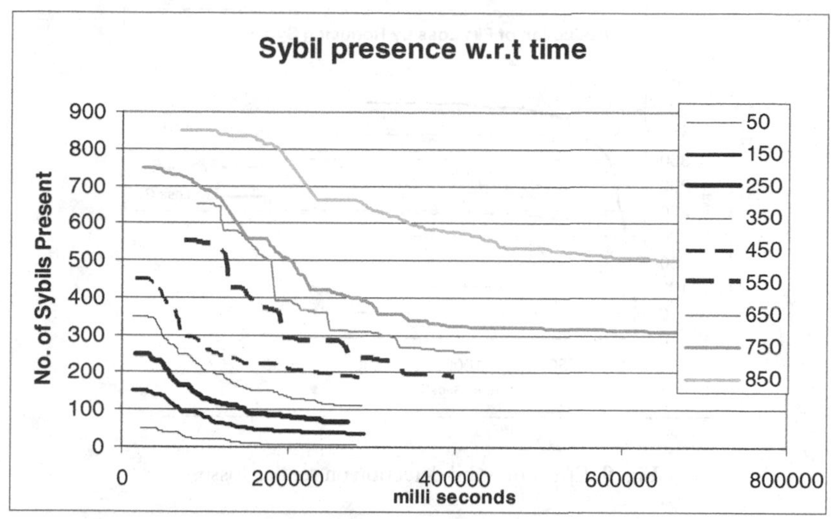

Fig. 7. Detection pattern of Sybils for different % of Sybils in the network

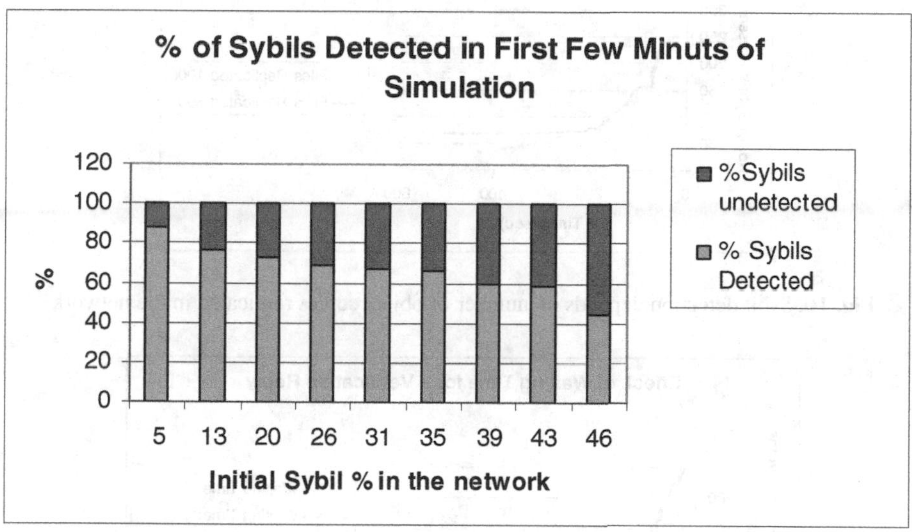

Fig. 8. Effect of % of Sybils on detection algorithm

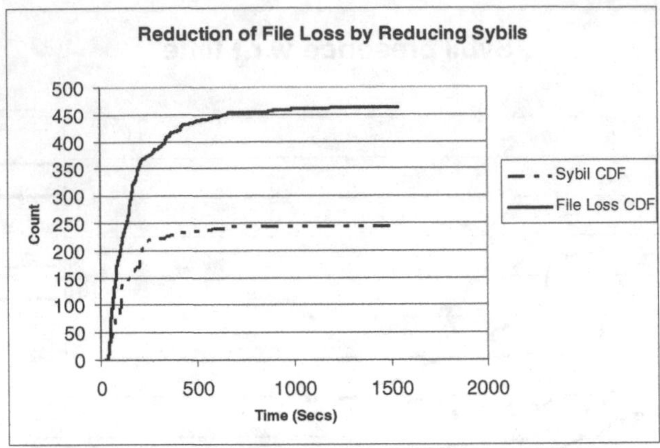

Fig. 9. Effect of Sybil detection on replica losses

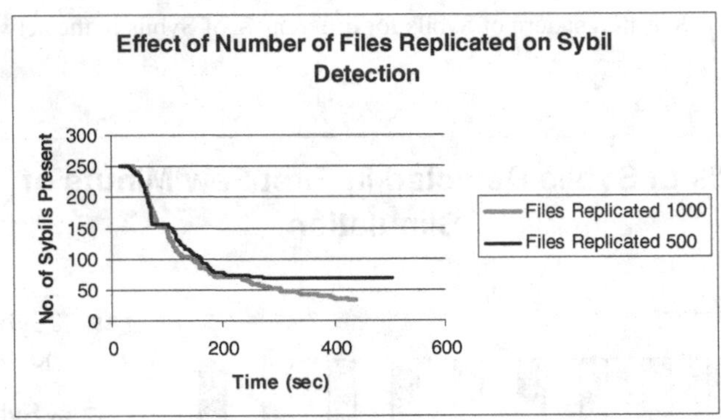

Fig. 10. Sybil detection depends on number of object copies replicated in the network

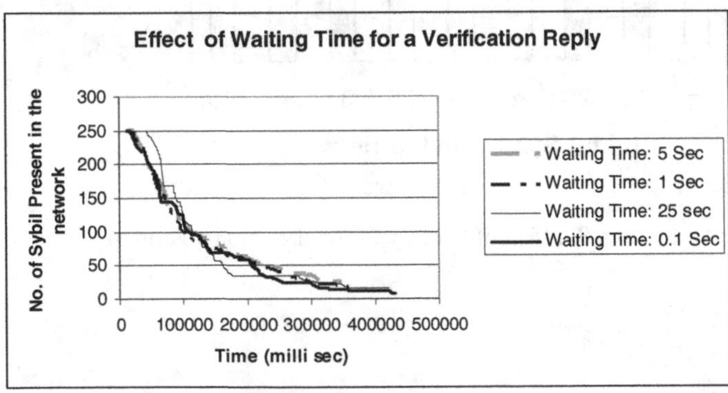

Fig. 11. The effect of verification waiting time on the Sybil detection is almost nil

5 Conclusion

This paper presented a novel decentralized protocol for limiting the corruptive influence of Sybil attacks on replication system in peer-to-peer networks by detecting Sybil identities and there by avoiding storing replicas on them. This approach relies on the principle that Sybil doesn't scale its storage capacity to the factor of its identities. Also unlike the other challenge-response approaches, this approach is more reliable because the storage is persistent. Here it is not difficult to simultaneously test the storage capacity of most identities because it can be done over a period of time. Experimental evaluations on this approach have shown that Sybil identities were detected to the extent of 90% of initial Sybil identities. Also the effect of parameters like initial percent of Sybil identities, total number of objects replicated in the network, waiting time for a verification reply is analyzed. Still the approach may suffer if the Sybil identities chose to store the replicas on another node. Our future work will focus on a fool proof 100% Sybil detection protocol with simulations on a larger network.

References

1. Gnutella Protocol Specification Version 0.4, `http://www9.limewire.com/developer/gnutella_protocol_0.4.pdf`
2. Kazaa, `http://www.kazaa.com`
3. Ratnasamy, S., Francis, P., Handley, M., Karp, R., Shenker, S.: A Scalable Content Addressable Network. In: Proceedings of the 2001 ACM Annual Conference of the Special Interest Group on Data Communication (SIGCOMM), pp. 161–172. ACM Press, New York (2001)
4. Stoica, I., Morris, R., Liben-Nowell, D., Karger, D., Kaashoek, M.F., Dabek, F., Balakrishnan, H.: Chord: A Scalable Peer-to-Peer Lookup Service for Internet Applications. IEEE/ACM Transactions on Networking 11, 17–32 (2003)
5. Rowstron, A., Druschel, P.: Pastry: Scalable, decentralized object location and routing for large-scale peer-to-peer systems. In: Guerraoui, R. (ed.) Middleware 2001. LNCS, vol. 2218, pp. 329–350. Springer, Heidelberg (2001)
6. Haiying, S., Brodie, A.S., Xu, C., Shi, W.: Scalable and Secure P2P Overlay Networks. In: Wu, J. (ed.) Theoretical and Algorithmic Aspects of Sensor, Ad Hoc Wireless, and Peer-to-Peer Networks. CRC Press, London (2005)
7. Douceur, J.R.: The Sybil attack. In: Druschel, P., Kaashoek, M.F., Rowstron, A. (eds.) IPTPS 2002. LNCS, vol. 2429, pp. 251–260. Springer, Heidelberg (2002)
8. Wallach, D.S.: A Survey of Peer-to-Peer Security Issues. In: Okada, M., Pierce, B.C., Scedrov, A., Tokuda, H., Yonezawa, A. (eds.) ISSS 2002. LNCS, vol. 2609, pp. 253–258. Springer, Heidelberg (2003)
9. Dinger, J., Hartenstein, H.: Defending the Sybil Attack in P2P Networks: Taxonomy, Challenges, and a Proposal for Self-Registration. In: Proceedings of the First International Conference on Availability, Reliability and Security (ARES 2006), pp. 756–763. IEEE Computer Society, Los Alamitos (2006)
10. Castro, M., Druschel, P., Ganesh, A., Rowstron, A., Wallach, D.S.: Secure routing for structured peer-to-peer overlay networks. In: Proceedings of the 5th USENIX Symposium on Operating Systems Design and Implementation, pp. 299–314. ACM Press, New York (2003)

11. Bianchini, M., Gori, M., Scarselli, F.: Inside page rank. ACM Transactions on Internet Technology 5(1), 92–128 (2005)
12. Viglucci, A., Tanfani, J., Getter, L.: Herald special report: Dubious tactics tilted mayoral votes. Miami Herald, February 8 (1998)
13. Anderson, D.: SETI@home in Peer-to-Peer: Harnessing the Benefit of a Disruptive Technology. O'Reilly & Associates, CA (2001)
14. Larson, S.M., Snow, C.D., Shirts, M., Pande, V.S.: FOLDING@home and GENOME@home: Using distributed computing to tackle previously intractable problems in computational biology. Computational Genomics (2002)
15. Miller, J.: Jabber: Conversational technologies in Peer-to-Peer: Harnessing the Benefits of a Disruptive Technology. O'Reilly & Associates, CA (2001)
16. Danezis, G., Lesniewski-Laas, C., Kaashoek, M.F., Anderson, R.: Sybil-resistant DHT routing. In: di Vimercati, S.d.C., Syverson, P.F., Gollmann, D. (eds.) ESORICS 2005. LNCS, vol. 3679, pp. 305–318. Springer, Heidelberg (2005)
17. Fiat, A., Saia, J., Young, M.: Making Chord Robust to Byzantine Attacks. In: Brodal, G.S., Leonardi, S. (eds.) ESA 2005. LNCS, vol. 3669, pp. 803–814. Springer, Heidelberg (2005)
18. Liang, J., Kumar, R., Xi, Y., Ross, K.: Pollution in P2P file sharing systems. In: Proceedings of. IEEE INFOCOM 2005, vol. 2, pp. 1174–1185. IEEE Computer Society, Washington (2005)
19. Yu, H., Kaminsky, M., Gibbons, P.B., Flaxman, A.: SybilGuard: Defending against sybil attacks via social networks. In: Proceedings of the 2006 conference on Applications, technologies, architectures, and protocols for computer communications, pp. 267–278. ACM Press, New York (2006)
20. Borisov, N.: Computational Puzzles as Sybil Defenses. In: Proceedings of the Sixth IEEE International Conference on Peer-to-Peer Computing, pp. 171–176. IEEE Computer Society, Washington (2006)
21. Aspnes, J., Jackson, C., Krishnamurthy, A.: Exposing computationally challenged Byzantine impostors. Technical Report, Yale University Department of Computer Science (July 2005)
22. Karger, D., Lehman, E., Leighton, F., Levine, M., Lewin, D., Panigrahy, R.: Consistent hashing and random trees: Distributed caching protocols for relieving hot spots on the World Wide Web. In: Proceedings of the 29th Annual ACM Symposium on Theory of Computing, pp. 654–663. ACM Press, New York (1997)
23. García, P., Pairot, C., Mondejar, R., Pujol, J., Tejedor, H., Rallo, R.: PlanetSim: A New Overlay Network Simulation Framework. In: Proceedings of 19th IEEE International Conference on Automated Software Engineering, pp. 123–136. IEEE Computer Society, Los Alamitos (2004)

Adaptive Clustering Method for Reclassifying Network Intrusions

Nehinbe Ojo Joshua

School of Computer Science and Electronic Engineering System
University of Essex, Colchester, UK
jnehin@essex.ac.uk

Abstract. The problems of classification and reporting of suspicious security violations often degenerate to other complex problems. However, efforts of system administrators to mitigate these flaws by reclassifying intrusive datasets so that realistic attacks can be substantiated are frequently unfruitful with swamped datasets. Also, the urgency required to process alerts has made validations of reduction criteria to be implemented with realistic attacks and unfortunately, these consistently endangering computer resources on the networks to more exposures. Consequently, the development of computer attacks that have been warned but still succeed is a classical problem in computer security. In this paper therefore, we have implemented a new clustering method to reduce these problems. Also, evaluation that we performed with synthetic and realistic datasets clustered alerts of each dataset to achieve a cluster of white-listed alerts. Moreover, the results obtained have indicated how system administrators could achieve prompt countermeasures to prevent realistic attacks.

Keywords: intrusion quarantining, intrusion blacklisting, intrusion white-listing, probing attacks.

1 Introduction

Internet technology and network protocols have numerous vulnerabilities that are frequently exploited by hackers [1], [8], crime syndicates and terrorists to perpetrate illegitimate activities across the globe. These have been widely corroborated by frequent cases of computer attacks such as Distributed Denial of Service (DDoS), virus, spam, buffer-overflow, e-data pilfering, deletion of audit trails, e-spoofing of sensitive information, probing attacks, e-masquerading, password cracking, etc across [1] the globe. Accordingly, this has necessitated the need to adequately secure computer networks and to constantly audit the security of the networks at a frequency of 24 hours per day. Hence, preventive technology such as Network Intrusion Prevention System (NIPS), honey pots, firewalls and routers are frequently [9], [18], [21] deployed on the networks to 18] disallow intrusive packets [21] from migrating into the networks.

Nevertheless, since authorized activities often change over time and computer attacks are becoming sophisticated everyday [15], these devices are often manipulated, electronically masqueraded and circumvented by attackers. Consequently, intrusion detectors are deployed as [8] an additional network layer of defensive mechanism to

D. Weerasinghe (Ed.): ISDF 2009, LNICST 41, pp. 135–146, 2010.

complement preventive measures. In essence, the premise behind this concept is that the tendency of achieving substantial reduction in the cases of successful attacks on the networks would be very high if attacks that cannot be prevented are promptly detected.

Fundamentally, there are serious obstacles that militate against the realization of these security goals in realistic networks. For example, network intrusions detectors exhibit classification and reporting problems [7], [8], [17], [20], [23] because they cannot accurately address the problems of intrusion quarantining, intrusion blacklisting and intrusion white-listing. The concept of intrusion quarantining is a method to rigorously isolate already reported intrusions on the networks and store them in a separate repository while intrusion blacklisting is seen as a method to deliberately avoid noisy events or attacks by putting them on a blacklist and intrusion white-listing is perceived as a process of reporting a list of approved intrusions on the networks. For these reasons, network detectors excessively report and log [8], [17] unnecessary details [23] that always constitute impediments to prompt intrusion analyses and clarity of security breaches. Consequently, the clarity of security violations in a realistic network is often lost and hence countermeasures that would prevent them are wrongly implemented.

Nevertheless, the methodology of substantiating reported alerts is another challenge that stems from the aforementioned problems. Most system administrators still spend wasteful time [9] and efforts to select appropriate filtering criteria that are used to corroborate the existence of realistic attacks in the audit trails. In essence, they manually cluster sophisticated attacks and hence the tendency that erroneous actions are taken against legitimate network activities is extremely high [21]. Therefore, analyses of attacks that have been warned beforehand are unduly delayed and they are not forestalled at the end of the day.

Nevertheless, out of the aforementioned problems, attempts that have been made to address the problems of classifications and intrusion reporting collectively exhibit [17] low success rates. For instance, intrusion blacklisting has been moderately implemented as alerts tagging in Snort whereby rules are designed to sequentially log packets that are triggered by the same rule [16]. Similarly, the problems of classification and intrusion reporting are also proposed to be controlled by disabling noisy rules and to default some rules to drop some generic events [9] so that few quantity of alerts would be logged and warned [16]. Additionally, the quantity and quality of alerts to be reported can as well be controlled by limiting attributes that should be reported at a given time and by personalizing [16] the detection rules to specific kinds of traffics such as personalization by packet size.

However, all these techniques have inevitable weaknesses. For example, the risk classification of changing the default settings of the detection rules is high because such modification would endanger ability to detect attacks such as buffer overflow that are tracked by the size of packet payloads. Also, it is impossible and computationally resource intensive for detectors such as Snort to automatically cluster alerts on the basis of many attributes other than the conventional six [16] attributes that are currently implemented in Snort. This implies that Snort can only improve on the quality of reported alerts on the basis of generation-id, signature-id, one of its three types of threshold at a time, source-ip or destination-ip (and not source-ip and destination-ip), count and time in seconds. Although, these strategies are efficient in reducing some proportions of false positives in the audit logs however, they tend to be vendor's specific or particularly restricted to Snort intrusion detector. In addition, Snort cannot cluster alerts [16] per port numbers or by combination of long sequence of selection criteria. Therefore, since different attacks tend to require different selection criteria to thorough ascertain their patterns, the ideas of limiting alerts or adopting restricted logging of security violations to interesting attributes are sources of potential dangers to the resources on the networks.

For these reasons, researchers [1], [3], [17], [23] over the years have automated some methods that indirectly reduced the problems of intrusion reporting. Consequentially, statistical methods have been proposed to reduce false positives [2], [22], automated strategies of attacks were proposed to preempt the intentions of attackers [14] and classification rules [4], [7], [11], [12] have been suggested to reclassify alerts into several clusters. However, each of these strategies has numerous [21] weaknesses as well. For example, they are frequently and widely criticized for poor detection capabilities [1], [8], [20], lack of adaptability [21] and poor performance tuning [18] to solve realistic network problems. Essentially, both the industrial and research designs are collectively flawed [15] and they have failed to enhance significant reduction of heightening cases of computer attacks across the globe. Therefore, the aim of this paper is to address these problems. We deployed Snort intrusion detector to sniff six different datasets that we have extracted from experimental, realistic and synthetic networks. After that, an automated clustering method was applied to succinctly cluster alerts of each dataset to expedite countermeasures that would prevent attacks that are signified by the alerts.

One of the essential contributions of this paper was an automated modeling of a practical approach that has bridged the wider gap that existed between research designs and industrial problems. We have been able to extensively validate the efficacies of our model in reducing the aforementioned problems with several kinds of datasets that broadly represented basic attacks that are encountered in everyday activities. Additionally, the results obtained have fully established the fact that the efficacy of our model is independent of the size of the dataset. Furthermore, our work has pointed out focal direction that stimulates future discussions in redesigning intrusion detection researches to be directly adaptable to solve realistic problems.

The remainder of this paper is organized as follows. Section 2 gives a review of closely related works. Section 3 gives an overview of experimental datasets that we have used to verify the performance of our model and section 4 gives an account of our model for reclassifying network intrusions. Section 5 gives an account of experimental results that we have conducted while section 6 gives conclusion and future research direction.

2 Related Works

The approaches for addressing the problems of classification and intrusion reporting [1], [3], [17], [19] and some of the associated problems that we have described above are diversified. For instance, consequence or collections of ordered alerts that are linked together by their respective duplicates have been implemented to reduce false positives. Examples of duplicates are alerts that originate from the same source IP address or source ports that migrate towards the same target IP address or target ports and within the same timestamp. In [7] for instance, duplicate alerts are merged with their consequence using algorithm that uses implicit rules. The algorithm then creates a new attack thread each time a new attack is discovered. However, this method will wrongly match attacks such as ping flooding and ping of death that exhibit closely related consequence and duplicates together.

Furthermore, AprioriAll-like sequential pattern mining rules [11] that use behavioural classification model to build a decision support system has been implemented to reclassify online alerts into false, unknown and normal alerts. Nevertheless, one of the major flaws of every behavioural classification model is that it is practically unfeasible to model all attacks. Also, Apriori-based models always exhibit low performance in processing long sequences of candidate generation alerts. In addition, apart from lack of objective evaluations that were not done with standardized evaluative datasets, this model is completely resource intensive to implement in corporate networks.

In addition, a formalized model that is proposed in [13] uses adequate knowledge of the resources on the network to eliminate false positives. Basically, the idea of this model is to isolate false alerts by reclassifying them as alerts that are not commonly reported by all the detectors on the networks whenever the alerts of all the detectors are correlated. Essentially, this model has rigorously established sound theoretical concepts that can be adopted to solve some intrusion detection's problems but then, it has numerous fundamental weaknesses. One of these is that it undermines the possibility of having some attacks that deliberately elude detections. Additionally, formalized approach suffers from lack of objective evaluation and hence, its efficacy in reducing redundant false alerts cannot be validated.

In addition, some attributes of alerts have been incorporated into expert [4], [12] systems to generate elementary (low level) alerts. In further reclassifying online alerts, this model validates each of the incoming alerts with its expert rules to determine their similarities. Thereafter, clustering is applied to cluster alerts that are generated by the same attack scenario while the proportions of the false positives in the datasets are reduced by selecting an alert per cluster. The uniqueness of different designs that adopt this approach is the mode of updating the expert rules. For example, expert system that is implemented in [12] automatically creates attack scenarios to update its expert rules unlike in [4] whereby the expert rules are manually updated by the system administrators each time a novel attack is discovered.

Support Vector Machine (SVM) method and multi-layer perceptron (MLP) are two examples of neural network [25] classifiers that are implemented to reduce false positives. The model automatically constructs graphs of attack scenarios from temporal relationships of alerts while correlation matrix procedure is introduced to eventually eliminate false alerts from alerts that temporally related. However, this method cannot process alerts of attacks that occur in multiple and unrelated phases.

Implementation of Queue graph (QG) [20] to extract patterns of multistep attacks that occur within different timestamps has also been designed to reduce false positives. In this approach, QG algorithm is used to search for the most recent alerts of each type that prepare for future alerts and they are then merged together on the basis of their timestamps. Like the attack-graph model, this method visually represents the distributions of alerts graphically. However, the interpretations of the output graphs are too complex to understand despite the timeliness that is necessary to counter intrusions.

The reduction of false positives is also achieved [24] with an exponentially weighted Dempster-Shafer theory that uses an alert confidence fusion approach. In this method, colored Petri-Net is used as an add-on to compute the probability of occurrence of each token and a specified threshold is applied to filter false alerts. Like all statistically based approaches, this model always produces low data reduction rate on datasets that contain lots of unrelated attacks. Essentially, apart from the inherent flaws of each of the existing models, they have indicated potential research gaps.

3 Overview of Datasets

We evaluated our method with simulated, realistic and synthetic attacks that were mainly DARPA 2000[6], DEFCON-8 and DEFCON-10 [5] standard datasets. Essentially, our assumption was that a wider coverage of different datasets [21] would give a good picture of realistic network attacks. The DARPA-1 (LLDoS.1.0) and DARPA-2 (LLDoS.2.0.2) were two traces of DARPA 2000 datasets that represented Distributed Denial of Service (DDoS) that were launched by novice and experienced attackers within 5 and 8 seconds respective intervals. Also, DEFCON-8 lasted for about 34 hours while DEFCON-10 lasted for about 47 hours. In addition, attacks in DEFCON-8 dataset were ports scan and buffer overflow while that of DEFCON-10 dataset were some probing and non-probing attacks that included bad packet, ports scan, port sweeps, etc. The UNI-DATA was a trace file that was obtained from one of the perimeters of a University's networks within 21 hours real-time monitoring of realistic events. Besides, a trace file from our experimental network that contained some probing attacks that were mainly ping, Xmas tree, UDP, SYN stealth scan attacks and attacks that explored versions and list of operating systems in the target machines was also extracted and labeled as TEST-DATA. Also, these attacks lasted for about 27 hours. Throughout this paper, we would constantly refer to probing attacks as attacks that seek for vulnerabilities in the target systems and non-probing attacks as attacks that exploit vulnerabilities in the target systems.

Specifically, the attacks in TEST-DATA occurred between 2009-04-28 at 12:45:45 pm and ended on 2009-04-29 at 15:21:38 pm while that of the UNI-DATA occurred between 2009-06-21 at 14:41:55 pm and stopped on 2009-06-22 at 11:38:05 am. Also, DARPA-1 occurred between 2000-03-07 at 16:27:51 pm and ended 2000-03-07 at 16:27:56 pm while DARPA-2 occurred between 2000-04-16 at 21:06:15 pm and stopped on 2000-04-16 at 21:06:23 pm. In addition, DEFCON-8 started on 2000-07-28 at 16:39:03 pm and lasted for 2000-07-30 at 02:11:15 am while DEFCON-10 that started on 2002-08-03 at 00:57:17 am stopped on 2002-08-04 at 20:56:00 pm.

4 Reclassification of Intrusions

Network intrusion detectors are not specifically designed to solve the problems of intrusion quarantining, intrusion blacklisting and intrusion white-listing. Instead, they moderately provide supportive information that can be adapted to lessen the problems of intrusion quarantining and intrusion white-listing. Essentially, we have identified three classes of suspicious network packets that commonly migrate across realistic networks (fig 1 below). These are packets that completely elude detections (i), packets that are blocked (ii) by the defensive devices (D) on the networks and packets that are reported by the detector (iii) that is positioned on the networks. Although, categories ((i) and (ii)) are beyond the scope of this paper, however they raise lots of questions [21]. For instance, it is imperative to understand the kinds of packets that have been blocked by the network defensive system to confirm whether they are legitimate or intrusive packets. Also, packets that elude detections are potential dangers to the network.

Hence, it is imperative to know what they are [21] and the impacts that they have on the networks. Nevertheless, the third category of suspicious packets (type-iii) is the main focus of this paper and hence, the security of a network is usually compromised by the existence of type-i and type-iii on every computer network. Basically, there are two classifiers in a compromised network that usually classify type-iii packets and they are mainly the higher level and the lower level classifiers. The higher level classifier (A) is a network detector such as Snort that classifies network packets at the packet level into normal and abnormal traffics during intrusion detections.

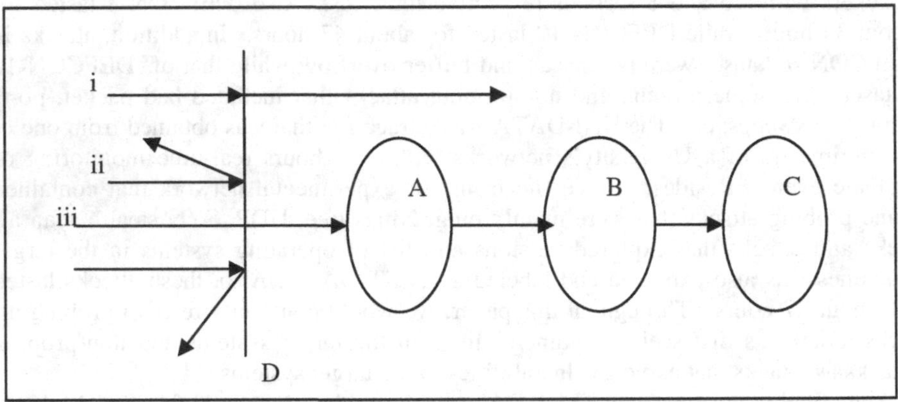

Fig. 1. Taxonomy of suspicious network packets

We have noticed that Snort is frequently regarded as the de facto standard for intrusion detection technology. The tool is an open source-code intrusion detector that uses rule-matching to perform protocol and packets' analyses, [16] logging and alerting suspicious events and it is a widely preferred choice for conducting most Network intrusion detection researches.

Accordingly, Snort validates each of the incoming packets that migrate across the networks with a database of its expert rules. Usually, a packet that does not match any of its rules is discarded while a match is appropriately tagged with reference identities or attributes [10] that have been extracted from the IP packet header. Thereafter, the packet is logged into two audit repositories. Some of these reference identities [16] are source-ip and source ports of the attacks, destination-ip and destination ports of the targets of the attacks and other attributes such as TOS, IPflag, TTL, IPprotocol, Timestamp, Priority, description, etc.

Simultaneously, an alert is sent to notify the system administrator about the presence of such event on the networks to complete the intrusion detection cycle at the higher level. Fundamentally, this is the origin of lots of issues that are facing intrusion detection technology since inception. However, we refer interesting reader to [10] and [16] for extensive discussions about network packets, alerts and their respective attributes.

In addition, the lower level classification is basically implemented by the system administrators (B). Ordinarily at this level, all notified warnings (output from higher level classifier) are reclassified and clustered into true and false positives (C).

S/N	Sequence
1	<timestamp>
2	<source-ip, destination-ip, timestamp>
3	<tos, ipflag, ttl, ipprotocol>
4	<source-ip, tos ,ipflag ,ttl, ipprotocol>
5	<destination-ip, tos, ipflag, ttl, ipprotocol>
6	<source-ip, destination-ip, timestamp, tos, ipflag ,ttl, ipprotocol>

Fig. 2. Selection criteria

Unfortunately, there are numerous challenges that disrupt these processes in reality and hence, to investigate these problems, we have used six sequences of alerts' attributes that are shown in fig 2 above as selection or filtering criteria.

4.1 Automated Reclassification of Alerts

We automated a clustering program that was implemented in C++ language to cluster alerts of each dataset on the basis of each of the six selection criteria in fig 2 above and the arrival time of the attacks in each dataset. Since each dataset has different arrival time, we standardized the clustering intervals in an increasing order of 5mins, 10mins, 20mins, 40mins, 80mins, 160mins, 320mins, 640mins, 1,280mins, 2,560mins, etc. Hence, the time to cluster each dataset in each experiment was computed as the summation of each interval and the starting time of the attacks in the dataset. For instance, in DEFCON-8, the attacks started on 2000-07-28 at 16:39:03 pm and lasted for 2000-07-30 at 02:11:15 am.

So, the first arrival time was 16:44:03 (i.e. 16:39:03 + 5mins later), the second arrival time was 16:49:03 (i.e. 16:39:03 + 10mins later), the third was 16:59:03 (i.e. 16:39:03 + 20mins later), etc until the last arrived time which was 02:11:15 on 2000-07-30. Furthermore, the automation processes were divided into two basic phases. In the first phase, for each dataset at each arrival time and a selection criterion, our model quarantined each alerts within the arrival time and clustered them into clusters of repeated alerts and white-listed alerts. Subsequently, an advanced clustering procedure was then applied to further reclassify both intrusive categories into a meaningfully condensed dataset to achieve succinct white-listed alerts. The above procedures were repeated for each of the six selection criteria and for every evaluative dataset.

```
[Priority: 3]
[**] [123:8:1] (spp_frag3) Fragmentation overlap [**]
[Priority: 3]
[**] [123:8:1] (spp_frag3) Fragmentation overlap [**]
[Priority: 3]
[**] [123:8:1] (spp_frag3) Fragmentation overlap [**]
[Priority: 3]
[**] [123:8:1] (spp_frag3) Fragmentation overlap [**]
[Priority: 3]
[**] [123:8:1] (spp_frag3) Fragmentation overlap [**]
[Priority: 3]
[**] [123:8:1] (spp_frag3) Fragmentation overlap [**]
[Priority: 3]
[**] [123:8:1] (spp_frag3) Fragmentation overlap [**]
```

Fig. 3. Analysis process of defco8alerts

Furthermore, fig 3 above is an example of a stage of our model that quarantined DEFCON-8 dataset during the process of clustering on the basis of <timestamp>. However, it is not feasible to individually report other processes for each of the dataset due to space limitations. In addition, all the results that we have obtained in the entire experiments before and after the automation were recorded and they are presented in section 5 below.

5 Experimental Results

The original quantity of alerts per evaluative dataset is as follows. TEST-DATA generated 67,469 alerts, UNI-DATA generated 16,087, DARPA-1 generated 834, DARPA-2 generated 816, DEFCON-8 generated 917,221 while DEFCON-10 generated 5,372 alerts.

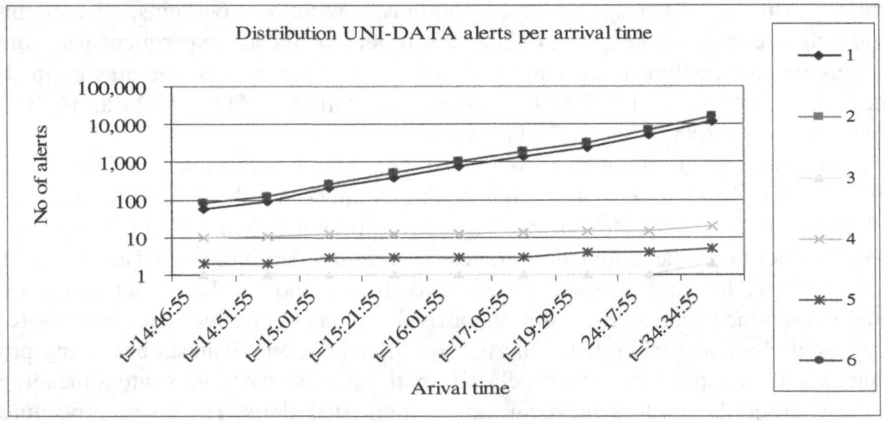

Fig. 4. Evaluation of UNI-DATA datasets

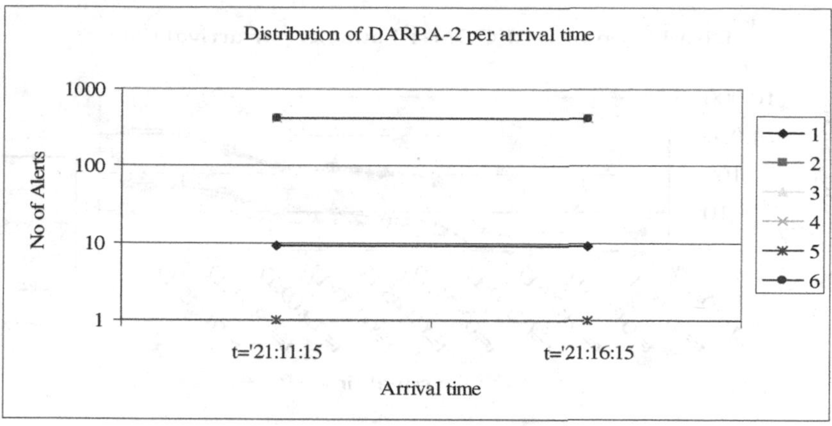

Fig. 5. Evaluation of DARPA-1 datasets

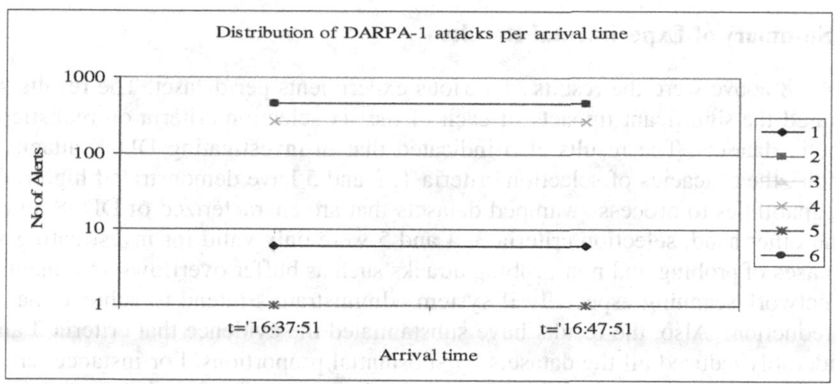

Fig. 6. Evaluation of DARPA-2 datasets

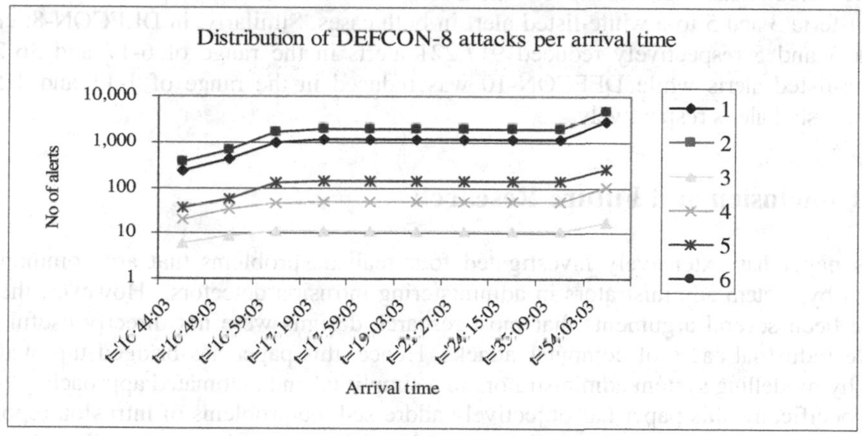

Fig. 7. Evaluation of DEFCON-8 datasets

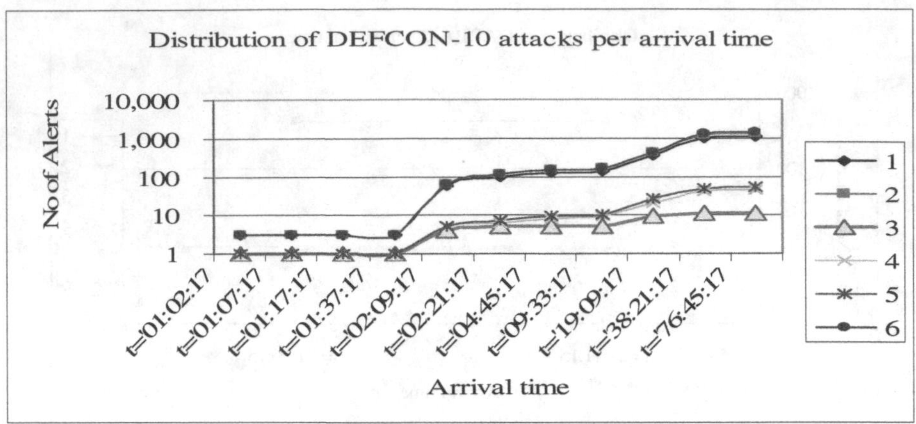

Fig. 8. Evaluation of DEFCON-10 datasets

5.1 Summary of Experimental Results

Figs 4 - 8 above were the results of various experiments per dataset. The results substantiated the significant impacts of each of the six selection criteria on realistic and synthetic datasets. The results also indicated that in investigating DDoS attacks for example, the efficacies of selection criteria 1, 3 and 5 have demonstrated high reduction capabilities to process swamped datasets that are characterized of DDoS attacks. On the other hand, selection criteria 3, 4 and 5 were only valid for investigating specific cases of probing and non-probing attacks such as buffer overflows and unauthorized network scanning especially if system administrators intend to achieve massive data reduction. Also, the results have substantiated the evidence that criteria 3 and 5 considerably reduced all the datasets by substantial proportions. For instance, criteria 3 and 5 respectively reduced UNI-DATA in the range of 1-2 and 2-5 white-listed alerts while TEST-DATA was respectively reduced in the range of 9-10 and 11-15 white-listed alerts. Also, DARPA-1 and DARPA-2 datasets were respectively reduced by criteria 3 and 5 to a white-listed alert in both cases. Similarly, in DEFCON-8, criteria 3 and 5 respectively reduced 917,221 alerts in the range of 6-17 and 36-25 white-listed alerts while DEFCON-10 was reduced in the range of 1-11 and 1-54 white-listed alerts respectively.

6 Conclusion and Future Research

This paper has extensively investigated four realistic problems that are commonly faced by system administrators in administering intrusion detectors. However, there have been several arguments that most research designs were not directly useful to solve industrial cases of computer attacks. Hence, this paper has bridged this wider gap by modelling system administrators in a simplified and automated approach.

Specifically, this paper has objectively addressed the problems of intrusion reporting, methodology of intrusion review, inability and inappropriateness of filtering criteria by automatic clustering of repeated alerts to synthesize a cluster of white-listed alerts that enhanced prompt countermeasures. Hence, our central focus was to also extend intrusion detection researches to add value and to be operationally relevant in achieving immediate solutions to some fundamental problems in real-world.

However, we have not been able to extend this model to address some other critical intrusion detection problems such as intrusion that elude detections and intrusion blacklisting that we have briefly discussed in this paper. Hence, our opinions about them are to detect them and subsequently isolate them from migrating within the networks. One of the methods of achieving these goals is to extend our ideas about intrusion quarantining, intrusion white-listing and intrusion blacklisting into cooperative expert modules. The implementation would incorporate functionality that has the ability to expel subsequent white-listed attacks that do not provide additional information to the system administrators from the networks. Hence, these are potential research areas that we plan to extensively investigate in our future research.

References

1. Aleksandar, L., Vipin, K., Jaidep, S.: Intrusion detection: A survey, Computer Science Department, University of Minnesota (2005)
2. Alfonso, V., Keith, S.: Probabilistic alert correlation. In: Lee, W., Mé, L., Wespi, A. (eds.) RAID 2001. LNCS, vol. 2212, pp. 54–68. Springer, Heidelberg (2001)
3. Chyssler, T., Burschka, S., Semling, M., Lingvall, T., Burbeck, K.: Alarm Reduction and Correlation in Intrusion Detection Systems, Department of Computer Science, Linkoping University, Sweden (2004)
4. Cuppens, F., Miege, A.: Alert correlation in cooperative intrusion detection framework. In: Proceedings of IEEE symposium on security and privacy (2002)
5. Capture The Flag Contest-Defcon datasets (2009), http://cctf.shmoo.com/data/
6. DARPA.: Intrusion Detection Scenario Specific Data Sets (2009), http://www.ll.mit.edu/mission/communications/ist/corpora/ideval/data/2000data.html
7. Debar, H., Wespi, A.: Aggregation and correlation of intrusion detection alerts. In: Proceedings of international symposium on recent advances in intrusion detection, Davis, CA, pp. 85–103 (2001)
8. Fatima, L.S., Mezrioui, A.: Improving the quality of alerts with correlation in intrusion detection. International Journal of Computer Science and Network Security 7(12) (2007)
9. Hartsein, B.: Intrusion Detection Likelihood: A Risk-Based Approach SANS Institute (2008)
10. Internet Protocol: Internetworking Technology overview (1999) (2009), http://www.cisco.com/en/US/docs/internetworking/technology/handbook/Internet-Protocols.pdf
11. Jan, N.Y., Lin, S.C., Tseng, S.S., Lin, N.P.: A decision support system for constructing an alert classification model. Journals of Expert Systems with Applications (February 2009)
12. Kabiri, P., Ghorbani, A.A.: A Rule-Based Temporal Alert Correlation System. International Journal of Network Security 5(1), 66–72 (2007)
13. Morin, B., Me, L., Debar, H., Ducass, M.: M2D2: A formal data model for IDS alerts correlation. In: Wespi, A., Vigna, G., Deri, L. (eds.) RAID 2002. LNCS, vol. 2516, pp. 115–137. Springer, Heidelberg (2002)

14. Ning, P., Cui, Y., Reeves, D.S.: Constructing Attack Scenarios through correlation of alerts, department of computer science, NC state University, USA (2002)
15. Paxson, V.: Considerations and Pitfalls for Conducting Intrusion Detection Research, International Computer Science Institute and Lawrence Berkeley National Laboratory Berkeley, California USA (2007)
16. Roesch, M.: Snort Manual version 2.8.4 (2009), `http://www.snort.org/assets/82/snort_manual.pdf`
17. Sadoddin, R., Ghorbani, A.: Network Security Laboratory, University of New Brunswick, Fredericton, Canada (2006)
18. Scarfone, K., Mell, P.: Guide to Intrusion Detection and Prevention Systems (IDPS), Recommendations of the National Institute of Standards and Technology, Special Publication 800-94, Technology Administration, Department of Commerce, USA (2007)
19. Urko, Z., Roberto, U.: Intrusion Detection Alarm Correlation: A Survey, Computer Science Department, Mondragon University, Gipuzkoa Spain (2004)
20. Wang, L., Liu, A., Jajodia, S.: Using attack graph for correlating, hypothesizing, and predicting intrusion alerts. Science Direct, pp. 2917–2933. Elsevier, Amsterdam (2006)
21. Valeur, F., Vigna, G., Kruegel, C., Kemmerer, R.A.: A Comprehensive approach to Intrusion Detection Alert Correlation. IEEE Transactions on Dependable and Secure Computing 1(3) (2004)
22. Xinzhou, Q., Wenke, L.: Discovering Novel Attack Strategies from INFOSEC Alerts, College of Computing Georgia Institute of Technology, Atlanta, GA 30332, USA (2004)
23. Yusof, R., Sulamat, S.R., Sahib, S.: Intrusion Alert Correlation Technique Analysis for Heterogeneous Log. International Journal of Computer Science and Network Security 8(9) (September 2008)
24. Yu, D., Deborah, F.: Alert Confidence Fusion in Intrusion Detection Systems with Extended Dempster-Shafer Theory, Department of Computer Science, University of Idaho (2005)
25. Zhu, B., Ali, A.G.: Alert Correlation for Extracting Attack Strategies, Faculty of Computer Science, University of New Brunswick, Fredericton, New Brunswick, Canada (2006)

Technology Perspective: Is Green IT a Threat to IT Security?

Dimitrios Frangiskatos, Mona Ghassemian, and Diane Gan

School of Computing and Mathematic Sciences, University of Greenwich, UK

Abstract. Industries are pushed by the regulations to reduce the CO2 footprint of their production lines. According to the latest statistics 3% of the CO2 footprint is generated by the IT industry. Currently a high percentage of the information being accessed by the users is produced and managed centrally. With the growth of data generation by users, e.g. social networking and YouTube websites, the storing and managing of the data will demand more energy on the networks.

One of the solutions to reduce the energy consumption in ICT is introduced by virtualisation technology. While virtualisation can help to reduce the energy consumption, it has introduced other complexities to the environment, such as scalability, resource management, security and management.

This paper focuses on the security issues created by the use of virtualisation technology which is being promoted to make computing Green. We also aim to highlight the system vulnerabilities which are a direct result of pushing computing to become greener by using virtualisation technology. We discuss the research challenges and directions needed to be further investigated in this field.

1 Introduction

Lately there is a lot of discussion around the reduction of greenhouse gasses and environmental and energy consumption issues. New legislation to regulate businesses' environmental impact has been introduced. The Waste Electrical and Electronic Equipment (WEEE), the restricted use of hazardous substances (RoHS) and the battery directive, have been adopted by the EU in an attempt to reduce the risk presented to the environment and human health by hazardous materials when incinerated or put into landfills. Retailers are trying to reduce excessive packaging, the air-freighting of food long distances and to providing alternatives to plastic bags. With regards to the latter, some will say that although allegedly these last for hundreds of years, most usually decompose before you get your shopping back home. Well they may be aware that in some places even bottled water was banned [5] to reduce the environmental impact.

It is not a secret that the IT industry, i.e. ICT (Information and Communication Technologies) uses vast amounts of energy to power the systems it uses to provide its services. Google's data centre's energy requirements have attracted the attention of environmentalists after it was claimed that the amount of energy required for two typical searches could boil a kettle [6]. Google's response was that each search takes approximately 0.0003 kWh [7].

D. Weerasinghe (Ed.): ISDF 2009, LNICST 41, pp. 147–154, 2010.

As the concept of green has an impact on the way people think about computing these days, big IT firms (IBM, HP, Sun and Google) are implementing major green schemes and environmentally friendly solutions. Google has embarked in a solar program for its headquarters, which since 2007 has produced 4,427 megawatt-hours [8].

It has been suggested that PC work places are under utilised, with less than 1% of the CPUs being used in any 24 hr period. Since PC hardware is distributed, each runs an OS and numerous applications, which are duplicated many times and each PC consumes electricity. There is also no resource pooling [15].

Having discussed the energy consumption means and the cost for it, there are number of solutions that the IT industry can use to reduce energy costs and protect the environment; i.e., replace paper with digital copies for business processes, adopt service oriented approaches, optimise systems and opt for virtualisation solutions.

Re-using old equipment is also a way to greener IT. Reusing old equipment for less demanding applications, can save up on raw materials (and thus energy) and reduce landfill waste. The rule is however that before donating or recycling used equipment, the hardware must be thoroughly cleansed of all data, not just data protected by privacy and security regulations. In a recent article [11] it was revealed that a security expert discovered that a VPN device bought on EBay automatically connected to a local council's confidential servers. The alternative to this is to use virtualisation.

Virtualisation is widely adapted today as a mainstream technology in IT. Virtualisation works by inserting a thin layer of software directly on the computer hardware

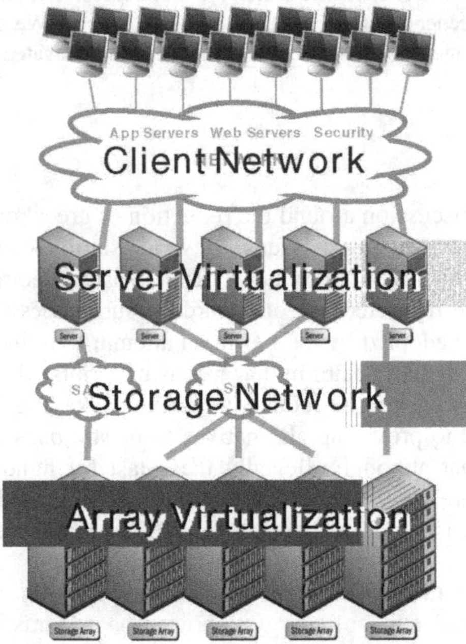

Fig. 1. Virtualisation is everywhere [13]

or on a host operating system. This contains a virtual machine monitor or "hypervisor" that allocates hardware resources dynamically and transparently. Pool common virtual infrastructure resources break the legacy "one application to one server" model with server consolidation, which dramatically improves the efficiency and availability of resources and applications in every organization.

Fewer servers and related IT hardware means reduced physical infrastructure, reduced power and cooling requirements and improved server to admin ratio. However there are voices of concern: can something be overlooked? After all, each VM is another server that an administrator must manage. Security updates must be applied and global configuration changes now need to be propagated to all of these new machines.

Virtualising a single physical computer is just the beginning. The four key elements that can be identified for virtual infrastructures are: clients, storage, servers and networks as depicted in Figure 1.

An automated data centre, built on a virtualisation platform responds to market dynamics faster and more efficiently than ever before. Management of a data centre on a virtual network architecture is a new dimension of research that is discussed and proposed in this work. Beside the flexibility, availability, efficiency and scalability features, a virtual data centre is green. According to VMware statistics [12] their customers typically save 50-70% on overall IT costs by consolidating their resource pools and delivering highly available machines with VMware Infrastructure.

Today's data centres consume a lot of electricity. A recent report by the Environmental Protection Agency claims data centres in the U.S. consume 4.5 billion kWh annually, 1.5% of the country's total. Perhaps more importantly, this figure has doubled from 2000 to 2006, and is likely to double again in the next few years. This trend is affecting data centres around the world and is likely to continue, given how central computing is to today's businesses and current lifestyles.

A virtualisation layer takes care of resource allocation from different data centre locations and all specifics when service instances are allocated in a particular data centre. Virtualised data centres provide a consistent operating environment spanning multiple physical data centre locations for the whole family of service instances [3].

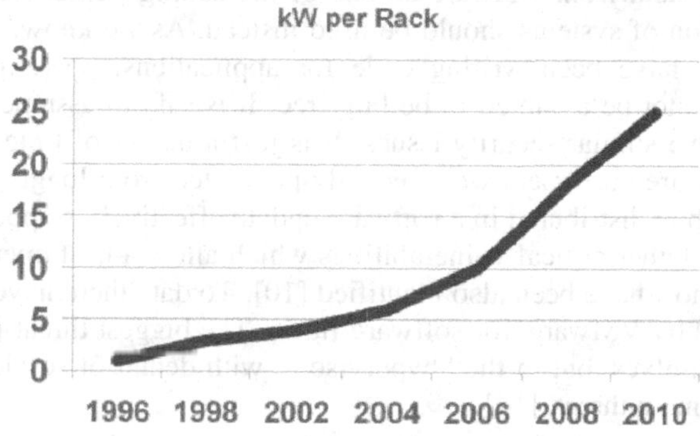

Fig. 2. Rising Energy Consumption in the Data Centre [1]

2 Research Challenges

While virtualisation technology has developed quite a long way from the basic elements in IT (machines, storage and networks), new research challenges have been turning into an increasing problem.

Most of the existing research work related to network virtualisation is discussed in [4], namely, interfacing, signalling and bootstrapping, resource and topology discovery, resource allocation, admission control and usage, virtual nodes and virtual links, naming and addressing, mobility management, monitoring, configuring and failure handling, security and privacy, interoperability issues and finally economics. Virtualisation is about sharing across IT domains, and that is often the problem. In this work we focus on the problems of security and management of virtualisation.

A. *Virtual Network Security and Threats*

In this section we investigate additional complexities and security threats as a result of using virtualisation.

Virtualisation is seen by many as a way of achieving green security. A growing number of security professionals are also considering the cost-cutting benefits of green security. Companies who have gone over to green security have found that having a smaller carbon footprint may not necessarily be a hindrance to maintaining their defences. Shrinking the number of boxes reduces costs and at the same time saves the planet by cutting the company's carbon footprint. The money saved can be used to spend on virtual security devices. There are currently a number of these devices on the market which reduce power consumption without compromising security [18].

Some organisations use virtualisation as a security substitute. Consolidating the data centre using virtualisation saves power, but integrating it to existing systems introduces many significant security challenges. Deploying virtual servers means that the physical cables that connect the original servers are no longer present. If security gateways were present between these servers then they no longer exist in the virtual world. If one virtual server in a data centre is compromised this could potentially put the rest at risk. Although virtualisation vendors have used the fact that their products will protect your data from malware as one of the selling points for their products, physical separation of systems should be used instead. As we know, for a number of years developers have been writing code for applications, operating systems and hardware that cannot be assumed to be bug free. It is safe to assume that virtualised solutions will have similar security issues. It is just a matter of time before they are discovered. VMware customers were recently prevented from logging onto their virtual servers as a bug distributed in a software update effectively stopped systems from powering up [9]. Other critical vulnerabilities which allow a host operating system to run code on the host have been also identified [10]. To date there have been a number of patches issued by VMware, for software flaws. The biggest threat is not to the virtual servers themselves, but to the "hypervisor", with denial of service attacks being perceived as the main threat. [14]

Security issues with server sprawling: Server sprawling although good for the environment can be responsible for virtualised solutions that are inappropriate for a number of reasons. The problem lies with the fact that servers can be created with the click of a button, without the usual physical constraints. This can lead to reduced efficiency which contradicts one of the key benefits of virtualisation. While the well-meaning administrator may be seeking to achieve objectives such as research or recovery, "extra" copies of VM environment can possibly sit dormant, not receiving the operating system or application patches needed to keep the VM secure. This creates vulnerability should these VMs, which are not up to the security standard, be re-introduced into the production environment [17].

Application performance on top of VM: Running virtual machines on a physical machine requires a lot of hardware resources, and unless properly configured, performance will be noticeably slow. With that in mind, certain parameters of applications running on top of a VM can be overlooked and that can lead to poorly configured applications. Problem diagnosis in VM servers might not be as straightforward to detect as in a non virtualised system.

Tracing of security incidents: With virtualised solutions the insider threat is greater than ever. In the past it wasn't easy for a disgruntled employee to take a server home, compromise it and then take it back to work. Now it is easy for someone to copy a number of virtualised machines on a USB, alter them at home and then copy them back to the company's network the following day.

Encryption standards in VM encryption

A provider may allow multiple customers to administer virtual machines on the same physical host but how well do different virtualisation environments protect or isolate one virtual machine from another? Especially when considering that there is not yet a standard for encrypting VM environments.

"Isolation between coexisting VNs can only provide a certain level of security and privacy through the use of secured tunnels, encryptions and so on; but it does not obviate the prevalent threats, intrusions, and attacks to the physical layer and VNs. In addition to that, security and privacy issues specific to network virtualisation must also be identified and explored. For example, programmability of the network elements can increase vulnerability if secure programming models and interfaces are unavailable. All these issues require close examination to create a realistic NVE."[4]

Network segmentation: Internal virtual network segmentation within a host and between its various VMs is also possible with the virtualisation tools, but this flexibility runs the risk that internal virtual segments cannot be reached from the external network. This could hamper traditional ingress security techniques, such as antivirus updates or operating system updates, or egress security techniques such as monitoring/alerting or log consolidation [17].

B. Virtual Network Management

Unlike the established and distinct roles for managing physical systems, networks and storage, virtualisation is not owned by a specific role. Rather it cuts across the three domains. Virtual elements are often not even considered as managed entities since they do not exist physically and are not inventoried. The Management Information

Base (MIB) is required to be compiled into the virtual management system. Consequently, management practices are often not applied to virtual entities such as change, configuration and release management processes.

Due to the fact that virtual resources, in the end, rely on sharing physical resources, estimating workloads, planning capacity and achieving predictable behaviour is becoming much harder with little evidence or experience from past providing guidance.

Most established management systems are not prepared and are of no help in dealing with virtual elements. One reason is that virtual entities can be created in an ad hoc manner and may only exist for a short time [2]. They also may not be active all the time and rather exist in a saved state which can be resumed at any time to recreate a virtual entity. This leads, in many cases, to the fact that virtual entities cannot be discovered, uniquely identified and registered in configuration and management databases. Hence, they are often unknown to management systems which rely on the information in those databases.

The benefits of virtualisation are undeniable. However, the virtual world residing in that clean and organized physical world can easily become unaggregated, fragmented and unmaintained leading to high management overhead, unpredictable risk of failure and chain effects.

Management software for virtual infrastructures, such as Virtualisation 2.0, is now in its second phase. This places an additional layer of software on the virtual platforms. The various layers of software (applications, protocol layers, OS in VMs and the virtualisation platform) must all work together to provide a business service. [16]

VMs can be cloned with a complete collection of applications installed on top of an operating system. When the duplicate (or more) VM(s) are created, the organisation needs to ensure their licensing agreement with the vendors covers that type of instance [17].

Staff skills must grow to meet the complexity of the more centralized resource allocation duties placed on the administrator of the virtualisation tools. Physical server team members, while competent in networking concepts, are usually placed in a role where they may create multiple virtual switches, VLANs, and maybe deploy a VM with router capabilities. The server team members need a combination of increased training and increased communication with the physical network team as well as the information security team [17].

Cloud computing is one of the fastest growing segments in the IT industry with companies tapping into the cloud to boost their infrastructure resources at a low cost. The idea behind cloud computing is based on multi tenancy and decoupling between specific hardware resources and applications. However there are concerns regarding the security because of the multi tenant feature of the cloud and the fact that there are no standards for security or data privacy. There is a slight reluctance on the part of cloud providers to create standards as there are concerns that cloud computing remains at such an embryonic stage that the imposition of strict standards could do more harm than good. Certain companies try to adapt ISO27001 for use with cloud based applications however that is not a panacea. Experts' advice to companies is to invest in monitoring tools and keep systems updated. At the same time security policies should be thoroughly reviewed and service availability guarantees and penalties should be scrutinised. However, cloud security policies cannot always accommodate an individual company's needs. That creates gaps in the cloud pot of data that can be exploited by attackers. Recent examples include Gmail's service which collapsed in Europe [19] and Saleforce's phishing attack [20].

3 Summary

A significant amount of virtualisation is already implemented in IT industry, e.g. data centres which eliminates hard-wire association, server Consolidation and increase the energy efficiency. For this scenario, a virtualisation solution reduces the energy demands of running a data centre by server consolidation (one device can appear as many) and dynamic management of computer capacity across a pool of servers. However there are further questions remain to be investigated such as the extra added management complexity and security threat for the storage network.

Fundamental concepts of management such as determining the existence and the identification of virtual entities are unresolved. Existing management systems hence remain unaware and incapable of managing virtual entities.

The goals of monitoring and assessment of virtual environments are a continuous process and more ad hoc. Associations of virtual entities to underlying shared resources are also often not represented, making fundamental management tasks such as monitoring problematic. While data can be collected using current monitoring systems, correct interpretation is often not possible because the context of the measurement or probing was not captured, such as the association of virtual entities to underlying physical entities at a given point in time. While a compromised virtual server can easily be replaced with a clean copy, the question remains, how many organisations would be able to identify that there was a problem quickly enough to avert any further problems?

The bottom line is that in today's growing virtual networks, to avoid longer term and more costly issues, it is critical to assess the current state and to implement policies, procedures, and tools to evaluate mitigation of the risks of virtualisation [17].

A solution must be found that can continue to reduce power usage and hence energy costs, while at the same time solving the business needs of organisations. While this paper has possibly raised more questions than it has answered, this is an ongoing work. The security challenges of using virtualisation technology to address the Green challenges of the future cannot be underestimated.

References

[1] How VMware Virtualisation Right-sizes IT Infrastructure to Reduce Power Consumption, VMware White paper

[2] Graupner, S.: Virtualised IT Infrastructures and Their Management. In: Workshop on Virtualised IT Infrastructures and Their Management (October 2008)

[3] Graupner, S., Kotov, V., Trinks, H.: Resource-sharing and service deployment in virtual data centres. In: Proceedings of 22nd International Conference on Distributed Computing Systems, pp. 666–671 (2002)

[4] Mosharaf Kabir Chowdhury, N.M., Boutaba, R.: Network Virtualisation: state of the art and research challenges. IEEE Communications magazine 47(7), 20–26 (2009)

[5] http://enjoybottledwater.org/?p=37

[6] http://technology.timesonline.co.uk/tol/news/tech_and_web/article5489134.ece
[7] http://www.thenakedscientists.com/HTML/content/questions/question/2246/
[8] http://www.google.com/corporate/solarpanels/home
[9] http://www.networkworld.com/news/2008/081208-vmware-bug.html
[10] http://www.securityfocus.com/archive/1/archive/1/502615/100/0/threaded
[11] http://www.pcpro.co.uk/news/227190/council-sells-security-hole-on-ebay.html
[12] VMware website, http://www.vmware.com/pdf/vi3_monitoring_statistics_note.pdf
[13] Mellish, B.: Best Practices in Managing Virtualised Environments. Storage Networking Industry Association (May 2009)
[14] Saran, C.: Virtualisation Presents Security Challenges. Computer Weekly, posted 9, 45 (March 26, 2008)
[15] Virtual Workplace – White Paper (Fijitsu) (March 2008)
[16] Virtualisation 2.0 is all about Manageability – White Paper, http://www.eginnovations.com/whitepaper/Virtualisation2_0.pdf
[17] Hoesing, M.T.: Virtualisation Security Assessment. Information Security Journal: A Global Perspective (January 2009)
[18] Bill Brenner, Cost cutting through Green IT Security: Real or Myth? (June 2008), http://www.csoonline.com/article/print/410513
[19] http://www.theherald.co.uk/news/news/display.var.2491445.0.Google_apologises_to_millions_after_gmail_collapse.php
[20] http://www.computerworlduk.com/management/security/cybercrime/news/index.cfm?newsid=6058

An Adaptive Fusion Framework for Fault-Tolerant Multibiometrics

S. Chindaro, Z. Zhou, M.W.R. Ng, and F. Deravi

School of Engineering and Digital Arts, University of Kent, Canterbury, CT2 7NT, United Kingdom
{S.Chindaro,Z.Zhou,F.Deravi}@kent.ac.uk

Abstract. The use of multiple biometrics will work with greater efficiency if all the systems are capable of acquiring biometrics of adequate quality and processing them successfully. However if one or more of the biometrics fails, then the system has to rely on fewer or one biometric. If the individual biometrics are set to use low thresholds, the system maybe vulnerable to falsely accepting impostors. The motivation behind the proposed method is to provide an adaptive fusion platform where the software system can identify failures in certain algorithms and if necessary adapt the current rule to ignore these algorithms and adjust operating points accordingly. Results from experiments carried out on a multi-algorithmic and multi-biometric 3D and 2D database are presented to show that adopting such a system will result in an improvement in efficiency and verification rate.

Keywords: Adaptive Fusion, Multibiometrics, Face Recognitions.

1 Introduction

Biometrics is an increasingly advancing field based on an automatically measurable, robust and distinctive physical characteristic or personal trait that can be used to identify an individual or verify the claimed identity of an individual. Automatic biometric-based systems have the potential of playing a major role in various applications in the areas of security, access control and surveillance. Even though a number of modalities have been tested and deployed in various applications with some success, there are limitations to each of them which are environment dependant (for example, lighting and pose for face, noise for voice recognition, and cleanliness of a finger in fingerprints etc). This has given rise to a growing interest in the use of multiple modalities [1]. Fusion of diverse modalities may result in systems which are more robust to changing conditions through integration of complementary information [1][2][3].

However, the use of multiple biometrics will work with greater efficiency if all the systems are capable of acquiring biometrics of adequate quality and processing them successfully with the correct configuration. However if one or more of the biometrics fails (fails to acquire or acquires an image of inadequate quality), then the system has to rely on fewer or one biometric. If both biometrics are set to use low thresholds, then the system has to adjust its configuration accordingly to avoid a false accept. Adaptive fusion is one solution to avoid such a scenario. The motivation behind the method is to provide an adaptive fusion platform where the software system can identify failures in certain algorithms or biometric modalities, and adapt the current rule to optimize the system performance.

D. Weerasinghe (Ed.): ISDF 2009, LNICST 41, pp. 155–162, 2010.

This work is part of the European Project, '3D Face' [4] whose aims are to (i) improve the performance of classical face recognition techniques by extending it to 3D, (ii) integrate privacy protection technology to safeguard the biometric information and (iii) deploy the secure face recognition system at airports for employee access control.

Even though there are several biometrics on the market today, the use of the face has gained prominence since the adoption of the ePassport by the ICAO as a standard for future passports [5]. The system adopted by the ICAO is mainly based on 2D face recognition. The disadvantages of developing an automatic authentication/verification system based on 2D include its sensitivity to changes in acquisition conditions such as lighting and the absence of liveness detection mechanisms [6] [7].

The integration of 3D models promises significant performance enhancements for border controls. By combining the geometry and texture-channel information of the face, 3D face recognition systems provide an improved robustness while processing variations in poses and problematic lighting conditions when taking the photo [6].

The work presented in this paper is based on fusion 2D and 3D facial biometrics in an adaptable fusion framework to optimize the system performance and improve efficiency, in addition to the robustness brought about by fusion. An experimental evaluation of the proposed system is presented and results are compared to non-adaptive systems. Results show that adopting such a system will result in an improvement in the verification rate. It also improves the efficiency of the system by reducing the number of rejections without compromising the security of the system.

In Section 2, the adaptive fusion framework is described. The experimental set-up which includes the database and the 3D and 2D face recognition algorithms used in these experiments are described in Section 3. Results and the analysis is presented in Section 4. Finally, the conclusions reached are presented in Section 5.

2 The Adaptive Fusion Framework

The use of multiple biometrics has seen a growing number of fusion frameworks being proposed using different modalities. There have been wide-ranging research in the fusion of various modalities such as speech and face, face and fingerprint [1] and more recently 2D and 3D face information [6][7]. In these investigations, the advantage of using fusion is not in dispute. However what is not clear is how this systems deal with failure to acquire images or to acquire images of adequate quality, or failure to process in one of the modalities is dealt with. Such systems have fixed thresholds and would be liable to falsely accepting users or reject users when one modality or algorithm fail (fails to acquire or process a particular biometric, for example) therefore reducing both accuracy and efficiency.

The motivation behind the method is to provide an adaptive fusion platform where the software system can identify failures in certain algorithms and if necessary adapt the current rule to ignore these algorithms and adjust thresholds accordingly. In the field, a configuration switch can be embedded in the software to adopt certain configurations according to the pattern of failure, with each configuration constituting of a pre-defined combinations and operational settings. This is depicted in Figure 1.

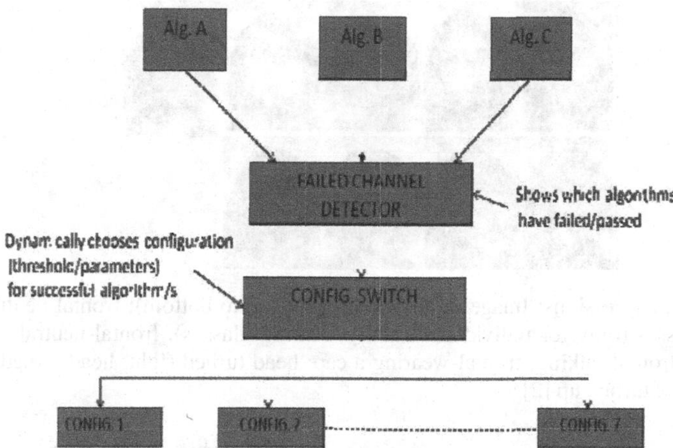

Fig. 1. An Adaptive fusion framework for multibiometrics

In the depicted system, the output of a set of different algorithms (Alg. A –C), which process different biometrics modalities indicates whether the acquisition and processing of the acquired biometric has been successful or not. Each algorithm outputs a code, say '1' or '0'. The code produced is then interpreted by the configuration switch, which then chooses the optimum configuration settings to employ.

Testing of such a system in a laboratory setting is a challenge, if the aim is to produce ROC curves which show different operating points. This is because of the difference in the thresholds required for each configuration. You can therefore not adjust a uniform set of thresholds for the whole system, which makes the plotting of ROC curves impossible. However figures relating to the verification rate, FAR and FRR at certain predefined thresholds can be obtained. In the next section experiments carried out using 4 different 2D and 3D face recognition algorithms and 2 sets of combinations are described.

3 Experiments

3.1 Database and Test Scenarios

The experiments we carried out on a database collected by the 3D Face project [4]. One hundred subjects were used for this phase of testing; containing a total of 2200 images. 3D images and 2D images were obtained using the ViSense Scanner [8] developed within 3D Face.

The tests were designed to address three application scenarios created using 3 different masks for selecting the appropriate scores from the scores and decision matrices [2]. **Scenario 1 (S1)** tests the performance of the system. Only neutral expressions are considered that is, *Neutral v/s Neutral.* **Scenario 2 (S2)** tests the realistic operational conditions, which takes into account the fact that expressions might differ during verification. It therefore tests the neutral expressions against other expressions (smiling and talking); that is, *Neutral vs. Expressions*. **Scenario 3 (S3)** tests the robustness of the system. It therefore compares neutral expressions against all other expressions and poses (see Figure 2); that is, *Neutral v/s All.* Results in this paper are presented for this challenging scenario (S3).

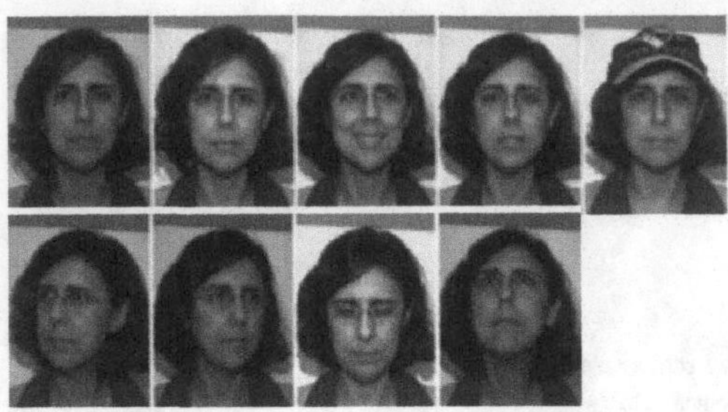

Fig. 2. Poses and expressions: Images from left to right(top to bottom); frontal-neutral expression without glasses (only for individuals usually wearing glasses), frontal-neutral expression, frontal-smiling, frontal-talking, frontal-wearing a cap; head turned right, head turned left, head turned down, head turned up [2]

3.2 3D and 2D Face Recognition Algorithms

Four face recognition algorithms provided by three members of the consortium were utilized in the experiments. Three 2D and one 3D face recognition algorithm were utilized in the combinations. Brief descriptions of the algorithms are provided in this section. The names of the providers are withheld for commercial purposes; acronyms will be used.

A2D (2D Face recognition algorithm) –In this algorithm after normalization, face features are extracted by applying local image transforms at a set of predefined image locations. These features are then concatenated from these components to form a raw feature vector. A global transform is then applied to the raw feature vector to produce the final vector which is used for the matching step.

B2D (2D face recognition algorithm) – This 2D algorithm represent the facial geometry by means of a flexible grid which is adjusted to the specific facial pose and expression by adjusting the size, position, and internal distortion. A set of specific filter structures is assigned to each node of the graph and analyzes the local facial features. Approximately 2,000 characteristics are used to represent a face and an individual identity and are used for matching.

C2DHR (high resolution 2D face recognition algorithm) - This algorithm is based on a multi-resolution analysis of the skin texture. After normalization, several pre-processing steps are performed in order to emphasize the skin texture singularities (features) in the high informational zones of the face. These features are then associated with 2D template for the matching phase.

A3D (3D face recognition algorithm) - In this algorithm, firstly face localization, normalization and smoothing is performed. From the smoothed data, shape descriptors are determined which form the raw vectors. These are transformed by a global transform into templates maximizing the ratio of inter-person and intra-person variance. The similarity between two 3D faces is obtained by applying a simple function on their templates.

These four algorithms were used in two combination set-ups to evaluate the fusion framework. The experiments are described in the next section.

3.3 Adaptive and Non-adaptive Fusion

The following combinations were tested; *A2D-A3D-B2D* and *A2D-B2D-C2DHR*.These combinations were picked because the individual algorithms had significant failure to acquire rates. Two fusion methods were used, the Sum and Weighted-Sum. The weights for the Weighted Sum Method were calculated using the equal error rates for each algorithm obtained from a disjoint fusion training set.

Table 1. Possible output patterns for a 3-algorithm fusion combination and corresponding thresholds (F – fail, S = success)

Output Pattern	P1	P2	P3	P4	P5	P6	P7	P8
Alg1	F	F	F	S	F	S	F	S
Alg2	F	F	S	S	F	F	S	S
Alg3	F	F	F	F	S	S	S	S
Thresh.	R	T1	T2	T3	T4	T5	T6	T7

The target performance set for the 3D Face Project was an FAR = 0.0025 at an FRR = 0.025 [2]. Therefore the operating points (thresholds) for the fusion system were set at these targets. These operating points were obtained from a disjoint training set. For each possible output pattern (P1-P8) for the fusion set-up, corresponding thresholds (T1-T7) were obtained and stored as shown in Table 1. R' means a complete rejection.

4 Results

In S3, the database had a total of 223 849 imposter scores and 3 287 genuine scores (a total of 22 7136). The confusion matrices in Tables 2-5 show the results obtained for the two different approaches; adaptive and non-adaptive fusion for the two different combinations and two fusion methods.

Table 2. Sum Result: A2D-A3D-B2D

Adaptive	Gen	Imp
Gen	3131	156
Imp	340	223509

Non-Adaptive	Gen	Imp
Gen	3089	120
Imp	340	217854

Table 3. Weighted Sum Result: A2D-A3D-B2D

Adaptive	Gen	Imp
Gen	3123	164
Imp	958	222891

Non Adaptive	Gen	Imp
Gen	3106	103
Imp	958	217236

Table 4. Sum Result: A2D-B2D-C2DHR

	Adaptive Gen	Adaptive Imp
Gen	3173	114
Imp	276	223573

	Non-Adaptive Gen	Non-Adaptive Imp
Gen	3127	82
Imp	276	217918

Table 5. Weighted Sum Result: A2D-B2D-C2DHR

	Adaptive Gen	Adaptive Imp
Gen	3199	88
Imp	2252	221597

	Non-Adaptive Gen	Non-Adaptive Imp
Gen	3157	52
Imp	2252	215942

In these tables, the first row (Gen) indicates the number of genuine users accepted correctly (under the 'Gen' column) and those falsely rejected (under the 'Imp' column) respectively. The second row (Imp) illustrates the number of imposters falsely accepted by the system (under the 'Gen' column) and the number of impostors correctly rejected by the system (under the 'Imp' column) .

In each case the number of genuine users rejected completely by the non-adaptive system is 78 (that is, for example in Table 2: (3287 – (3089+120)); which is a failure rate of 2.37%. This means in a large airport, processing for example 100 000 people per day, 2 370 are completely rejected. The number of imposters rejected by the system in each case is 5655 (that is, for example in Table 2: 223 849 – (340+217854)) a failure rate of 2.53%.

The adaptive system in this case, processes all users. It increases the number of genuine users who successfully uses the system, who otherwise would have been rejected by the non-adaptive system. For example, of the 78 genuine users rejected by the non-adaptive system for A2D-A3D-B2D-Sum (Table 3), 42 are successfully processed (column A in Table 6), that is 54% (column B in Table 2) of these. In all cases, the 5655 imposters rejected by the non-adaptive are successfully processed (and correctly rejected). All the corresponding figures for the other combinations are given in Table 2. These figures are hugely significant in large scale implementations.

Table 6. Scale of rejected genuine users by non-adaptive system who are successfully processed by the adaptive system

	A	B
A2D-A3D-B2D-Sum	42	54%
A2D-A3D-B2D WSum	17	22%
A2D-A3D-B2D-Sum	50	64%
A2D-A3D-B2D WSum	42	54%

From these results it can be observed that using the adaptive system, the number of users accepted by the system is increased, therefore increasing the efficiency of the system. In this case all users are processed successfully by the adaptive system.

It can also be observed that despite the increase in the number of users being processed by the system in the adaptive framework, the number of imposters falsely accepted is not increased, therefore security is not compromised.

Table 7. The verification rates of the two systems

	Verification Rates	
	N-Adaptive	Adaptive
A2D-A3D-B2D-Sum	0.94	0.95
A2D-A3D-B2D WSum	0.94	0.95
A2D-A3D-B2D-Sum	0.95	0.97
A2D-A3D-B2D WSum	0.96	0.97

Table 7 shows the verification rates of the two systems. There is an increase in the verification rate in each case when using adaptive fusion (number of genuine users correctly accepted).

5 Conclusion

Multiple biometrics fusion can be efficient if all the biometrics are working correctly without failure. However if one or more of the biometrics fails, the system's accuracy and efficiency is compromised. Adaptive fusion is one solution to handle such a situation. From these experiments, the advantages of using the adaptive fusion approach has been shown to improve the performance of the 3D and 2D face recognition system in terms of verification rate and efficiency without compromising the security of the system (no increase in false acceptance) and presents a framework for utilising multi-biometric fusion in a more efficient way. Even though experimental results are presented for 2D and 3D facial biometrics fusion, the proposed system is generic and can be employed in any multi-biometric scenario.

Acknowledgments. The authors would like to acknowledge the support of 3D FACE, a European Integrated Project funded under the European Commission IST FP6 program contract number 026845.

References

1. Ross, A., Nandakumar, K., Jain, A.: Handbook of Multibiometrics. Int. Series on Biometrics. Springer, Heidelberg (2006)
2. Castro Neves, M., Chindaro, S., Ng, M., Zhou, Z., Deravi, F.: Performance Evaluation of Multibiometric Face Recognition Systems. In: Proceedings of the Special Interest Group on Biometrics and Electronic Signatures (BIOSIG 2008), Germany. Lecture Notes in Informatics (LNI), vol. P-137, pp. 47–58. Springer, Heidelberg (2008)
3. Veldhuis, R.N.J., Deravi, F., Tao, Q.: Multibiometrics for face recognition. Datenschutz und Datensicherheit – DuD 32(3), 204–214 (2008)
4. 3DFace, `http://www.3dface.org/home/welcome`

5. International Civil Aviation Organization Technical Advisory Group 15 Machine Readable Travel Documents/New Technologies Working Group, Biometrics Deployment of Machine Readable Travel Documents,Version 2.0 (May 2004)
6. Chang, K.I., Bowyer, K.W., Flynn, P.J.: Face recognition using 2D and 3D facial data. In: Proceedings of ACM Workshop on Multimodal User Authentication, pp. 25–32 (2003)
7. Cook, J., McCool, C., Chandran, V., Sridharan, S.: Combined 2D/3D Face Recognition Using Log-Gabor Templates. In: 2006 IEEE International Conference on Advanced Video and Signal Based Surveillance (AVSS 2006), p. 83 (2006)
8. Neugebauer, P.J.: Research on 3D Sensors - Minimizing the Environmental Impacting Factors. In: Workshop on Biometrics and eCards (2007)

Cross-Enterprise Policy Model for e-Business Web Services Security

Tanko Ishaya[1] and Jason R.C. Nurse[2]

[1] The University of Hull, Scarborough Campus, Filey Road, Scarborough, YO11 2AZ, UK
[2] Department of Computer Science, University of Warwick, Coventry, CV4 7AL, UK
T.Ishaya@hull.ac.uk, jnurse@dcs.warwick.ac.uk

Abstract. Contemporary e-Business applications comprise of dynamic extensible and interoperable collection of services, Web Services and information shared by collaborating entities performing various transactional tasks. Securing these services offerings is therefore of crucial importance. To address security requirements, there has been a plethora of proposed solutions, ranging from hardware devices and security specifications to software applications. Most of these security solutions are largely technology focused with little or no evaluation and integration of policies and procedures of these collaborating entities. This research investigates the use of an approach that integrates documented cross-enterprise policies with current security technology, to enhance the overall security requirements of businesses that decide to use web services. A policy model for enhancing web services security is developed evaluated and presented.

Keywords: security, security policies, security model, web Services, cross-enterprise, e-Business, web-based applications.

1 Introduction

Electronic Business (e-Business) has undoubtedly become the fastest growing means of doing business in today's economy. An assessment of the UK e-business field in [15], noted that over two-thirds of UK companies are doing business online, a 50% increase from 2002. There is also a considerable increase in the level of collaboration between e-businesses, with service offerings such as e-banking, online order processing and even e-payments –particular through the use of Web services (hereafter referred to as WS) technology. An example of e-Business use of WS is the streamlined communications between airline, hotel and car rental companies discussed in [12]. Using WS technology, the interactions between these distinct companies is dynamically available in real time and possibly all through one single interface to the customer.

Electronic Data Interchange (EDI) has enabled cross-enterprise interactions (see [9]) before the existence of WS; main benefit available with WS is their ability to facilitate interoperability between heterogeneous systems due to their use of standardized protocols and open technologies. WS provides the ability to allow for seamless integration of services and business processes across disparate types of enterprises.

D. Weerasinghe (Ed.): ISDF 2009, LNICST 41, pp. 163–171, 2010.

While WS presents e-Business with dynamic and interoperable service integration, the security dilemmas that they pose are enormous. As noted in [13], WS presents a new avenue for attack not addressed by current security infrastructure. This security issue is compounded by the fact that an individual, isolated approach to security by each e-Business is no longer sufficient as each one's approach must now readily interoperate with the others' at any moment in time. The seriousness of this security issue is stressed by numerous authors in [2], [11] and [14] with [6] linking this issue as the limiting factor on widespread deployment of WS. Hartman et al. (2003) proposed a 'structured approach' to achieving secure joint WS offerings. This approach requires each e-Business to clearly define a set of security requirements for its services; the level of functionality that needs to be exposed; and then the special mechanisms to be put in place to fulfill each participating entity's needs. Essential to this proposed solution is also the concept of Enterprise Application Security Integration (EASI) techniques as they aid considerably in providing a common security framework for integrating many different technology solutions (Hartman et al., 2003). A shortcoming of this approach is that it places so much emphasis on the mechanisms/technologies to be used (e.g. the EASI framework), but not the overarching requirements that must be fulfilled to enable the highest security level of WS intercommunications. In addition to technology implementations, one key requirement for secure service interactions is the need for overarching cross-enterprise business policies. This requirement is especially crucial in arranging and supporting these sometimes complex and highly sensitive intercommunications.

Policies that focus on a higher level than the technology solutions to be implemented form another protective layer. The benefit of these policies is that once established they help to maintain a high level of trust between all participating companies. This trust is sustained by enabling the exchange of information to always occur in an expected and understood manner. The presence of this trust is a crucial requirement to the realisation of the seamless integration of services promised by WS technologies. While, there are considerable developments in WS security policies, these developments consider policies at the technology layer and thus do not address the higher-level policy layer, which was introduced in the paragraph above.

Given the significance and value of an additional way to secure WS, the focus of this research is to investigate whether an approach to WS security oriented on agreed-on cross-enterprise policies can significantly aid in providing protection against fraud, lawsuits and other business risks. The approach adopted for the research is a combination of empiricism and hermeneutics research methodologies. A specific WS-based scenario (in the form of a case study) that demands an extremely high level of trust between entities is presented. Members of this scenario include an e-university, an e-bank and an e-hotel (which is defined as a provider of temporary accommodation for students). The purpose of this particular case scenario is to allow this research to identify some of the most crucial aspects that should be considered in the creation of any reliable WS security model. The model has been implemented through a proof of concept prototype, which is currently being evaluated.

The remainder of this paper is organized as follows: Section 2 presents related work and suggests shortcomings that could be overcome by enterprise policies; in Section 3, the case study developed in this paper is described and the proposed policy model presented. Finally, Section 4 concludes this paper and outlines future work.

2 Related Work

This research is based on three related areas of work, e-Business and its security concerns, the adoption of WS for e-Business, and current approaches used in securing WS. These have been reviewed and presented in the following sections.

2.1 e-Business and Its Security Concerns

e-Business is undoubtedly one of the most discussed topics in the business and information technology (IT) fields today. Interestingly however, there seems to be no globally accepted definition with some authors linking e-Business primarily with internal operations [9] and others with both internal and external business processes [5]. The latter perspective conveys a more complete and accurate description of our view of e-Business. IBM is one of the many entities that support this internal and external orientation, thus defining e-Business as: "The process of using Web technology to help businesses streamline processes, improve productivity and increase efficiencies. Enables companies to easily communicate with partners, vendors and customers, connect back-end data systems and transact commerce in a secure manner". This definition highlights key constituent elements such as the use of Web technologies, internal and external communications and the overarching concept of the requirement for security.

e-Business has experienced a phenomenal growth over the last decade. The large-scale integration of business processes within the UK has experienced a massive 40% increase from 2002 [15]. Similarly, this considerable increase is being experienced all over the world. For example, the US e-Business sector estimates an average increase of 18.6% per year in online retail sales between 2005 and 2009 (eMarketer-b, 2006). As advancements in technologies enable easier online integration between companies, an increasing number of businesses have embraced the use of Internet technologies in order to gain competitive advantage. The wide adoption of these technologies comes with significant challenges- including security [7].

Web security has been broken into three components [3], namely the clients, the servers (or more generally, the server-side) and the communications pathways. These three components constitute the vulnerable areas thoroughly analysed in [9] also identifies six requirements that must be addressed and then the appropriate mechanisms implemented to fulfill. From a business perspective, one common temptation in the pursuit of security is simply to find and implement the latest range of highly rated security technologies. These could range from new intrusion detection systems to the installation of complete antivirus packages. This approach however is inadequate as technologies by themselves do not and cannot solve the security problem. To successfully address these threats a more complete and layered approach is necessary which takes into account laws and industry standards, policies and procedures and also, technology solutions (see [9]).

2.2 Approaches to Web Services (WS) Security

Web services have been defined using different terms and terminologies. For example, as a standardized way of integrating web-based applications using XML, SOAP,

WSDL and UDDI [6] and [13] and as a platform-independent, loosely coupled, self-contained programmable Web-enabled application that can be described, published, discovered, orchestrated and programmed using XML artefacts for the purpose of developing distributed interoperable applications [11]. However, all varying definitions of WS, emphasizes on interoperability, machine-to-machine or service-to-service interaction, mechanism for service description and discovery, platform-independence and the fact that they are self-contained (i.e. expose functionality not implementation (Hartman et al. 2003). In addition to the interoperability characteristics, WS are easy and inexpensive to implement since they use open technologies; and (b) they can significantly reduce the cost of business-to-business (B2B) communications.

While, the use of WS has substantial advantages to e-Business, they also come with many challenges – one of which is the security vulnerabilities that e-Businesses are exposed to in [1] and [11].

Until recently, technology mechanisms were the main approach for achieving WS security [8]. Technology solutions were quickly needed to respond to immediate security threats. With the wide adoption of WS in e-Business and other large-scale web-based applications, a holistic approach to WS security became apparent because of the inter-business integration allowed by WS, plus the high level of communications now readily expected, the use of agreed-on cross-organisational policies becomes an even more critical consideration. As increasing amounts of e-Businesses adopt WS and thus open their precious internal processes and workflows, trust between organisations is a crucial requirement. Thus frameworks such as the Web Services Security roadmap proposed by IBM, Microsoft and VeriSign became a roadmap for research and development in WS where policy component including the overall system design and implementation mechanisms all play critical roles (Hartman et al., 2003). A model-driven approach to define WS security architecture was proposed and explained in Nakamura et al. (2005). This approach does not provide a method with which to produce software requirements.

The main aim of this research therefore is to investigate the use of agreed-on, cross-enterprise policies in Web services (WS) security, to determine whether they can significantly aid in enhancing the security currently provided. The next section presents the proposed security model.

3 Web Services Security Model

Section 2 examined Web services (WS) security and assessed the role and use of policies in these security solutions. Given the significance and the need for the use of policies, this section describes a policy-based WS security model. To achieve this aim, the main approach adopted has been a careful definition of a specific WS-based case scenario followed by a detailed analysis of its interactions and requirements.

The case features an e-university, its e-bank and an e-hotel and by its very nature, demands an extremely high level of trust between all entities. With these aspects as a basis, the proposed high-level model is then defined with emphasis placed on some generic cross-enterprise policies. These policies act to provide a more clear illustration of the model's focus, but also to provide general policies that can be applied to most WS scenarios.

Section 3.1 presents the case scenario and its analysis followed by a detailed analysis of requirements in Section 2.2. Section 3.3 presents a proposed model.

3.1 e-Business Case Scenario

The business scenario used in this research consists of the various transactions that occur between four main entities - a student, an e-University, the e-University's e-Bank, and an e-Hotel. For completeness, two other entities are highlighted, these being the student's e-Bank and the e-hotel's e-Bank.

Figure 3.1, is a graphical representation of all these entities followed by a basic description of each participating entity. This scenario assumes that e-University did have previous business relations with e-Bank and the e-hotel. However, previous communication did not use WS technologies to facilitate the cross-organisational communication.

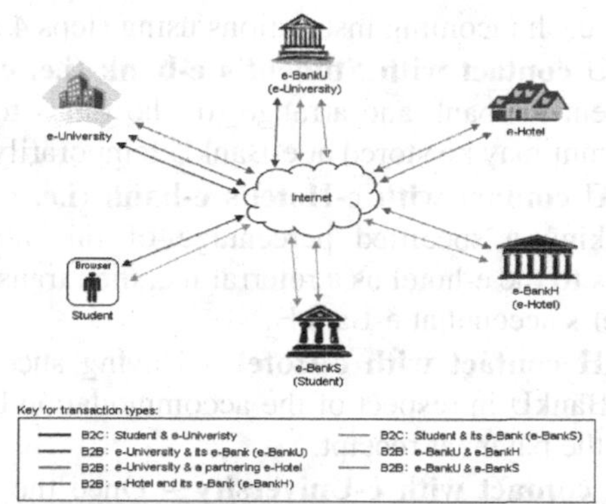

Fig. 3.1. Graphical Representation of the case Scenario

- Student and his/her e-bank (e-BankS). A student represents a person who is either a prospective student applying to the e-university or a current student of the e-university. A student uses the university's site to: (a) apply, register and access course content online; (b) to arrange for course fee payments; and (c) to find and arrange payment for temporary accommodation.
- E-University and its e-bank (e-BankU). E-University is a university (or more generally, an e-business) that offers online education to students. It also acts as an interface for students that allow them to do task (b) and (c) above. Its e-bank plays a critical role in enabling and handling the payment instructions received at the university's web site. In effect, all these instructions are passed to the e-bank for processing. Once completed, it is expected to inform the e-university and other necessary parties.
- E-Hotel and its e-bank (e-BankH). E-Hotel is essentially a business that holds information on a number of accommodation properties available for rent to students of e-University. Its e-bank's purpose is to support its online transactions especially the receiving of payments in lieu of student accommodation fees.

Having identified the main entities, the following steps are a walk-through of how these entities work together:

- **Step 1: Student contact with e-University** – Students may be required to be at the e-university campus for either examinations or for a prescribed residential course. To find temporary accommodation for the duration of their stay, they access the university's website and login using a username and password. By logging in, they are able to browse; upon logging in they see a list of properties available for temporary rental.
- **Step 2: E-University contact with e-Hotel** –Once a property has been selected; a payment instruction is made by the student at the university's web site to start the booking process. This instruction primarily uses the student's bank details, which are stored on e-University's records.
- **Step 3: E-University contact with its e-bank (i.e. e-BankU)** – Upon receiving this payment instruction, e-University passes the student's and e-Hotel's bank account details to e-BankU with the instructions for processing. e-BankU validates and verifies each incoming instructions using steps 4 and 5 below.
- **Step 4: E-BankU contact with Student's e-bank (i.e. e-BankS)** – E-BankU contacts the student's e-bank and arrange for the funds to be taken from their account. The amount may be stored at e-BankU temporarily.
- **Step 5: E-BankU contact with e-Hotel's e-bank (i.e. e-BankH)** – The next step involves taking a specified percentage of this amount, which the e-university charges to the e-hotel as a referral fee, then transferring the remaining amount to e-Hotel's account at e-BankH.
- **Step 6: E-BankH contact with e-Hotel** – Having successfully received the payment from e-BankU in respect of the accommodation booking, e-BankH informs e-Hotel of the payment receipt.
- **Step 7: E-Hotel contact with e-University** – Once the e-Hotel receives this confirmation for accommodation fee payment; it contacts the e-university to verify that the booking for a specific student (identified by name) and property is now complete. It also updates it records to show this that this property is no longer available.
- **Step 8: E-BankU contact with e-University** – Upon completion of the payment process originally instructed by the e-university, e-BankU sends an acknowledgement to the university.
- **Step 9: E-University contact with e-Hotel** – This acknowledgement in addition to the verification received from the e-hotel acts to confirm the booking process. Now, the full accommodation booking details (e.g. specific property and time of stay) and the necessary student's details (e.g. name, contact information) are sent from e-University to e-Hotel for it to update the necessary records.
- **Step 10: E-University contact with Student** – Finally, the e-university notifies the student of the successful booking of the selected accommodation by email.

With the general case scenario outlined, functional requirements for each of the entities have been analyzed leading to the definition of the main security requirements presented in the next section.

3.2 Security Requirements

Based on the functions of each entity's system and the main services it should provide an assessment is now made into where exactly, aspects of security would be needed. From a policies point of view perspective, all e-businesses (or organisations) must typically have their internal policies. Below is an outline of five top-level, security-specific policies for e-University, e-Bank and e-Hotel. The list is not intended to be exhaustive but to focus on the specific areas that will be considered for this scenario.

1. All of e-University's information and services is categorized into two main classifications:
    a. Public – declared public knowledge by someone with the authority to do so
    b. Confidential – all other information. This information is further divided into:
        i. HIGH priority – declared at this level by someone with the authority to do so. Very sensitive information that must be highly secured
        ii. LOW priority – all other information. Security here is also required but at a reduced and basic level

    For all confidential information, it should be secured whether in storage or in transit.
2. Remote access to the company's internal information and services (web site being an example) which deemed to be confidential must be accessed in a secure manner and by authorised entities.
3. An e-business and thus always open via the Internet, measures should be taken to ensure persistent and consistent availability of services.
4. All personnel are to be classified into specific user groups that link to their job roles and responsibilities in the organisation.
5. Measures should be taken to ensure that persons can only access the accounts, data, information, system capabilities to which they have been strictly authorised.

These general policies have been analyzed into specific low-level security requirements for each participating organization – e-University, e-Bank, and e-Hotel used to define the proposed model in the next section.

3.3 The Model

The first policy is to ensure that each business has its own security policies, A layered approach defined in [7] and [9] has been adopted to secure each individual business entity according to their defined requirements.

Having secured the individual e-business Business, the next aspect is to secure communications between entities. One option to address this aspect is to simply perform the necessary service bindings to the consumer/provider's service and let the business's security setup interact with the consumer/provider's Web service. However, as highlighted in the literature review section, this approach only focuses on the technology solution to service interactions. Thus, an approach that allows participating organisations to partner and define a framework (agreed-upon policies) with which the security of the entire communications (internal and external to each business) is proposed. External communications are defined as everything that goes on external to an e-Business within the service interactions.

The goal of this policy oriented security framework would be to give each entity some level of assurance for security of the overall WS communications especially those outside their own control. By partnering and defining cross-enterprise policies, one substantial achievement to be made is that of a new level of trust between all entities. These agreed-on policies would clearly outline requirements for the overall WS communications and purport a level of trust beyond that attainable with technology solutions. Figure 3.2 is a diagrammatic representation of the proposed model.

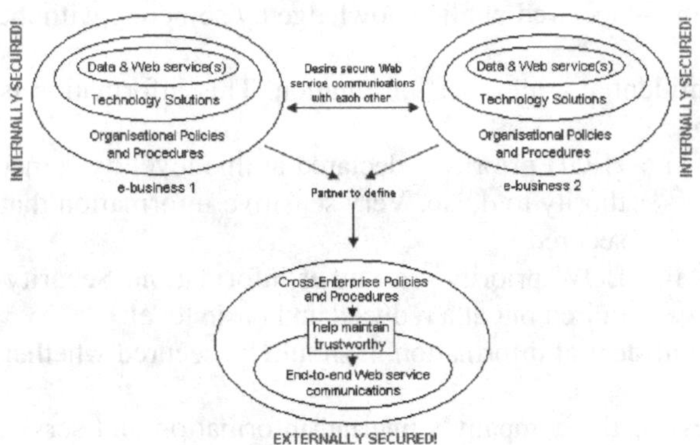

Fig. 3.2. A Model for enhancing WS security

From Figure 3.2, each business entity is required to ensure that their businesses are internally secured. Once this is done and they are ready to offer their services externally they essentially 'Desire secure Web service communications'. At this point, they then move to partner to define cross-enterprise policies and procedures that help maintain trustworthy end-to-end WS communications. The process of partnering to define cross-enterprise policies may require that additional security policies and mechanisms be in place for some or all organizations. The model also defines a set of generic Cross-Enterprise Policies and procedures applicable to a wide range of WS scenarios.

4 Conclusion and Future Work

The proposed model is currently being implemented and evaluated in a two-step process. The first step assumes that each business has its own internal policies, procedures, and technology solutions to protect its data and now, Web services. The next step is the definition and application of the cross-enterprise policies and procedures that will enhance the overall security of the WS communications. These policies can be seen to provide a wrapper to allow for this enhanced level of security.

The vast benefits attainable through Web services (WS) usage in e-business will undoubtedly make this pair a force in the future. As show however, one hindrance to WS widespread adoption is the new security concerns it introduces. Unless concerns are adequately addressed, the advantages possible with WS will be remain as theory and never put into widespread practice. This WS security formed the basis of this report paper and its research investigated into the use of cross-enterprise policies for enhancing the currently provided security solutions

Future work considers two specific areas: (a) continued development of the proposed Web services security model, especially the generic cross-enterprise policies; and (b) the critical and thorough evaluation of this model.

References

1. Bebawy, R., et al.: Nedgty: Web services Firewall. In: IEEE International Conference on Web Services, ICWS 2005 (2005)
2. Boncella, R.: Web Services for E-Commerce. Communications of the Association for Information Systems 4(11), 4–14 (2000)
3. Boncella, R.J.: Web Services and Web Services Security. Communications of the Association for Information Systems 6(14), 344–363 (2000)
4. Cavanaugh, E.: Web services: Benefits, challenges, and a unique, visual development solution, `http://www.altova.com/whitepapers/webservices.pdf` (accessed 3 June 2006)
5. Chaffey, D.: E-Business and E-Commerce Management, 2nd edn. Pearson Education Limited, Essex (2004)
6. Chatterjee, S., Webber, J.: Developing Enterprise Web Services: An Architect's Guide. Prentice Hall PTR, New Jersey (2004)
7. Davidson, M.A.: Security for eBusiness. Information Security Technical Report 6(2), 80–94 (2001)
8. Krawczyk, K., Weilgus, M.: Security of Web Services. In: International Conference on Dependability of Computer Systems (DEPCOS-RELCOMEX 2006), pp. 183–190 (2006)
9. Laudon, K.C., Traver, C.G.: E-commerce: business, technology, society, 2nd edn. Addison Wesley, Boston (2004)
10. Nakaruma, Y., Tatsubori, M., Imamura, T., Ono, K.: Model-driven based security based on web services security architecture. In: IEEE International Conference on Services Computing (SCC 2005). IEEE Computer Society, Orlando (2005)
11. Papazoglou, M.P., Ribbers, P.M.: e-Business: Organizational and Technical Foundations. John Wiley & Sons Ltd., West Sussex (2006)
12. Pulier, E., Taylor, H.: Understanding Enterprise SOA. Manning Publications, California (2005)
13. Rowan, L.: Security in a Web Services World in Network Security, June 2005, vol. 2005(6) (2005)
14. Steel, C., Nagappan, R., Lai, R.: Core Security Patterns. Prentice Hall PTR, Englewood Cliffs (2005)
15. Young, K.: UK firms surf the e-business wave (2005), `http://www.itweek.co.uk/vnunet/news/2144211/uk-business-internet-soaring` (accessed 29 May 2006)

Challenges of Identity Management – A Context in Rural India

Rajanish Dass and Sujoy Pal

IIM – Ahmedabad

rajanish@iimahd.ernet.in, sujoypal@iimahd.ernet.in

Abstract. An efficient identity management has been an aspiring and dream for many nations and organizations. The objectives for uniquely identifying individuals have been different for different entities. For some, the need for better security had been the driving factor, while for others identity management would mean better transparency and improved efficiency. The challenges in implementing an efficient identity management mechanism in a country like India are immense. In this paper we have tried to identify the challenges and factors effecting identity management in rural India at a micro level by studying the membership management of Self Employed Women's Association (SEWA) an organization working in rural districts of India.

Keywords: Identity management, Rural Organization, Factors affecting identity managemen, NGO.

1 Introduction

Managing the identity of individuals has been a challenge for different nations and organizations since years. There have been different reasons for identifying people uniquely. Enhancement of security through detection of fraud, guard against terrorism and illegal immigration are some of the prime objectives for providing unique identification to the citizens [1]. Another important use of national ID cards is to authenticate a person's entitlement to government services [2]. Even though in real life there are enough dimensions for unique identification of different entities, but when it comes to managing identity of individuals within an organization or a nation, the decision need to be made solely based on the captured dimensions. In many cases the dimensions captured may not be enough to provide unique identification to individuals. There are two different problems related to identity of an individual, absence of identity of an individual and existence of multiple identity of the single individual.

Around one hundred nations including Argentina, Belgium, Brazil, Bulgaria, France and Spain have implemented national ID cards for their citizens, while some countries like Indian, Bangladesh and China are taking initiatives for providing their citizens with ID cards. Considering the Indian context, a nation with 1.1 Billion population and huge amount of diversity in terms of terrain, culture and religion is expected to face huge challenges in achieving this mammoth task. Considering the fact that more than seventy percent of Indian population residing in the rural parts, it won't be unfair to say that actual India can be seen in the rural areas.

D. Weerasinghe (Ed.): ISDF 2009, LNICST 41, pp. 172–183, 2010.

In order to understand the complexities involved in managing identity in rural parts of India, we decided to investigate about the challenges and their probable solution at a micro level. We conducted this study in order to understand and address the challenges of identity management faced by Self Employed Women's Organization (SEWA) which is a Non-Government Organization (NGO) working since 1972 towards the empowerment of poor self employed women. SEWA is registered as a trade union and has more than five hundred and sixty thousand members in Gujarat out of which more than fifty four percent members reside in the rural areas.

We have conducted an exploratory study to identify the factors effecting the efficient management of unique identification of members at SEWA. Through this study we were able to determine various factors affecting the identification management exercise both in positive as well as in negative terms. Certain factors were found to be under the control of the organization, while some factors the organization had absolutely no control. Through this study we were able to suggest a decentralized process of data digitization and verification for resolving the issues of identity management at SEWA. Further we proposed to enhance the service delivery structure by implementing identity verification of members during service delivery in order to convert the process of enrollment from a push based system to a pull based system.

2 The Problem

SEWA being a trade union, as per the norms of the Labour Ministry of India, mandates its members to renew their registration every year. Hence, the organization needs to maintain accurate records of its members and get them audited by the Ministry. Moreover, the organization provides various types of products and services, conducts various activities and extends facilities to its active members. This mode of working also requires proper identification of active members in order to ensure that the facilities and services reach the right individuals.

In order to serve the members, various branches of SEWA have evolved during the years. Each branch provides different types of services to the members of SEWA. The existence of unique identification of the members would also help these branches to consolidate information related to each member and provide better services through proper coordination. Despite of taking various Information and Communication Technology (ICT) initiatives, the organization has failed to provide unique identity to its members.

This study was conducted to evaluate the challenges of the organization in the identity management of its members and propose a suitable solution. The study was conducted with the following objectives:

- Identify the challenges of identity management within an organization working in rural parts of India
- Determine the drivers at various levels of the organization for generating and maintaining unique identification.

3 Related Research

Identity management is a much larger issue than purely personal identity management. Identity management involves systems for the identification of a variety of objects supporting societal behavior: people, goods, places, etc. [3]. In information society an individual may take on a number of different identities. As a consequence an individual may accumulate a vast array of personal identifiers for different services. Hence, multiple identity management is a significant issue for individuals and organizations, both in public and private sectors [4]. Beynon-Davies [3] has used a semiotic framework [5] for building an holistic account of the issue of personal identity management in the sense that it is seen as consisting of three inter-related processes – authentication, identification and enrolment – that bridges between the realm of ICT systems and that of human activity systems [6].

An identifier is a symbol or a set of symbol that can be used to identify something. Authentication involves validating the association between the identifier and the person [7]. The term identification is defined by Concise Oxford Dictionary as "the act or process of establishing the identity of or recognizing something. Personal identification concerns the practical way in which individuals are identified in various contexts [8]. The process of enrolment (a term adopted from actor-network theory [9]) performed by a validated identity serves to enroll the individual in some defined human activity system [6] that comprises a logical collection of activities performed by some group of people in pursuit of some goal [3]. The sequence of processes followed during first interaction is: enrolment, identification and authentication [10].

4 Methodology

In this type of study, understanding the context of the organization becomes very critical. Hence, we adopted various methods for understanding the context and analyzing the data obtained to determine the dimensions of the problem. The methods adopted in this study are as follows:

Review of existing data and documents
Data for the year 2006 and 2007 were extracted from the existing membership management system in order to get a better insight of the existing processes and its drawbacks. Various documents like annual reports and organization website was referred to understand the organization and the context of the existing problems related to identity management.

Interviewing the decision makers of SEWA
One-to-one interviews as well as group interviews were conducted with the decision makers of SEWA in order to understand the views and challenges of the top level management. During these interviews we also focused on the critical success factors of the top level management and their dependability on efficient identity management of the members. In such an exercise, the support of the top level management towards the implementation of strong system for identity management becomes very critical.

These interviews also enabled us in determining the degree of interest among various layers of top management in supporting the introduction of such a system.

Focused group discussions
Around five focused group discussions were conducted among the district coordinators (who are responsible for coordinating various activities in their respective districts) and aagewans (leaders who are responsible for collecting membership details fees from the members every year). These focused group discussions gave us complete insight about the challenges and bottlenecks at various levels of the organization. These discussions provided a complete picture through the perspectives of the various stakeholders of the organization and helped us in identifying the grass root issues related to identity management of the members.

Analysis of the identified dimensions
After collecting the relevant data, we analyzed it to determine the factors effecting the efficient identity management of SEWA. We further went ahead to analyze the identified dimensions and tried to determine the relationship of each dimension with the exercise of identity management.

5 The Study

Through detailed discussion with various stakeholders of SEWA and review of the existing documents, we were able to determine the processes that were followed in the existing membership management system at the organization.

5.1 Existing Processes for Membership Management at SEWA

The membership receipt books are generally printed once in a year with each book containing forty membership receipts. As the books need to be distributed district-wise, they carry a serial number on them for each district along with a unique district code. While, serial numbers from one to forty are printed on each individual receipt of each book. In case of shortage of receipts books, reprinting is done based on the demand for the same.

The receipt books are issued centrally for all districts from the SEWA reception centre (SRC) situated in Ahmedabad. The district coordinators, local district coordinators or karyakartas collect the books from SRC. At the SRC a manual register is maintained to keep track of the issued books. The receiver of books is supposed to sign across each record on the register which records the book number, name of the receiver and issue date. The books normally exchange few hands before reaching the aagewans. During each such exchange, manual records are maintained about the receiver of the books along with the date and signature of the receiver.

After receiving the membership receipt books, the aagewans collect the membership details along with annual membership fee from new as well as existing members of SEWA. After filling all the relevant details, the receipts are given to the members as a proof of membership while, the counterfoil is safely retained by the aagewan.

The total number of members registered by an aagewan normally demonstrates her capability and strength within the organization. Each aagewan is normally responsible for registering members only from a single village/area, but may vary depending upon the local scenario.

After registering the members, the membership receipt books along with the collected fees need to be returned back to SRC. The aagewans normally sends the filled receipt books back to SRC through the same channel by which they had received the books. Still in many cases the books reach the SRC through a different channel. The decision about who would deposit the books and the fees to the SRC is based on convenience rather than any rule. During this process, the details of pending books (i.e. the books that are issued but not been received) at the SRC is also fetched and conveyed to the receiver.

After accepting the membership fees at the SRC, the collected fees are deposited in the bank on daily basis. The deposit receipts are maintained and are later audited at the end of the year against the acknowledgement receipts that were issued to the depositors of membership receipt books. In order to facilitate the audit process, list of received book numbers are maintained on the hind side of the bank deposit receipt counterpart.

At the SEWA reception centre, a three member back-office team is responsible for digitizing the membership management data using FoxPro based software. The digitization of manually maintained data of issued and received membership receipt books is done on daily basis. This data is used to generate various types of information. Firstly, this data is used to calculate the current status of total membership at any point of during the year. Secondly, this data is used to keep track of the membership receipt books that have been issued and not yet been received.

5.2 Analyzing the Existing Membership Data

In order to gain a better insight about the existing membership management at SEWA, we analyzed the membership data of the year 2006 and 2007. The dimensions stored in the database included name of the member, age, gender, residential address (including area/village, taluka and district), member's primary trade, member's secondary trade, primary trade address, secondary trade address and the name of the leader who collected the membership details. In addition to these dimensions, provision for capturing activity related details were also provided which were never filled.

Along with the digitized data, we also had copies of their annual report mentioning the total number of members across various trades. We first compared the aggregate values of the digitized data with the values of the annual report and found the result to match with each other. On further analysis we found high frequency of duplicate values across various dimensions. First we tried to determine the number of records have same value for member's name (including first name, middle name and last name) and reside in the same location (i.e. same district, taluka and village). The summery of the findings is given in Table–1.

Table 1. Frequency of Membership Records with Same Name and Location

No. of Records with Same Value	Total Instances Found
2	14,419
3	1,878
4	409
5	143
6	58
7	21
8	12
9	2
10	2
14	1

As shown in the table, fourteen thousand four hundred and nineteen instances were found where the same values were repeated twice and one thousand eight hundred seventy eight instances were found where the values were repeated thrice. Most amazing was the fact that one instance was found where the same values for name and location was found to be repeated fourteen times. On further investigation, we included member's trade as a dimension along with the name and location to see the effect on the duplicate records. This reduced the frequency of duplication by some amount, but the resultant values were still significant. The result is presented in Table – 2.

Table 2. Frequency of Membership Records with Same Name, Location and Trade

No. of Records with Same Value	Total Instances Found
2	11,760
3	1,320
4	263
5	85
6	31
7	12
8	4
9	1
10	2
14	1

We further went on to check the uniqueness of book numbers and slip numbers that were used for membership collection. As each printed books contained a district code and a serial number unique for that particular district, we tried to find out whether there exists any record with similar values for district code, book number and slip number. The output of the query is given in Table – 3.

Table 3. Frequency of Records with Same Book Number, Slip Number and District

District	No. of Records with Same Value	Total Instances Found
Ahmedabad City	2	285
	3	5
Ahmedabad Dist.	2	170
	3	9
Anand	2	15
Gandhinagar	2	36
Kheda	2	15
Kutch	2	1
Mehsana	2	16
Panchmahal	2	3
Patan	2	19
Sabarkantha	2	14
Surendranagar	2	28
Vadodara	2	8
	3	2

The above table shows that in Ahmedabad City, there were two hundred and eighty five instances where the combination of book number and slip number were repeated twice, where as in five instances, the values of the fields were found to be repeated thrice. In almost all districts, duplicate values were found for book number and slip number.

5.3 Facts Revealed from the Interviews and Group Discussions

The interviews and focused group discussions with various stakeholders of SEWA revealed that there were members residing in the same location who were having completely same name and even involved in the same trade. But still there were chances for some amount of data being incorrect considering the fact that most of the aagewans responsible for collection of membership details were uneducated and had to take help from for filling the membership receipts. Hence, in order to save effort, certain data might be unduly duplicated. Moreover, discussion with the district coordinators revealed that the aagewans were given targets for membership generation every year and during the year end, they would create duplicate records in order to meet these targets. For example, the case where there were fourteen records with the same name, location and trade can be an instance of such case. Further discussion revealed that this case can also be a result of a membership book being lost by an individual and in order to compensate the same, duplicate entries were being made.

Discussing about the fact of duplicate membership book and slip numbers within the existing data, it was found that there were instances where the records of membership receipt books that were either not received or digitized in the current year, were enter in the subsequent year. As the receipt books did not have any mention of the year of membership, records were generated with the same values for book number and slip number.

5.4 Challenges Encountered during De-duplication of Data

We tried to perform a de-duplication exercise on the data for the year 2006 and 2007 in order to distinguish between the member who reregistered themselves in 2007 and the ones who joined as new members. Given the fact that duplication existed in almost all dimensions of the existing data, there were hardly any combination of dimensions that could be used for uniquely identifying the members even within a single year. Moreover, the interviews and discussions with various stakeholders of SEWA revealed many interesting facts about the characteristics of members as well as the leaders responsible for collecting data which made the de-duplication task much more difficult.

The discussions surprisingly revealed that even the basic data regarding the members like name, age, location does not remain consistent for a member across years. As all the members of SEWA are women, their middle name, last name and residential address are subject to change after marriage. Moreover, in certain casts in India, there is a tradition of changing even the first name of a woman after marriage. As the members are self employed and related to unrecognized sector of trade, they also change their location as well as trade in search of better livelihood. It was also found that the values recorded for age of the members were not consistent as the majority of the members were uneducated and could not correctly reveal their date of birth. Even the age mentioned by them across years were found to be inconsistent.

In addition, there were traces of typographical errors within the existing data. As the data entry operators used to manually enter all the details of membership during the process of digitization every year, it was found that they used different spellings for the name of the same members in subsequent years. For example, a member whose name was registered as "Menaben" in one year might be registered as "Meenaben" in the subsequent year. This also happened due to the fact that the data originally recorded on the registration slips were in the local language (Gujarati) while the digitization process happened in English. Using techniques to identify the similar sounding words, we were able to resolve the issue of inconsistency in the spelling of members' name up to certain extent. But the fact that almost all the captured dimensions in membership details showed different degrees of volatility, made the task of de-duplication very difficult. In the absence of any supporting data (like voter identity list, list of ration card holders, etc.) from some authentic source the task of de-duplication seemed impossible. However, when an extracted list of duplicate data were sent to the district offices for verification, it was found that the district coordinators and the aagewans were able to identify the discrepancies and authenticate the data quite easily.

6 Findings of the Study

Through this study, we were able to identify various factors affecting the process of identity management at SEWA. These factors could be classified based on two dimensions: its effect on identity management and whether the dimension is under control of the organization. The identified factors and their role towards efficient identity management are as follows:

Table 4. Factors Affecting Identity Management at SEWA

Factor	**Description**	**Effect on Identity Management**	**Under organization's control (Yes / No)**
Business Needs	This is a factor that can determine the support of the top level management in the identity management exercise. The degree of business needs in maintaining unique identity for the members is also expected to determine the level of effort the organization would put in the whole exercise.	Positive	Yes
Cost of Operations	Cost is found to be one of the major constraints towards efficient identity management. High cost of operations of such system could act as a deterring factor in the path of identity management exercise.	Negative	No
Reachability and connectivity	Reachability and connectivity to the members both in terms of geographical terrain as well as technology has been found to be a factor in determining efficiency of identity management exercise.	Positive	No
Skill of Personnel	Capability of the people involved in implementation of the identity management exercise was one of the major factors in its successful implementation. In this case the lack of capability of the aagewans in reading and writing the membership details had proved to be a hurdle for identity management.	Positive	Partially Yes
Motivation of Personnel	Motivation of the people involved in implementation of the process also plays a major role in successfully implementing an identity management system. In this case, the electoral structure of the organization provided a positive motivation to the aagewans towards identity management, while meeting the intended target of membership proved to be a negative motivation towards the exercise.	Positive	Yes

Table 4. (*continued*)

Factor	Description	Effect on Identity Management	Under organization's control (Yes / No)
Benefits for the members in retaining identity	Determining the relationship between the benefits for the members in retaining identity with the organization and an efficient identity management is a tricky issue. On one hand, if the benefits received is very low the members may not show enough interest in retaining identity with the organization. While on the other hand, in the presence of very high benefits for the members, there may be inclinations for maintaining multiple identities with the organization. In case of SEWA, there was a lack of motivation for the members in retaining their identity as there was no authentication of membership conducted while extending various services to the members. This was also a reason for the process of identity management of SEWA being push based rather than a pull base approach.	Both Positive and Negative	Yes
Availability of resources for checking validity of identity	Once the member is enrolled, availability of proper resources for authenticating the identity at the time of service delivery would act as an important factor in the implementation of identity management for the organization. This factor would also provide sufficient control over the entire process.	Positive	Yes
Volatility of captured dimensions	In our study we found high degree of volatility even for the very basic dimensions (like name, address, age) that were captured. This provided a huge challenge in efficient identity management for the organization.	Negative	No
Availability of supporting data from other authentic sources	This factor can act as a source for cross checking the validity of data captured about the members.	Positive	No
Distance between source of data and place of validation	The study revealed that the data that was hard to validate from the central location could be very easily validated at the districts where they had originated. This shows a very important fact that complexity of data validation actually increased due to centralization of data. Hence, reducing the distance between the source of data and location of validity could play a significant role in identity management.	Negative	Yes

Table 5. Relationship of Identified with Identification Management Exercise

	Positive	Negative
Controlled	• Business Needs • Skill of Personnel (partially controlled) • Motivation of Personnel • Benefits for the members in retaining identity • Availability of resources for checking validity of identity	• Benefits for the members in retaining identity • Distance between source of data and place of validation
Uncontrolled	• Reachability and connectivity • Availability of supporting data from other authentic sources	• Cost of Operations • Volatility of captured dimensions

7 Conclusion and Further Research

The study revealed various factors effecting identity management at SEWA, an organization working for the rural population of India. Out of the determined factors some were found to be in control of the organization, while others were to be out of control of the organizational boundaries. Some of the dimensions were found to be related to the identity management exercise while others were found to have negative effect on its efficiency.

Through the study we found that due to close social contacts between the members and leaders at the local, the validation of data worked much more efficiently when the task of verification is decentralized and brought near the source of data. This fact led us to suggest a decentralized process for digitization of membership data within the organization. After the data gets digitized at the local level, it can be transferred to a central server. Once the data is collated at the central server, a second level of verification at the central level can be performed and can be referred back to the local agents in case of any discrepancy. This would provide two levels of check on the data being used for unique identification of members.

It was also found during the study there were absence proper motivation for the members in retaining the proof of membership as there were no existing procedure to check the validity of member's identity during service delivery. Further, there was no existing process in place that could track the participation of the members in various activities or services received or rendered by the member. Hence, there were urgent need to implement a mechanism for consolidating the data generated due to the participation (or non-participation) of the members in various activities of SEWA and provide them with enhanced facilities with the help the knowledge that would be generated from the consolidated data. Initiatives towards this direction would enable the organization from shifting the identification management from a push based system to a pull based system where the members themselves would approach the organization with valid data for registration.

This study was conducted for resolving the issues of identity management of a single organization working for the rural population in Gujarat, India. As the study had a fixed scope, the determined factors would be limited. Further research can be conducted in order to understand the factors that would effect the identity management when looked from the perspective of the nation as a whole. Moreover, research can be conducted to determine the degree and nature of relationship among various factors and their overall contribution towards the efficiency of identity management.

References

1. LSE, The Identity Project: an assessment of the UK Identity Cards Bill and its Implications. London School of Economics and Political Science (2005)
2. Dass, R., Bajaj, R.K.: Creation of Single National ID: Challenges and Opportunities for India, Indian Institute of Management, Ahmedabad (2008)
3. Beynon-Davies, P.: Personal identity management in the information polity: The case of the UK national identity card. Information Polity 11, 3–19 (2006)
4. Graham-Rowe, D.: Privacy and Prejudice: whose ID is it anyway? New Scientist (2005)
5. Stamper, R.K.: Information in Business and Administrative Systems. Batsford, London (1973)
6. Checkland, P.: Soft Systems Methodology: a thirty year retrospective. John Wiley, Chichester (1999)
7. Zorkadis, V., Donos, P.: On biometric-based authentication and identification from a privacy-protection perspective: deriving privacy-enhancing requirements. Information Management and Computer Security 12(1), 125–137 (2004)
8. Clarke, R.: Human identification in information systems: management challenges and public policy issues. Information Technology and People 7(4) (1994)
9. Bijker, W.E., Hughes, T.P., Pinch, T.J.: The social construction of technological systems: new directions in the sociology and history of technology. MIT Press, Cambridge (1987)
10. JRC, Biometrics at the Frontiers: Assessing the Impact on Society, in technical report. EU Joint Research Center (2005)

Author Index

Printed in the United States
By Bookmasters